# Breve˰
# a Parachuting
# Odyssey

## DOUG PEACOCK

*In 1945 Royal Air Force Parachute Jumping Instructors were awarded honorary aircrew status by virtue of their role as despatchers on Airborne Operations in the European and Far East theatres during the Second World War.*

PARACHUTE TRAINING SERVICES
ABINGDON 2014

## ALSO BY THE AUTHOR

*Skydiving Basics*
Parachute Training Services 1996

# Contents

Published in the United Kingdom by Parachute Training Services

© Parachute Training Services 2014

British Library Cataloguing in Publication Data
Data available

ISBN: 978-0-9525825-1-9

Typeset by Hope Services, Abingdon Ltd
Printed and bound in Great Britain by
TJ International Ltd, Padstow, Cornwall

# List of Plates

**Section Three** *between pp. 92–105*

# *Preface*

It was on a bleak afternoon in February 1957 when I was marched into the sanctum of the Officer Commanding, No. 1 Parachute Training School, RAF Abingdon, and stood smartly at attention before the desk of Wing Commander J.R.W. (Jimmy) Blyth AFC. Flanked as he was by School Warrant Officer Jock Fox and my course instructor Sgt Ben Cass, I was faced by a formidable triumvirate who were to determine my whole future career. I was a qualified Physical Training Instructor in Her Majesty's Royal Air Force, and had just completed a sixteen-week Parachute Jumping Instructor course. I had made twenty parachute descents, and was fiercely keen to achieve the coveted PJI brevet.

The interview was brief – I was informed of my varied shortcomings in pithy military language and mentally prepared myself for a rapid return to life in the Sports Section from whence I came. Salvation arrived from an unexpected source. "What do you think, Mr Fox?" queried the Wing Commander. "I think we should give him a chance sir," replied the Warrant Officer. The Wing Commander paused, eyed me for a long moment, and came to a decision. "Very well Corporal, here is your brevet, but remember we shall be watching you very carefully for the next six months". I saluted, about turned, and marched out. I was totally elated; the moment was sufficient in itself. I had little idea of what the future was to hold.

Those six months have been extended fifty-seven years to the present day. Time adds perspective, and it is with a sense of mild disbelief that I realise the Parachute School had only been in existence a mere fifteen years when I qualified. Sitting at my desk at home, one short mile from the headquarters building where the interview took place, dusting off the logbooks and surrounded by mementos of a lifetime shaped by jumping out of aeroplanes, I decided that now was probably as good a time as any to share that experience with any interested parties.

I have been totally privileged to enjoy each day of my working life, privileged to have worked at the No.1 Parachute Training School, and doubly privileged to have shared that life with my wife Helen. For her unsparing and selfless support over all these years, I remain forever in her debt.

Abingdon
February 2014

**Chapter 1** | # *Basics*

*1957 - 1960*

I qualified as a Parachute Jumping Instructor in February 1957 and was immediately taken on the strength of the Parachute School and put to work on a Territorial Army (TA) course. These courses were shortened versions of the Regular Army eight-jump courses, which lasted one month. The TAs did the course in two weeks, with seven descents only, missing out on the night jump. Whereas the Regulars carried out seven days ground training with the first jump scheduled for the Tuesday of the second week, the TAs trained in the hangar for three days and started the parachuting programme on the Thursday of the first week. This fast track schedule was normally popular with most instructors, as we were quickly into the jumping phase. My logbook for 4th March 1957 shows that I was flying and despatching for six consecutive Hastings lifts from 14.30 to 20.15, the last two being night sorties. My education proper had begun.

There was always a tremendous buzz about the place, a pervasive enthusiasm and a sense of purpose. We were very busy at that time, there were always two Regular Army courses running concurrently, one intake in the parachuting phase and another two weeks behind. There would invariably be a TA course at the same time, along with sundry other specialist courses, AQMs, AMOs, APJIs etc. Our home was C Hangar at Abingdon, an area of some 30,000 square feet, which contained a plethora of synthetic training equipment – coir matting (very dusty) high ramps, low ramps, wheel trainers, slides, flight swings, block and tackle trainers, mock doors, fuselage mockups, a parachute storeroom, a maintenance section (STESS), fitting racks, plus six fan descent trainers high in the roof. At the other end of the hangar, suspended on high and gathering more dust, were full-scale replicas of Garnerin's(1797) parachute and Robert Cocking's ill-fated (1837) contraption. Offices, crew room, standby room, and parachute section were shoehorned in along the airfield side. When there was no parachuting programme running, this place was bursting at the seams. Of necessity, the vocal cords of your average PJI rapidly became extremely well developed.

Regular courses were usually about eighty strong, divided into two syndicates, each with its own Syndicate Officer and Flight Sergeant. Thus, a forty-man Syndicate would typically be split into five sections of eight soldiers, each under the charge of a Sergeant or Corporal instructor. This was an ideal student/instructor ratio and, because of the confidence factor, there was always a special relationship between the soldier and "his" instructor. The soldiers themselves were (generally) young, extremely fit and highly motivated. They came to us straight from P Company, pre-para, the Parachute Regiment's selection process. The P Company dropout rate at that time was around fifty per cent, which left us with the very best material to work on.

The seven-day ground training phase was extremely comprehensive. Most days on the first week the Syndicate Officer would deliver a formal lecture on each particular aspect to be taught – Flight Drills, Aircraft Drills, Malfunctions etc. and training films would be shown. The troops were then returned to the hangar floor where the theory was put into practice. We each worked with our section for seven days, teaching parachute landing falls from progressively increasing heights – standing, low ramp, high ramp, progressive landing trainer (steps), slides; and at progressively increasing speeds – standing, walking, running, then swinging from the wheel trainers, (giving the order to release at the high end of the swing, but if confident of the student's ability, or feeling mildly sadistic, at the bottom of the swing). Six directional landings were drilled into the student: forwards, sideways and backwards, both left and right. By the end of the ground training phase we were confident that our jumpers could absorb the horizontal and vertical impact of a parachute landing at any windspeed up to 15mph (13kt), and from any directional approach.

Flight drills were conducted in those days from a huge platform of swings, which dominated the centre of the hangar. The parachutes we were training to use were 28ft flat circular X types, with a descent rate of about 18ft/sec and which were inherently prone to oscillation. This oscillation was damped out by pulling down either front or rear lift webs (risers), depending on the direction of drift. Drifting backwards, front lift webs: this directed some of the pressure inside the canopy in the opposite direction, thus slightly reducing the backwards speed and at the same time releasing the build-up of internal pressure which caused the canopy to oscillate. We practised steering techniques, reserve techniques, water landing techniques both with and without equipment until these drills became second nature.

Exit technique was particularly critical. Dropping speed from the Hastings was about 115 mph, and the soldier had to make a forceful controlled exit from either port or starboard door. These exits were initially taught from the mock doors, then reinforced by jumping from the fan exit trainer, some thirty feet high just under the hangar roof. Further sessions were conducted from the outdoor exit trainer, a high wire apparatus jocularly known as the knacker cracker as a warning to the uninitiated who neglected to ensure a correctly fitting harness. Once individual exit techniques had been mastered, stick jumping was introduced. The speed and length of sticks was progressively increased, culminating in simultaneous sticks of fifteen from port and starboard doors of the fuselage mockup. The final sessions were almost invariably conducted by the Syndicate Flight Sergeant and it was a miniature education to observe Flight Sergeants such as Bill Coad or George Richardson take aircraft drills, achieving a cadence and precision worthy of the Brigade of Guards on parade.

The overriding consideration was safety; this was instilled into us from the very outset. It is my firm conviction that parachuting is as safe or as dangerous as one cares to make it oneself, and that the most important safety factor is one's own attitude. Ground training was carefully progressive, and practical parachuting followed the same pattern. The first two descents were made from a static balloon from a height of eight hundred feet (more accurately, from eight hundred feet cable length, actual height depending on the cable angle). First was a door exit, whilst the second was a floor aperture exit. This aperture was a rounded, coffin-shaped hole in the floor of the balloon cage some five and a half feet long by three feet wide, originally to duplicate the size of the exit aperture in the Albemarle, which had been used as a jump aircraft in exercises and operations during 1943–44. This aperture exit training was retained with the introduction of the Blackburn Beverley aircraft in 1957 (see under). Refusal to jump was a rare occurrence. PTS operated a zero tolerance policy toward refusals; the soldier either jumped or he did not, there were no second chances. The rationale was that if he had refused once, he might well refuse again at any stage, and there was no room for uncertainty. The student was returned to his unit within twenty-four hours as refusals were considered potentially contagious. Refusals were usually confined to the first balloon jump; naturally we were not allowed physically to assist anyone out of the cage, although on occasion a jumper might have his position in the door slightly adjusted. The two balloon descents were followed by aircraft descents with progressive increase in stick length and speed, leading up to a qualifying descent of simultaneous 15s from the Hastings. The Hastings was the main jump aircraft in 1957, the Valetta was on its way out and the Beverley was just being introduced. The latter had both lower and upper decks, with forty troops downstairs while the upper deck, or boom, held twenty troops who exited in a single stick through a rear aperture (hence the balloon training).

The foregoing notwithstanding, these activities did not always proceed totally smoothly and according to plan. I recall particularly a balloon incident which certainly grabbed our attention. This was during the Dropping Zone (DZ) phase of our course at Weston on the Green when we were covering the DZ under supervision for a Hastings sortie. It was January, the weather was pretty murky, the plume from Smokey Joe four miles west was horizontal and the Hastings called down to report a seven hundred foot cloud base;

they were hence unable to drop, as a minimum of eight hundred was required. OC PTS, the aforementioned Wing Commander Jimmy Blyth, was on the DZ and decided the aircrew were mistaken, and announced his intention to put up the balloon to check the cloud base. OC Weston on the Green tentatively mentioned a lightning risk two, but, being comprehensively outranked, had this well-intentioned information ignored. The cable paid out, up went the balloon with the cage unmanned. Pennants were attached to the cable every two hundred feet. Just after the third pennant had been attached, a dozen flashes of lightning from all angles of the sky converged on the metal vent valve at the rear end of the hydrogen-filled balloon. The conflagration was spectacular, with the balloon coming down in flames, eventually settling, neatly draped over the cage, in front of the Control Tower and burning away merrily. The fire section arrived with commendable alacrity, whilst the OC jumped into his staff car and departed in similar fashion. It started to rain. The Hastings decided to run in anyway and drop the drifter, I believe it was Ron McKail, who landed, totally ignored, at the far end of the field at a great rate of knots. The rain poured down, the Tower fired a red Verey, the Hastings disappeared into the lowering cloud and we all went home.

On another occasion, we were running a night descent programme using the Beverley freight bay (downstairs). I was the starboard door despatcher, and hence merely an interested bystander. Before dropping troops, it was standard procedure to drop an experienced instructor on the first run to act as drifter to confirm the exit point. It was also standard procedure to carry out a lights check prior to a live jump run (Red on, Green on, Go). Port door was open; drifter at action stations, Murphy's law ensured the inevitable outcome. Out went the drifter, Jerry Cording, on the lights check, which the navigator had switched on shortly after passing the Bicester Ordnance Depot at Graven Hill, some two miles short of the DZ. The face of the number one despatcher, Jock Brown, on headset with the rest of the aircrew, was a mixture of horror and disbelief. Jerry was located some thirty minutes later trudging across hedge and ditch on his way back to Weston. Needless to say, SOPs were re-drafted with some haste.

Before the students made their first balloon jump, there was always a demonstration cage of five instructors, each of whom would demonstrate a particular aspect of the flight drills as had been taught in the hangar. It was possible to steer the X type to some degree by pulling down one lift web in the desired direction of travel. It was also possible to slip the parachute by hauling down several handfuls of rigging (suspension) lines. This resulted in a noticeable increase in rate of descent. On this occasion, I was detailed to demonstrate steering and slipping to the basic course. I knew that Flight Sergeant Alf Card was reputed to have pulled down so far as to have reached the periphery of the canopy and I accordingly decided to put this to the test. I grasped one set of lines and kept on hauling down until the canopy had had enough and partially collapsed, putting about ten twists in the lines in the process; all this from an open canopy height of about seven hundred feet. I let go in a hurry, making sure the lines did not catch on my reserve on their way back up, and made a rather spectacular crash landing a dozen yards from the assembled troops waiting to make their first descent. Despite this (to me, anyway) perfectly convincing demonstration, my Syndicate Officer immediately grounded me for a couple of weeks, leaving me to explain matters to my own section; I certainly learned about parachuting from that. Those were indeed the days... we were young, dynamic and unsuccessful... all for an extra six shillings and ninepence (34p) per day.

The powers that be must have been satisfied with my progress as, six months following my original interview, I was promoted to Sergeant. In total, I spent four years from 1957 through the whole of 1960 learning my trade on the hangar floor. I remember particularly one of the courses, the RMA Sandhurst entry of September 1958. George Richardson was the Flight Sergeant; the instructors were Ron Ellerbeck, Bob Uden and myself. One member of my section was Officer Cadet John Ridgway, the first direct Sandhurst entrant into the Parachute Regiment, he who later achieved fame in 1966 by rowing across the Atlantic with his platoon sergeant Chay Blyth. We also gained valuable experience by frequent deployment on airborne exercises, both in the UK and overseas. Hutton Moor, Hankley Common, Methwold, Netheravon, Larkhill, Imber, Everleigh, Studland Bay, Morfou; these Dropping Zones were all overflown, low level formation for an hour or two, followed by fifteen minutes stick stand up and culminating in a twenty second blur of movement as the sim. 15s or sim. 20s left the door, each man encumbered by a ninety-pound weapons container. The regimented shuffle step as practised in the hangar became a headlong charge. Our job was to make sure the strops were clear and to act as a human buffer to divert the charge and literally manhandle the onrushing troops through the door.In May 1960 I flew for fourteen hours in a Beverley to reach Cyprus, via Malta, for a Brigade Exercise onto the Morphou DZ on the western coast of the island.

Interspersed with basic training and exercises were various types of demonstration jumping. My 200th descent, in June 1960, was in a sim. six static line at Topcliffe. Surface winds were in the region of twenty knots, we were blown sideways across the airfield and ten out of twelve of us landed on the (non active) runway. Bob Garrett failed to collapse his canopy in time and was dragged for a couple of hundred yards, with his backpack literally smoking and sparking in flames from the friction. On the same jump Roy Free suffered a head whip, which hospitalised him for some time; we had no hard helmets, only the original round canvas and rubber models, which had been standard issue since 1940. There were also visits from various film companies. We acted as stand-ins for Alan Ladd (The Red Beret), Virginia McKenna (Carve Her Name with Pride), George Peppard (Operation Crossbow) and Brigitte Bardot (Babette goes to War), the latter comedy involving a balloon programme on the airfield. It was blowing about 20 knots, the cable was at a ridiculous angle and the exit height was about six hundred feet, but we all survived the subsequent dragging and were each £5 better off for the experience. Brigitte was scheduled for the Officers Mess for lunch, but was hijacked by Jock Fox to No. 2 Sergeants Mess where she perched herself on a bar stool, surrounded by PJIs and press photographers, with a pint of bitter in her hand and listening to our chat-up lines until we all had to head off back to work.

The following month I was airborne in a de Havilland Comet from Lyneham, outward bound to Nairobi for an exercise with Special Forces. Our first leg was seven hours to Kano (Nigeria), refuelling at RAF Idris in Libya and was the first time I had been able to observe the world from 40,000 feet. I was totally fascinated by the transition from the blue Mediterranean to the dusty yellow Sahara merging into the dark green tropical forest of Central Africa, a fascination which lives on to the present day. The following morning we flew from Kano a further five hours to RAF Eastleigh, now Moi Air Force Base. I was the youngest of four PJIs on this three-week detachment, in support of Special Forces then on exercise in the area. Our detachment commander was Ringway veteran Flight Lieutenant Dally Duncan; the Chiefy was Hughie Bell, whilst Paul Hewitt and myself made up the party. As the aforesaid Special Forces were nowhere in evidence, we had a couple of days off visiting a game reserve in the National Park. We then went to work, travelling up country in a Pembroke, checking out various potential dropping zones. We finally settled for a game park near Nanyuki, situated right on the Equator and at 6,000 feet above mean sea level, one hundred miles north of the capital. The Special Forces contingent eventually put in an appearance and we gave them refresher training in Beverley aircraft drills, and, as the junior on his first overseas detachment and detailed for DZ duties, I was allowed to jump in as drifter. I still remember standing hooked up at the forward edge of the Beverley boom aperture, watching as we flew at eight hundred feet over native villages encircled by walls constructed of reeds, over native cattle, and over herds of zebra and giraffe. Sure as hell beats the Sports Store, I thought. I also noticed several dark patches of vegetation on the DZ boundary. Green on, smartly through the hole, check canopy, check drift. Drift turned out to be briskly sideways heading toward said vegetation, which I now identified as lion thorn bushes. Abandoning drifter protocol (no steering), and putting my previously castigated slipping technique to good use, I hauled down three or four handfuls of opposite riser and crash landed on the Equator only feet away from a dense thicket of natural tropical barbed wire. The exercise then proceeded without incident, the SAS disappeared into the aforementioned lion thorn, and we eventually returned to the UK by Beverley to Khormaksar (Aden) and from there to Stansted by civilian Britannia. I was living the PTS experience to the full, was learning all the time, and would have changed places with no one else on the planet.

As instructors, we were expected to maintain our own parachuting skills, both to demonstrate a technical standard to the students and, possibly more importantly, to engender a positive atmosphere regarding jumping generally. This appealed to me immensely and I set out to jump at every opportunity. I was determined to improve my personal parachuting and I volunteered for any parachute programme going, even on my days off. In November 1960 I was detached to Boscombe Down for a month to augment the trials team who were evaluating the replacement canopy for the X Type, which had been the standard assembly since the early 1940s. We jumped, often in marginal wind conditions, from a Valetta flying at 1200 feet, all exits being filmed from a Harvard flying alongside in formation. There were six canopies being tested, including a GQ 32ft shaped which was virtually oscillation free, and a beautiful canopy to handle. It had the unfortunate corollary of being also virtually impossible to collapse on the ground. On one occasion, following a rather ambitious standup attempt in a 20-knot wind, I was dragged across the Everleigh DZ for a full quarter mile. The canopy only came to rest by virtue of the fact that I had been rolled into the suspension lines from risers to periphery and became trussed in the lines up to the waist. The MOD final choice was the 32ft flat circular PX 1, which was introduced into service the following year. In all, I made twenty trials descents in four weeks at Boscombe, which bumped up my total to 237. We were also witness to a freefall descent made by Geordie Charlton and Jake McLoughlin, through cloud, and without personal oxygen, from 21,000 feet. This jump was to have tragic echoes some fourteen months later as we shall see.

Back at PTS there were many instructors on the staff to emulate: Tommy Moloney, Danny Sutton and Alf Card had been members of the British freefall team at the 1954 World Parachute Championships at St Yan in France. Bluey Lambeth was a particularly stylish exponent of standup landings. The most accomplished skydivers, however, were Jake and Geordie, who I had met at Boscombe Down, and Norman Hoffman, then on a temporary tour as a PTI at Shawbury. These instructors had formed their own freefall demonstration team, under Norman's leadership, calling themselves The British Skydivers, and using a de Havilland Rapide, operating out of nearby Thruxton. The three were augmented by Dennis Lee and PJI Mike McArdle. This team was way ahead of any other group in the UK, in terms of technique, experience and equipment. I already knew that freefall parachuting was the way forward for me.

Although *ad hoc* delayed opening descents had been made at PTS with manually operated parachutes in the early 1950s, (a flavour of which can be found in this fascinating narrative from John Saxby, OC 2 PTS in 1947:

> "– It seems a long time ago when Stannard and I tried out a freefall from 10,000 feet at Aqir in Palestine in 1947 using wrist watches. I was about to hand over command of No 2 PTS and proceed on demobilisation and it seemed a jolly end to my RAF career. Group Captain Geoffrey Wood was the Station Commander and took a bit of persuading. Before I left Stannard and I took a Dakota up to 10,000 feet over the station, Aqir – bloody cold – to let them all see what a drop looked like. Our usual DZ was Yibna some miles away. At 1000 feet as I remember the school instructors did a demonstration jump with Statichutes as usual, and at 10,000 feet Stannard and I baled out wearing standard Pilot Type parachutes. I spent a lot of the previous night trying to be sure that my maths was right – 120mph = feet per second??? = how long dare I wait ??? We used our wrist watches to time the drop before pulling the release. Knowing no better I adopted the standard exit position and reached TV in that position – surprised to feel myself 'standing' in the air with the wind whistling past but no feeling of

*falling–how naive we were. But then I began to tumble and was sick, remembering to keep my boots out of the way! Finally I saw Stannard's parachute deploy and decided to rely on his maths and deployed my own")*

... the first formal recognition occurred when Sir Raymond Quilter, co-founder of GQ Parachute Company, approached No 1 PTS in 1954 asking for jumpers to train for the forthcoming World Parachute Championships. After four weeks training (from scratch) in basic freefall techniques, six instructors were selected for the British team at this second WPC which was to be held at the former French National Parachute Centre, St. Yan, (Saône-et-Loire). They were Flight Lieutenant Doddy Hay, Sergeants Alf Card, Danny Sutton, Timber Wood, Norman Hoffman and Tommy Moloney. The team returned from France without any medals, but having gained valuable experience in terms of freefall techniques, canopy handling and freefall equipment. Disappointment ensued as the then PTS establishment showed little interest in developing these new ideas, it being felt that there was no requirement for freefall jumping in the Service. The parachutes were returned to GQ, and the cadre dissolved. Only two men had other ideas, which they were determined to put into practice.

The prime movers in taking freefall jumping forward at PTS were Alf Card and Norman Hoffman. http://www.telegraph.co.uk/news/obituaries/1443195/Norman-Hoffman.html On their own initiative, they formed a weekend group operating at Weston using the 47 Squadron Flying Club Tiger Moth as the sole jump aircraft. The pilot was Master Signaller Gerry Schellong, a Czech national, who had survived Russian internment, then escaped from occupied Czechoslovakia to serve in the RAF as a fighter pilot during WW2. The fledgling club attracted a lot of interest, mainly from the younger staff members, although the number of parachutes available was limited, as was jump altitude. Most unfortunately this venture survived only for a few months before they had a fatality and the club was forced to close. The jumper was ex Flight Lieutenant Neil Perry, recently retired as a PJI. He over-delayed from 2500 feet, pulling at about three hundred, with the inevitable consequences. Progress stagnated until 1959 when Alf started an operation at Kidlington airfield with Keith Teesdale and Pete Denley. Alf stored the parachutes in the coal shed of his Married Quarter. It was in the May of that year that I invested the sum of fifteen shillings (75p) to make my first descent freefall. The jump aircraft was a Tiger Moth, and the exit height was 1500 feet with a nominal three-second delay. Because of the bulky main container and a front-mounted reserve I could not sit in the front cockpit but had to take off with one leg inside and the other outside, straddling the door with my foot on the wing. My recollections are of a beautiful evening, and of a run in at 1500 feet toward the Woodstock Road. We crossed the airfield boundary; I glanced back at the pilot, received the thumbs up, and climbed out on to the wing with right hand across the chest holding the ripcord and left arm holding the forward edge of the door. I stepped off backwards, left hand came across to achieve symmetry (banana position), arched hard and watched the aircraft seemingly rise away, counted a rather brisk three seconds then pulled. The opening was smooth and on heading and I landed in front of the control tower with much satisfaction. I jumped again a couple of weeks later, then followed an enforced break as I was detached for two months to the School of Physical Training at St Athan on my Senior Trade Management course. Although I was unable to parachute for a few months, the benefits of this interlude were significant both in terms of trade qualifications and in personal performance. The course was run by Flight Sergeant Stan McCabe, who was to become highly influential in my thinking. He was fanatical about his job and a consummate professional. Under his guidance not only did I consolidate a high level of physical fitness but, more importantly, I came to adopt his training ethos which was to underpin my whole career.

The following year 1960 provided my chance for a breakthrough, in that opportunities had arisen for staff members to be trained in freefall techniques. There was now a Special Forces training requirement, and PTS had to quickly adapt to the task. The previous year (the then) Flying Officers Peter Hearn http://www.amazon.co.uk/Parachutist-Peter-Hearn/dp/0709154135 and John Thirtle, along with Flight Sergeants Alf Card and Tommy Moloney, had attended a freefall course at the French Airborne Depot (BETAP) in Pau and they formed the instructor cadre back at Abingdon. This time, as opposed to 1954, the benefits were immediate and permanent. Freefall was now firmly on the PTS agenda. From our point of view, although the opportunities to jump were there, parachutes were still in relatively short supply and training sorties were tagged on to the end of static line programmes. One needed persistence and a willingness to extend one's working hours to make progress. By now our main jump aircraft was the Beverley, exits being made from the freight bay port and starboard doors whilst the jumps were observed by the directing staff from the boom aperture. I made first my service freefall jump in January of that year, another three-second delay this time from 2500 feet.Dropping speed was about 110 mph, twice that of the Tiger Moth, and the side door exit technique had to be mastered. First time out of the starboard door, facing forward, again in the regulation banana position with both arms in, I turned and rolled simultaneously and, courtesy of my fashionably tinted goggles, found myself after a couple of seconds upside down in a yellow world. Two jumps later I was trusted to take my hand off the handle and open out in a conventional spread position and hold it for five seconds. On my fourth jump I nailed the exit; pivot with the leading shoulder angled into the airflow and just the right degree of push from the front leg. My logbook then showed a four-month gap during which time I was heavily engaged working on the floor with basic and TA courses and the Brigade exercise in Cyprus. I had a further break, on the Kenya detachment, but by September I had managed to fit in fourteen freefall descents, could hold a stable position, turn, and was cleared for 20 second delays. My final free fall of the year was a Battle of Britain demo at Halton. The logbook entry was "17 September 1960, Number 1 stick of 3. 4,000 feet. Opening on altimeter 1500 feet." First demo completed, I knew that this was to be my way forward.

# Chapter 2 | *Trials*

*1961*

I returned from the Boscombe detachment three days before the Christmas stand down, and worked a further three months on the floor. In February I took a section of WRAF parachute packers from Upper Heyford on a two-jump balloon course, with Flight Lieutenant Stan Roe as the Course officer. I was told that these were the first female jumpers to be trained at the School since the war. My personal breakthrough came in March when I was moved from Basic Training Squadron onto trials flight under Flight Lieutenant Peter Hearn. John Thirtle was in charge of freefall training flight, already taking the SAS on basic courses, with Tommy Moloney as Flight Sergeant. We lost Alf Card, who had been posted to Akrotiri on the NEAF Rescue Team, and with him a lot of experience. Alf was a great character, the only man I ever saw spotting from the Beverley door with his beret firmly pulled over his ears. Alf was the total enthusiast, always willing to help, advise and encourage. His career as a jumper, and indeed in the Air Force, ended in 1963 when he suffered a badly broken leg following a canopy collision on a simple stick of three static line jump on to the Akrotiri Ladies Mile DZ. Alf was highly influential during the formative years of freefall at PTS from 1954 through to 1961 and his contribution should never be underestimated.http://www.telegraph.co.uk/news/obituaries/1394095/Flight-Sergeant-Alfred-Card. html Pete Denley and Keith Teesdale, of the Kidlington Club, had been posted; Norman Hoffman remained at Shawbury, Geordie and Jake were still at Boscombe, but the training tempo accelerated unabated. We had a lot of catching up to do.

There were three of us coming through the system on trials flight; Dave Francombe, Snowy Robertson and myself. We had all been cleared to jump from 5,000 feet and began our progression training acting as supernumerary instructors to the SAS courses now arriving at PTS. I knew Snowy very well; we had played football together for the station team and for Transport Command as well as for Abingdon Town for the last four years. Snowy was what is usually referred to euphemistically as an extremely competitive midfielder, as well as a useful 400 metre runner, and we became close friends. Service football in those days was at a very high standard as many junior professionals were doing National Service. Brian Clough had just left Watchet, Tony Macedo, the Fulham keeper, was playing in our London League, whilst at Abingdon we had Ron Atkinson, later to become manager at Manchester United, playing midfield for us.

From the beginning of 1961, however, football became a secondary consideration and I set my mind to learning my new trade. The AFF type coaching, which we now take as a matter of course, was still far into the future in the UK, and, the exits apart, our descents were largely unobserved. We jumped at every available opportunity, pooled our information and shared it with our students. It was a steep learning curve. Over the course of another ten jumps, through trial, error and self-critique the three of us were all cleared to make 45 second delays from 9,000 feet. (At that time, 9,000 feet was the maximum altitude we were allowed by the RAF, the aviation medics fearing we would all succumb to anoxia if we went any higher. It was not until March of the following year that we were given clearance to 12,000 feet). All basic techniques had to be mastered. We taught ourselves upper body turns and leg turns. We lost stability, we regained position, and tried again. We taught ourselves a delta position, which we then finessed into an aerofoil track. We practised what was then termed a Canarrozzo position (no lift dive) after the Italian show jumper of that name, head down, body straight, arms crossed over the chest, legs wide apart. We pulled out of a Canarrozzo into a track and marvelled at the exhilarating speed and lift we could achieve.

We studied books of the period, "*Birdman*" by Leo Valentin, http://www.britishpathe.com/workspaces/birdman/leo-valentin

and "*Chute Libre*" by the French camera jumper André Suire. http://
www. priceminister. com/mfp/12830/chute-libre-suire-andre#pid=
161244955 Geordie Charlton returned from the 1960 WPC with a
rare prize, a 1956 Russian skydiving manual, translated into German
as "*Sportsprünge mit dem Fallschirm*".http://www.abe books.co.uk/
Sportsprünge-Fallschirm-Theoretische-Grundlagen-Fallschirms
portes-Anwendung/5765613124/bd, We watched 16mm movies of
the French jumpers at their National Centre in Biscarosse,
immaculate in white jumpsuits putting together an eight-way above
the woods fringing their drop zone on the coastal Landes of
southwestern France.http://patrimoine-memoire.aviation-civile.
gouv.fr/flb/04-02_Biscarosse-memoire-parachutisme-civile/files/
assets/basic-html/toc. html.

We absorbed as much information as was available, from whatever
source, tried out techniques, discarded, adopted or adapted them,
and after a couple of months or so, could claim to be comfortable in
our aerial environment.

In 1961 there was no formation skydiving in the UK, although the
French were already well versed in *vol relatif.* Our first exposure to this
new discipline came from the Golden Knights US Army Parachute
Display Team, in the form of a baton pass. One jumper would exit
with a twelve-inch wooden relay baton, which he would pass to a
colleague in freefall, thus demonstrating manoeuvrability, closing
and docking techniques. The Golden Knights came over to the UK in
1961 and Gerry Borquin successfully exchanged a baton with SAS
jumper Pete Sherman, from an Auster 9 over Middle Wallop. The first
all-British baton pass was on 18th July 1961 at Weston on the Green,
made by Peter Hearn and John Thirtle, jumping from a Beverley at
7,000 feet. Thereafter, we all tried it out, but practise time was limited
as team display techniques began to take precedence.

Inevitably, our main influence came from across the Channel.
The French had a formidable parachuting history. They had had a
parachutist licensing system in place since 1936 and, to put their
expertise into context, a full twelve years before Geordie and Jake
had jumped from 21,000 feet at Everleigh, Leo Valentin had

established a world record with a jump from 22,000 feet without personal oxygen. At that time, in 1948, the Brits were still falling off backwards from miscellaneous Tiger Moths at 1500 feet. In 1949, the French had established a new National Parachute Centre at St Yan, relocated to Biscarosse in 1952, and in the same year had also opened two regional centres. All these initiatives were backed by Government money. We were aware, from experience at World Meets, that the Soviets also were technically much further advanced than ourselves but Eastern bloc information was closely guarded. So it was to the French that we turned and, as we have already heard, four PTS instructors had attended a BETAP military course eighteen months previously. Over the next few years, several of us were to travel to French centres to improve our skills and extend our knowledge, more of which in a later chapter.

The parachute assemblies we used were manufactured by Irvin GB Ltd, with the factory then based in Letchworth. Most of the canopies were unmodified 28ft flat circular, white X-types. Whilst we were totally familiar with these, and they were fine for training, they were of little use when it came to competition or display jumping when landing precision was an absolute pre-requisite. They were gradually becoming replaced by the single blank gore canopy, which could at least be pointed in one direction, and had an airspeed of about 5 mph. The history of the blank gore canopy is worth almost a chapter of its own. The 1960 blank gore had its origins back in the early fifties and was used by the British team at the 1954 World Parachute Championships. Designed by GQ for static line use, this contraption was a flat circular 28ft canopy with one complete gore removed right up to the apex. This allowed internal air pressure to escape, thus eliminating oscillation. It also had the side effect of giving the canopy an inherent airspeed of about 5mph. In its original configuration, as then used, it was pretty ineffective as an accuracy canopy as the blank gore was positioned at two o'clock, in the forward right quadrant of the canopy, in accordance with its original purpose of cutting down drift for a static line jumper. It was consequently virtually impossible to steer in any useful direction. This configuration was subsequently modified to a three-quarter cut and the blank gore re-positioned at six o'clock. Control lines were fitted, with small rings as toggles, and it was brought into service at PTS in 1960 as our first steerable canopy. We were still jumping them at least up to the end of 1962.

A sleeved deployment system was standard. Originally, freefall canopies had been packed in the container with the extractor parachute, and were deployed canopy-first, which of course led to severe opening shock at terminal velocity. The sleeve was introduced into Great Britain by Jake McLoughlin, then at Boscombe Down. In 1958 Jake was the only PJI member, in fact the only Service member, of the British team for the Fourth WPC held at Bratislava, in the erstwhile Czechoslovakia. Sleeves had been used by the Russians at least as far back as 1954, but it was not until Jake brought one back to this country that they became adopted by a British manufacturer. The first company he approached turned him down flat, saying a parachute would never open with a sleeved deployment. http://www.parachutehistory.com/process/deployment/sleeve.html. Irvins, however, recognised the concept and copied the sleeve exactly from the Czech pattern. Initially the sleeves were unattached, drifted free on opening, and had to be retrieved from the surrounding countryside. Soon thereafter they were attached by a retaining line with no adverse effect on deployment or on performance.

There was also an issue with the positioning of the ripcord handle. Classically, this had always been on the left side of the harness, which made sense as it was better protected and also gave maximum leverage. This positioning dictated the closed (banana) exit body position taught by the French on the early short delays. There was always a strong tendency to roll in this position. To improve stability whilst still retaining a grip on the handle on exit, we experimented with the handle repositioned on the right, the so-called outboard pull. Now initial jumps could be made with the elbows extended to give more lift to the upper body whilst the legs were positioned wide apart. For experienced jumpers the handle position remained according to personal preference, but by early next year, we had standardised this to positioning on the right. This became adopted by Irvins, and by 1964 had also become standard on American-manufactured sport assemblies. As with many innovations this idea was not without precedent, as early as 1948 Willans had jumped freefall with the handle on the right because of the obstruction imposed by a high-mounted reserve.

With regard to instruments, a stopwatch was considered essential, and was indeed mandatory at PTS at the time. We had tables which gave distance fallen each second in a flat stable spread to terminal velocity and beyond; from these we worked backwards from an opening height of 2,000 feet. The stopwatch was originally regarded as our main instrument, with small two-inch diameter Casella mountaineering altimeters as a backup. Both instruments were mounted in small pockets on the top of the side pull Irvin reserve. The Casellas were virtually unreadable in freefall and were rapidly discarded in favour of aircraft altimeters – Mk 17a's – which were already in common use by all sport jumpers. The requirement for a stopwatch persisted however for many years, mounted alongside the altimeter on a metal plate.

In mid-June our work was suddenly brought into extremely sharp focus with the establishment of a Royal Air Force parachute display team, and the directive that this team was to make its official debut at the Society of British Aircraft Constructors (SBAC) Farnborough Air Show in September. Many matters remained to be resolved: what should be the display format? How many in the team? How could we guarantee landing accuracy onto a restricted area? How were opening and exit points to be determined? These were the major issues to be addressed, and time was getting short. Our most experienced jumpers at the time were the directing staff – Flight Lieutenants Hearn and Thirtle and Flight Sergeant Tommy Moloney. In contention for a team place were the rest of trials flight – Sgts Stan Phipps, Brian Jones, Paul Hewitt, George Hill, Dave Francombe, Snowy and myself.

Early indications were not propitious, as a June rehearsal at Farnborough did not go well. The exit point, as determined by the forecast winds, was incorrect and the jumpers were scattered widely, nobody made the designated target area. The single blank gore canopies were plainly lacking sufficient drive to compensate for a bad spot. Things had to change, and our very participation in the big show in September remained unconfirmed. Maybe I was fortunate not to be involved on this sortie, as John Thirtle, Dave Francombe and myself were over in Germany competing in the European Championships.

The first issue to be addressed was the spot. In the sport jumping world, the opening point was determined by throwing a wind drift indicator (WDI) at opening height directly over the target, noting its landing point then running in the requisite distance past the target on the reciprocal. We also had to reckon with the then little understood phenomenon of freefall drift. In those days, drift from altitude was compensated for (by those in the know) by tracking to the opening point. Those who were not in the know were frequently confronted by a long walk back to the clubhouse, trying to work out what went wrong. The WDI was fine for normal club jumping, but was simply not possible at a major air show. The difficulty at Farnborough was that each event had a precise time-slot and there was no allowance for the Beverley to remain in the circuit at 2,000 feet for an extra couple of minutes to see where the streamer landed. Our experience in June had highlighted the inadequacies of a met. forecast, so we made our own local arrangements. The DZ party were equipped with met. balloons and theodolite, and radioed up the actual wind readings from surface to exit height at 30 minutes and 10 minutes prior to drop. Freefall drift was calculated, and the exit point was laid off from the opening point accordingly. All these details were copied onto two air photographs in the Beverley, one for the navigator and one for the jumpers. Major credit for this innovation must go to Ron Ellerbeck, who used a slide rule to transcribe the balloon readings into distances and bearings. The responsibility for spotting the aircraft was solely in the hands of the navigator, from his position forward in the nose. At that time we were also given a dedicated aircrew, who flew us on all shows and rehearsals.

Next issue was the canopies. Our single blanks were woefully inadequate, with an airspeed of maybe 5mph and a corresponding opening zone radius at best of 200 metres. We learned at the time that the SAS team were also scheduled to jump at Farnborough and that they would be using TU canopies from Irvins (marked experimental). http://www.parachutehistory.com/round/combo.html. This canopy modification, albeit still in a 28ft flat circular, gave an airspeed approaching 10mph with a corresponding increase in opening zone radius to 400 metres. The rate of descent was also increased, but remained acceptable. We rapidly obtained permission to purchase the same, and took delivery about four weeks before the show. With these canopies we were totally confident that we could achieve the landing accuracy which was the first pre-requisite of a successful parachute demonstration. The landing area at Farnborough was a triangular stretch of grass some 200 metres long and 80 metres at its widest, about 150 metres from the crowd line. We marked out a similar area at Weston with tape, with the (then) ten-metre diameter accuracy sand pit in the centre. This was our private DZ from now on.

Concomitant with an accurate group landing, the second requirement was to demonstrate control and movement in freefall to the spectators some two miles below. We were all able to track fast and far, and we had already ensured that our movement across the sky could be traced by a stream of French chalk released from zipped bags attached to our ankles. John Thirtle came up with the idea of a tight linked group exit from the Beverley tailgate to build up a thick chalk trail to be held for twenty seconds, then for us to break and track outwards for ten seconds which would give a spectacular bomb-burst effect. The movement would be further enhanced by the group then turning in the track and converging on the opening point and pulling at two thousand feet. To this end, early in July, we started experimenting with linked exit techniques. We started with groups of three, with the centre man on his back, an idea which, although hilarious to jump, was quickly discarded as impractical for our purpose. We then went to fours and fives, all facing forward which worked, albeit with some spectacular funnels. By the middle of

August we were making clean sill exits in a forward facing line of six, arms locked and the whole group flying stable. Six was the maximum number that could stand in line on the Beverley tailgate. The Big Six* was born… . By the end of the month we had taken delivery of our new TU canopies, Jake McLoughlin was posted in from Boscombe and we felt we were in business. The selected team was Hearn, Thirtle, Moloney, McLoughlin, Snowy Robertson and myself.

Although there were only six jumpers, the Beverley freight bay was quite crowded. On the two minute call, we ducked under the lashing tape strung at waist height and linked arms with feet poised for the step-off. Kneeling in front of us were three assistants, one helper for each two jumpers, whose job it was to unzip the chalk bags on the red light and to start the stopwatches on the green. The AQM (loadmaster) was hanging to one side, halfway up the bars on the wall. It was his job to co-ordinate the exit by giving the GO signal on the navigator's green. Such was the novelty there were invariably at least half a dozen photographers straining on their safety belts. The exit at 9,000 feet was a step backwards, arch, and try immediately to lock legs. We held on for the full twenty seconds, which took us down to 6,000 feet, broke on time and tracked outwards for ten seconds, turned in the track for the opening point and opened at 2,000 feet on altimeter. My logbook shows nine group six exits in total before the show, three of which were carried out at Farnborough itself. The final rehearsal was at Weston on 1st September 1961, group exit in six from 9,000 feet for Pathe News. We used Pains Wessex orange smoke canisters on this occasion, although chalk bags still continued in use for some time.

The SBAC Farnborough Air Show opened for us on Tuesday 5th September. Cloud restricted us to 3,000 feet, we jumped side door sim. 3s and all made the area. We jumped again on the Thursday and Friday, from 4,500 and 5,000 feet respectively. Although we were disappointed we could not demonstrate the high show, it was nevertheless useful experience and confirmed our canopy handling

---

* Coined during training. Groups of three, four and five, leading up to the "Big" six.

capabilities. Saturday 9th September was the first open day, the weather was brilliant and in front of an estimated audience of 120,000 we performed the bomb burst from 9,000 feet. Two and a half minutes after stepping from the sill our six white canopies were overlapping the orange target cross in the middle of the triangle. This was the culmination of eight months hard work and was one hell of a buzz. It was my 72nd jump. Next day, Sunday, we were restricted to 7,000 feet, but still put in the bomb burst and were all on target.

We jumped together for the rest of the season, giving demonstrations at Abingdon and at Cranwell. On 15th December we flew out to the French Airborne parachute school (BETAP) in Pau, with the Command rugby team who had an away fixture there. In the morning, we jumped from 8,000 feet on to their DZ from the Beverley as a five group, our linked exit arousing only a mild curiosity from our French Army counterparts. That afternoon their team jumped from the Nord Atlas into the downtown rugby stadium prior to kick-off. It was a perfect day, wall-to-wall blue, and the team of six came streaking out of the sky from 10,000 feet trailing chalk, heading for the far end of the stadium. The DZ party lit a smoke flare, showing a 180-degree wind shift. From about 5,000 feet, the formation swept round in the track and hurtled for the new opening point on the upwind edge. They smoked it down to about 1200 feet and landed their EFA 653 single T blank gore canopies in the centre of the pitch. All, that is, save one who opened a little lower and finished up on the road outside the stadium only to be triumphantly escorted back inside by a couple of gendarmes who had halted all the traffic to ensure him a safe landing. This was a demo *par excellence* from our mentors, but, in display techniques at least, we felt we were now not too far behind them.

Although trials flight had been fully occupied all season, Peter Hearn actively encouraged us to build up experience by jumping outside the PTS environment. Pete had already competed at international level and recognised the value of our learning to spot and to improve our accuracy under canopy. In consequence, throughout the year, I spent whatever spare time I had jumping out at Kidlington. I entered for the National Championships, held there in May, and as a result was selected along with Dave Francombe for the British junior team at the European Championships to be held in Germany the following month. John Thirtle and Jake were in the senior team. Three weeks later the four of us flew out, courtesy of Transport Command, to the competition venue at Leutkirch, a small town in the Allgäu region of southern Bavaria. The airfield was situated a couple of miles to the north of the town where we found a grass strip, control tower, a couple of hangars and an absolutely immaculate Flying Club. The airstrip was dominated by a steep wooded hillside to the northwest, on the slopes of which stood the ancestral castle of Schloss Zeil, home to the Flying Club patron, the Duke of Waldburg-Zeil. Bavarian cattle chewed the cud in the neighbouring meadows, to the accompaniment of clanging cowbells, whilst some forty miles away the Bavarian Alps ascended on the southern horizon. A more tranquil and picturesque setting for a drop zone it would be hard to imagine. It was a relatively small competition, with seven teams entered – France, Italy, Austria, Switzerland, Germany, the UK and an American Special Forces team.

The aircraft in use were three two-seater Piper Cubs from the Burda Advertising and Publishing Company, the *Burda Staffel*, each of which carried one jumper. The main jumpship was a German Army H 34 Sikorsky helicopter. Before the first round started one of the local jumpers acted as drifter (*windspringer*), using a Kohnke triangular canopy with a blank gore. My first jump was from one of the Cubs, running in at 1600 feet. I remember it particularly as being the first using a parachute I had packed myself. This was on the mats in C hangar and had been checked (I felt in somewhat cursory fashion) by Jake the previous weekend. On jump run any misgivings evaporated and I hopped off the strut quite happily. I landed inside the 25 metre scoring circle 2 metres from the target centre. The canopy had a double blank modification, adequate for the light wind conditions which prevailed throughout. We all made five jumps each and, whilst not in the medals, managed to finish in the top ten individuals. I was to return to Leutkirch again in a couple of years, to complete unfinished business. Next month in July we entered a three-way competition against the SAS and the US Army Golden Knights at Hereford racecourse. Pete Hearn distinguished himself jumping a C9 double L canopy and scored 1.3 metres on the first jump and 0. 76 metres on the second. This, on a homemade parachute onto a hard target, was a British accuracy record in 1961. The boss was leading from the front.

The year had also seen a significant development in the wider organisation of sport parachuting in the UK. Early that year the British Parachute Association had been formed, emerging from the previous Royal Aero Club Parachuting Committee. This committee first convened in February of 1959, under the chairmanship of Dumbo Willans http://www.independent.co.uk/news/obituaries/ terence-willans-6161561. html. Jake and I had travelled down to London in his vintage Morris Minor convertible to attend a couple of these meetings. In those days you could just drive down to central London and park on virtually any kerbside. The first chairman of the new BPA was Mike Reilly, who had been the leading light in the sport since 1958 when he first represented Great Britain at the WPC in Bratislava. Mike competed also in Bulgaria 1960 and organised and jumped at the British National trials in Thruxton (1960) and the National Championships at Kidlington. http://www.amazon. co.uk/Alone-sky-Mike-Reilly/dp/B0000CLMRU.

The SAS had formed their own freefall team, under the leadership of the CO, Colonel Dare Wilson, and had already qualified several HALO jumpers with American Special Forces at Fort Bragg in North Carolina. They had also sent jumpers to the French centre at Chalon-sur-Saône for basic and advanced civilian training. Several of their jumpers coming through PTS early in 1961 had over 100 freefalls to their credit. The year 1961, in short, was the year in which everything started to come together, on the military scene and also on the civilian sport front.

1. *PTS C Hangar 1958. Slide landing trainers.*      *Crown Copyright*

2. *Flight Swing Trainers.*      *Crown Copyright*

3.  *Static Balloon.*

4. *Blackburn Beverley Exits* c. 1960.                    *Crown Copyright*

5. *British Skydivers team Thruxton 1959. Left to right: Norman Hoffman, Jake McLoughlin, Dennis Lee, Geordie Charlton, Mike McArdle. Note Norman, Jake and Dennis are wearing American B4 assemblies with 2-shot Capewell releases. Geordie and Mike have Irvin assemblies. All have handles positioned on the left (cross pull). Note also altimeter plates mounted on the reserves. Dennis has a Mk 17A aircraft altimeter fitted with tube into reserve flap to measure static pressure.*

**6.** *PTI Senior Trade Management Course, RAF St Athan 1959. I am back row first left, Stan McCabe is front row seated first left. Other PJIs are Norman Pilling, back row extreme right and Red Summers, middle row second left. Seated front row second right is Flt. Lt. Bill Roden, later on the staff at No 1 PTS, who tragically lost his life in the Hastings crash at Toot Baldon in 1965.*

**7.** *Waiting to emplane in the Beverley at RAF Abingdon in 1960. Self, John Thirtle back to camera, Graham Micklewright, Geoff Watters with X type parachute, Alf Card, Peter Hearn (half hidden behind Alf).*

29

**8.** *Abingdon Town FC 1960. Snowy is second right front row, I am third left back row (goalkeeper). PJI Jesse Pye is centre front row.*

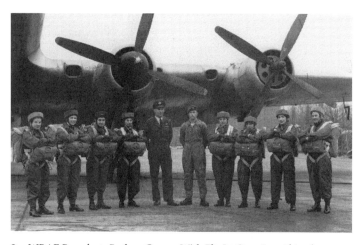

**9.** *WRAF Parachute Packers Course. With Flt. Lt. Stan Roe, Abingdon February 1961. Note standard issue sorbo rubber jump helmets.*

*Crown Copyright*

10.  *Pete Sherman (left) with Gerry Borquin, USA Golden Knights.*
*First UK baton pass over Army Aviation Centre, Middle Wallop 1961.*
*Photo courtesy Pete Sherman*

11.  *Royal Air Force Parachute Display Team 1961.  Hearn, Moloney, Self,*
*McLoughlin, Robertson, Thirtle. PTS C Hangar RAF Abingdon.*

**12.**  *Original GQ Single Blank canopy in freefall mode. Note position of the blank gore.*

**13.** *Peter Hearn, briefing George Hill and Stan Phipps on board the Beverley, 1961.*

**14.** *RAF Team, Beverley tailgate exit. French Airborne School DZ Pau, December 1961.*

**15.** *With Snowy, Jake and Dave Francombe (kneeling). French Airborne School Pau, December 1961.*

**16.** *John Thirtle waiting to emplane in the German Army H34 Sikorsky. European Parachute Championships Leutkirch, June 1961. Les Howe is sitting in the foreground.*

**17.** *French Army Team with EFA 653 canopies. Stadium demo Pau December 1961.*

18. *Kohnke Triangular blank gore canopy. Windspringer at Leukirch 1961.*

# Chapter 3

# *The Sorcerer's Apprentice*

*1962–1963*

I first met James Edward McLoughlin at A&AEE Boscombe Down in the winter of 1960 when on detachment from PTS as part of the team evaluating the replacement X Type canopy. It was Jake who helped me out after my quarter-mile dragging episode through the Everleigh ovine ejectamenta, mentioned in Chapter One; a small kindness which was much appreciated at the time. I was there when he jumped with Geordie Charlton through cloud from 21,000 feet a week later, landing on target in the middle of Everleigh DZ on a grey cold December afternoon. Snowy was with me, and we examined the freefall equipment, the thermal gear and the modified canopies with professional curiosity, and returned to PTS with a renewed respect for these two parachuting masters. Jake was one of the true parachuting pioneers. He went through No 1 PTS, then at Upper Heyford, in 1950 before moving to Boscombe Down on the trials team; had completed an advanced freefall course at Chalon under the tutelage of Sam Chasak; had represented Great Britain at the 1958 World Parachute Championships, and had spent three months at Woomera assisting GQ on the Folland Gnat ejector seat trials. Later in 1958 he made two live ejections from a modified Gloster Meteor at Netheravon as part of the same project. We next met the following summer when Jake was posted in to PTS to augment the Trials team and the Display team. Jake was noted for an inexhaustible

37

stock of one-liners, which he frequently employed, mostly to keep Snowy in his place. Prior to the Leutkirch competition, he loaned me a rig and gave me a couple of packing lessons. We returned from the trip together and from then onwards worked virtually in tandem. My apprenticeship was under way.

Following the Farnborough shows, Jake had suggested we should restart the parachute club at Kidlington, which had lapsed when Alf Card and Keith Teesdale were posted. This sounded like a great idea to me, and, at the end of September, we drove down to the airfield to meet Battle of Britain ace pilot Tim Vigors, who was running the Piper agency on the airfield. Tim had one parachute jump to his credit, having baled out from his Brewster Buffalo fighter in northern Malaya in 1941. During the descent he was strafed by attacking Japanese aircraft and took a bullet through the thigh. Despite this unfortunate introduction to the game, he retained sufficient enthusiasm for parachuting to listen to us sympathetically and agreed to lease us a building on the airfield to act as kit store/classroom. We also came to an agreement to use one of his Piper Tri-Pacers as a jump aircraft. Jake and I pooled our slender resources and bought six American government surplus B4 containers with C9 canopies, which we modified to double blank gores for student use. Our static line system was a normal freefall rig with the 4-pin ripcord removed and the container held closed by 50lb ties threaded through the cones and tied round the static line. Temporary pins were inserted and removed on the flightline check. This break-tie system with sleeve deployment was to remain in use until 1974. In order to project a more professional personal image, we bought ourselves new French jumpsuits and parachute boots from the Au Fanion equipment store in Paris. We were ready to go.

Jake and I had christened the new Club "British Skydivers Parachute School." The British Skydivers team leader, Norman Hoffman, had been posted back in to PTS and I had now been elected to the erstwhile Thruxton based team. At the same time, I purchased my own personal rig from an outfit called Volume Sales based in California. With the end of the Korean War, there were thousands of aircrew parachutes on the market, and the cost to me was £10.00 including shipping. For that outlay I received a brand new 28ft C9 aircrew canopy, candy striped 1.1oz ripstop nylon, in an olive green B4 container. I modified the canopy myself by carefully cutting out two gores, five gores apart, from the rear of the canopy. The gores were removed up to 40 inches from the apex, leaving the high-pressure area intact. I then cut out an 18-inch bar between these five gores at the periphery, and two 18-inch turning windows outboard of the blank gores. The edges were reinforced by tape, and steering lines attached to the outside suspension line of each turning window. This gave me a five gore TU canopy with an airspeed of about 10mph, and descent rate of about 20 feet per second. http://www.parachutehistory.com/round/combo.html. I spent a further £5.00 on a sleeve, plus another five on a T7a 24ft side pull reserve. I had reserve D rings installed and was ready to go. One important feature of these American freefall rigs was that they all featured Capewell canopy releases, which were designed for aircrew to cut away the canopy if they were being dragged after landing. http://www.capewell.com/capewell-releases.

The parachuting year of 1962 did not start well. In the first month we had two high-profile fatalities. On the tenth of January, BPA Chairman Mike Reilly himself was drowned in the English Channel. He was jumping from a B17 Flying Fortress as a stunt double for Robert Wagner in the film "The War Lover", starring Steve McQueen. On hitting the water his canopy remained inflated and Mike drowned as a result of dragging; his rig was not equipped with Capewells. Four of us attended his funeral at a little country church in deepest Surrey. He was twenty-nine years old. http://www.flightglobal.com/pdfarchive/view/1962/1962%20-%200078.html. On the thirtieth of the same month Peter Hearn, Snowy and myself were on a liaison visit to Boscombe Down. It was a pretty gloomy January afternoon, with the cloud base down to about fifteen hundred feet. Before returning to PTS later that afternoon, we heard rumours of a parachute fatality in the area, involving the SAS team. There was simultaneously a complete news blackout from Hereford and it was not until two days later that the facts emerged. A team of eight SAS jumpers had taken off in a Handley Page Dart Herald from Boscombe to attempt a new British altitude record. Under the leadership of Dare Wilson, they left the aircraft at a height of 34,350 feet, with personal oxygen bottles, jumping on to Imber DZ. Problems arose with icing of goggles and altimeters and Keith Norry, who had over two hundred descents at the time, failed to arrive at the RV. He was found on the ground shortly afterwards, with neither his main nor his reserve handle pulled. The Board of Inquiry was unable to establish any specific cause of the accident, whilst the rest of the parachuting world could only surmise the factors involved. I knew Keith from his course at Abingdon, he now lies at rest in Tidworth military cemetery and each year I join his remaining teammates there in a brief remembrance ceremony. There was, in fact, an ironic connection between these two accidents in that Colonel Wilson took over from Mike Reilly as BPA Chairman and was himself to prove a highly influential figure in the organisation and development of the sport between 1962 and 1966.

On a less tragic note, a few weeks later in March, Geordie Charlton suffered a potentially career threatening injury. Geordie was involved in clearing the Beaver for freefall, using the Everleigh DZ. The area was criss-crossed by tank tracks, some of them two feet deep. It was also frozen solid and snow covered. Unbelievably, the target cross had been placed over some of these tank tracks and Geordie, naturally, in a fifteen knot wind was fine-tuning his accuracy. He landed backwards on target and smashed his right ankle landing in the trench. Complications ensued, and he was not to jump again until June of the following year. At that time, Crown indemnity precluded his taking action for damages, and it was not until much later that the Crown Proceedings (Armed Forces) Act of 1987 permitted such claims to be made. Today, he could well have had a case for substantial compensation. Ever the parachuting fanatic, he had spent most of his hospital time at Halton learning Russian so he could read their parachuting manuals on accuracy and style techniques. He regained full jumping fitness and started his comeback on the British Skydivers demo at Hucknall, more of which later.

Jake and I spent all our spare weekends running the Kidlington operation, which had opened with a jumping programme on the first of October the previous year. Our first students were three officers from the Royal Horse Guards, one of whom was the Lord Patrick Beresford, who was later to serve with No 1 (Guards) Independent Parachute Company and No 22 SAS. We trained all our students using the B4 containers with the double blank gore canopies. We started off using the Tri Pacers as jump aircraft, but toward the middle of the year we were offered the use of an eight place de Havilland DH 84 Dragon – the forerunner of the DH 89 Rapide. This was a venerable machine indeed, with an historic aircraft plaque attached to the forward bulkhead dated 1934. We also used this machine for static line students, as well as most of our demos. Film work, demos and training kept us busy during all our spare time for the rest of the season and all the money we earned was spent on training jumps and kit.

Back at the day job, spare time was at a premium as we still had a full training, trials and demo commitment at PTS. There had been a couple of changes, John Thirtle had been posted and Flight Lieutenant Peter Williams had taken his place as deputy leader. Also on board now as a regular was Paul Hewitt. On the second of February, having finally received altitude clearance, we made our first jump at Weston from 12,000 feet. We were also conducting freefall trials with new carrying straps for the Bergen. In March we went across to Netheravon to clear the Single Pioneer for jumping and get in some spotting practise, using the Everleigh DZ. This particular day was enlivened by the appearance of the Boscombe based Drop Zone Safety Officer (DZSO), a non-freefall jumper, who appeared round the side of the hangar to give the DZ brief wearing a jumpsuit, aircrew gloves, a yellow scarf and flying boots, with aircrew goggles pushed up on his forehead. Unbelievable…. In April we were still practising our "big six" exits from the Beverley sill. We could by now guarantee stability and were working on turning and tracking the group. This demo format was to stand us in good stead right until August, when the Argosy superseded the Beverley and we were forced to bid the Big Six a reluctant farewell.

At the end of April the Display Team were scheduled to give a demonstration at the Goodwood motor racing circuit on Easter Monday. The previous week, and at the same venue, the British National Parachute Championships were to be held. This was solely an accuracy competition, with the added incentive that the winners would represent Great Britain at the sixth World Parachute Championships to be held in August at Orange, Massachusetts. The RAF team was Tommy Moloney, Jake McLoughlin, Norman Hoffman, Brian Clark-Sutton and myself. Our main rivals were the SAS team and an invited US Army team. It proved to be a big wake up call for us all. Sufficient to say that the SAS took the team event and as a result were selected to go to the WPC. Our only slight consolation was that Geordie Charlton, still injured, was asked to go to Orange as team coach. Not to be completely outdone, however, Norman, Jake and Tommy decided to compete in Orange as the Irish team, more of which later. On Easter Monday, we reverted to RAF mode and made a group demo from 12,000 feet prior to the start of the main event, a 42 lap Formula One race. For the record, the race was won by Graham Hill, but was sadly marred by the crash which ended the career of Stirling Moss.

For us, then, it was back to the drawing board for competition accuracy. Our main work in May was jumping the Twin and Single Pioneer aircraft at Weston. We were all given intensive spotting practise, particularly valuable for those team members without sport jumping experience. As it was also envisaged the Single Pioneer would be used as a demo platform, we used chalk bags for practise on one occasion. This operation was swiftly discontinued after Norman opened the bottom zip inside the aircraft at 9,000 feet before climbing out on to the strut. The whole aircraft interior was instantly engulfed with a swirling white chalk cloud that covered us all, pilot included, prior to a rapid exit (us). The pilot, whose entire instrument panel was obliterated, managed to wipe off sufficient chalk to make a landing, then to treat us to a rather succinct debrief. Even less impressed was the Junior Tech crewman whose job it then was to clean up the mess. A couple of jumps later, *sans* chalk, Snowy and I progressed to a double baton pass from 9,000 feet.

At the end of the month three of us flew up in the Single Pioneer to Speke Airport on Merseyside to give a demo at the SSAFA airshow. Jumpers were Tommy, myself, and Flight Lieutenant Peter Williams, deputy team leader to Peter Hearn. Squadron Leader Dick Mullins, Ron Ellerbeck and Geordie Charlton were running the DZ. This was the first time we had used a light aircraft on a demonstration jump, and protocol demanded that the team leader, in this case Peter, remained on headset in communication with the pilot. The opening point was determined by balloon and theodolite and instructions passed up to be transcribed onto the airphoto exactly as per the Beverley routine. Tommy was spotting, I was two, and Pete was in the back. Run in was at 4,500 feet, with an eight hundred metre opening point. It was to be an important learning experience for all of us. Tommy got out smack over the opening point and I dived out right after him. We opened at 2,000 feet and landed on the target, nearly knocking over the theodolite. Pete finished up landing about five hundred metres deep on the threshold of the runway, being strafed by a low-flying Avro Shackleton firing off distress flares. We lined up to be presented to the local Member of Parliament, the formidable Bessie Braddock. The lady was kept waiting until Pete was able to join us, whereupon Bessie delivered a witheringly apposite Scouse comment, much to Pete's discomfiture. On the debrief we discovered that as Tommy and I had dived out, Pete had unplugged his headset, donned his jumping helmet, stowed the map, climbed out onto the strut and made a classic poised exit a good fifteen seconds behind us. It was an important lesson for us all, in that the rigid protocols applicable to a large aircraft cannot be so easily transferred to what was essentially a sport parachuting civilian demo. It also led eventually to the team leader at the door being given an aircrew bone dome with headset and throat mike incorporated. Peter took it all on board and went on to become a highly proficient and popular team leader.

The demo season was with us now with a vengeance, both with the British Skydivers and also with our day job. On the eleventh of June the two converged, as both teams were booked to jump at Hucknall on the same show. Six of us flew up from Abingdon in the Beverley for the RAF team demo; Pete Hearn, Paul Hewitt, Snowy, Tommy, Jake and myself. Cloud base was low; we made a routine stick of six from 3,500 feet and landed as directed on the target crosses in the middle of the airfield, on the far side of the runway and some three hundred metres from the crowd line. Team line-up, salute into the distance, and on board the Landrover aiming for the tea tent. Ho hum. Once across the runway Jake, Tommy and myself made for the car park where Norman and Geordie Charlton were waiting in Norman's Ford Zephyr. They had driven up from Abingdon to meet us, bringing our white British Skydiver jumpsuits, smokes and personal civilian parachutes. Norman had booked a Rapide and we laid out the target cross about five metres from the crowd line. We took off, climbed to 4,500 feet in broken cloud and ran in parallel to and about four hundred metres behind the crowd. We exited in a close stick of five, each with smoke and swooped in low to hook turn and stand up in a line five metres out from the spectators. It was a great show and a great comeback for Geordie, who had been out injured for fifteen months. The crowd were volubly appreciative, and we "civilians" were compared most favourably against the RAF who had preceded us. Pete Hearn took it all in good part, bound as he was by Service protocol and lacking the flexibility afforded to us as free agents to choose our own landing area.

On the sixteenth of June we jumped at RAF Upavon at the Air Show to mark the 50th Anniversary of the formation there of the Royal Flying Corps. My logbook records a good high show, group of six from the Beverley sill and pinpoint accuracy. A week later we flew over to France for our very first overseas demo at the Rouen Air Show. We were one of several parachuting items on the programme, which, as well as the French Army team, included French professional demo jumpers Gil Delamare and Micheline Violin. The surface wind was gusting to twenty knots, the upper winds were forty plus, and all the French jumpers, relying on a wind streamer, missed the airfield entirely. Our balloon/theodolite system gave us both freefall and canopy drift, the sill exit was stable, the bomburst spectacular against a clear blue sky. The white TU s landed, albeit backwards and at speed, all around the target cross, much to the appreciation of the assembled multitude. Gil Delamare made it back to the target area in time for the photo opportunity; Tommy, ever the diplomat, asked the leading French professional of the day if he were a sport jumper, a question that, judging from the response, lost nothing in translation. We would also have wished to compare notes with our French military colleagues but they had unaccountably returned to Pau. The French evening reception at the City Hall was a fine occasion; the champagne flowed, and we were presented with a most impressive and unexpected trophy, awarded to the best display team of the show. We returned to PTS the next day, slightly hung over, but reasonably content with our first foray into the continental demo arena. The month ended with a flurry of activity at Kidlington with the whole Skydivers team involved in the making of a movie for the Central Office of Information and a couple of local demos.

Meanwhile, Norman, Jake and Tommy had recovered from the setback at the Nationals and had decided to enter the WPC in Orange anyway as the Irish team. They included a young Mike Turner, Royal Engineers, who had only seventy-odd jumps at the time. In order to raise funds for the trip, Norman had organised a parachute rally at a site known as Farmer's Cross, which was a large field about a couple of miles from the end of the main runway of Cork International Airport. We made the journey from Abingdon to Holyhead by train, then by ferry to Dún Laoghaire, and night stopped in Dublin before catching the train to Cork the following day. The party was Norman, Tommy, Jake, Dave Francombe, Mike Turner and myself, and we were greeted at the station by Freddy Bond, chairman and founder member of the Irish Parachute Club. Arriving at the airstrip the following morning we caught up with three jumpers from Austria who had travelled by rail from Vienna to Calais, Calais to Dover, Dover by rail to Fishguard, then by ferry to Rosslare, followed by a bus ride to Cork. True dedication indeed, carrying their parachute rigs for two days, fifteen hundred miles across Europe for the sake of one jump from an antiquated Auster 9... .

That was, in actuality, the deal. We arrived at the airstrip on the Sunday morning escorted by Irish Parachute Club members to find the hillside overrun by an estimated nine thousand crowd. To control the multitude, and vainly trying to collect car-parking fees, were two volunteer stewards equipped with bus conductors' leather satchels. To keep the crowd entertained the Club had booked three motorcycle stunt riders riding through specially constructed wire mesh tunnels covered with burning straw. As for sustenance there was nary a hot dog stand, nor coffee stall, in sight. Arousing equal interest were the three jump aircraft, two elderly Auster 9s and a vintage Tiger Moth. We had arrived about ten in the morning, the cloud base was down, it was raining, and the wind was a steady twenty-five knots. In between the wall of fire show, Norman also kept the crowd entertained by conducting an interview with one of the Irish female team members. By three in the afternoon, the motorcyclists had had enough, the straw had all burned away, and Norman had run out of jokes. With still no jumping, the multitude were becoming a little restless. Norman decided we had to get going, wind limits notwithstanding. We started the show with a formation mass drop from 4,000 feet, Norman in the lead Tiger Moth, with Jake and Tommy in one Auster and Mike Turner plus one of the Austrians in the other. Takeoff was delayed as the crowd were milling about all over the runway; they could only be dispersed by one of the Austers revving up and taxying toward them. The bus conductors were nowhere to be seen. As Dave and I kitted up, waiting for the second lift, we watched as the mass formation exited about one thousand metres deep. As soon as the chutes opened, the crowd surged toward the landing area, only parting reluctantly as the jumpers came in. Jake arrived over a moving circle of humanity, which scattered just in time to allow him to touch down next to a perambulator complete with infant, which had been left in the middle of the circle. Dave and I had a shouted conversation with Tommy to confirm the opening point and off we went. Four thousand feet, fifteen second delay and I managed to locate the target cross surrounded by the fans. In the event, I contrived to land closest to it and was duly declared the winner. "What's it like jumping from all those thousands of miles up in the sky mister?" inquired one earnest young local... .

We spent a most convivial evening in downtown Cork, enjoying unlimited Irish hospitality along with our Austrian colleagues, before leaving by car after midnight to catch the 08.00 ferry from Dublin on the Monday morning. No chance. Dave and I arrived at Dún Laoghaire just in time to see the stern of the vessel leaving port and I spent the rest of the day conducting a guided tour of the Irish capital for our new-found Austrian friends, which was probably more a magical mystery tour as it was my own first visit there. Dave and I arrived back at PTS twenty-four hours adrift. Pete Hearn took one look at us and stood us down for the rest of the day. He was that sort of boss.

Meanwhile, Snowy was out of action with an arm injury. He had previously dislocated his left shoulder parachuting, and one morning, after a fan landing demo, the shoulder popped from its socket again. I had to hold his arm while he shucked it back in. That evening we were scheduled for a training jump on the airfield and of course Snowy went for it. I followed him out from nine thousand feet, and was mildly surprised to see his canopy deploy ten seconds later at about eight thousand. His shoulder had come out again in freefall; he could no longer maintain stability so he had to pull and settle for a long ride down. Enough was enough, so Snowy had his operation and was back in action again later following his posting to the Far East. If that was high, Dave Francombe went a bit low on one occasion, also on the airfield. This year we decided to distinguish our jumping helmets by covering them with orange dayglow tape. It just so happened that some of the Beverley aircraft had their noses similarly painted. Murphy's law operated again as Dave, whose vision was not of the sharpest, came whistling down from nine thousand feet above the 47 Squadron dispersal pans and took it down to about twelve hundred. He later explained he thought he was watching the man in front and was waiting for him to pull... .

On 23rd August we first used the Argosy in the freefall role. I already had a few static line jumps from this aircraft, the first being previously in May, at Everleigh on PX canopy trials. Now into August the Argosy was taking over the role of the Beverley for the upcoming Farnborough show and we were working out a high show consisting of an out and back follow the leader track pattern from the side doors, reminiscent of the spectacular movement displayed by the French team in Pau the previous December. We now had eight jumpers and first performed this routine in public with a demo at Benson on 5th September. We followed up at the SBAC two days later, one high show on the seventh for the Press day and a low show on the Saturday for the public. Whilst professionally satisfying, these two shows evinced, for me anyway, a certain feeling of *déjà vu* compared with the high profile events and sense of achievement of the previous year. We reverted to the Beverley the following Saturday for a Battle of Britain low show at Biggin Hill.

The next day, Sunday sixteenth, Jake and I were out at Kidlington again jumping the Rapide. It was to be my last jump for six full months. We got out deep at 8,000 feet and set out to track back just for fun, I opened normally and, under my own 5 gore TU, hooked in rather low for landing. My left leg slid away from me on the wet grass, all my weight went over my left knee, and I finished up with a grade three medial collateral ligament tear. That was me out of the game for six months, four weeks of which I spent at Headley Court. When I returned to PTS I was put to work in the hangar stores whilst undertaking relentless rehab exercises to rebuild the quadriceps. As it happened, my personal parachuting was not greatly affected, as from Christmas onwards PTS virtually closed down because of one of the worst winters of the century. Courses were suspended and the instructors went on cross-country marches along the Ridgeway on the neighbouring Berkshire Downs. In early

January tragedy struck as on one of these marches Jack Drinkwater collapsed on the hill in deep snow and succumbed to a heart attack. The very next week we lost a second instructor who died playing badminton in the hangar. The Station Medical Officer was so concerned at this coincidence that he considered banning physical exercise pending further investigation. The winter finally relented at the beginning of March and I returned to jumping on the twenty-sixth of that month with a static line jump at Weston, a confidence building soft stand up landing on a 32 foot PX.

During this long interlude I had already been planning for the new season. Geordie Charlton and I decided to book ourselves an advanced parachute course in France, and one week after my comeback at Weston I travelled with Geordie to the French regional parachute centre at Chalon-sur-Saône to complete my rehabilitation and get back up to speed. My suitcase had been packed for a week. We travelled overnight by train, arriving at the Centre on the morning of the third of April and were suitably impressed by the sight of the neat low-roofed white buildings of the airfield alongside the RN6, just north of the town. We booked in at reception, had our logbooks and licences checked, then were sent back down town for a medical. This achieved, we returned to complete the formalities and purchase the compulsory insurance. We were assigned to complete a course *(Perfectionnement)* of advanced manoeuvres; tomorrow we were to start.

It was immediately obvious to us both that the organisation and professionalism of this Centre was far in advance of anything we had in the UK. Chalon was one of the first regional centres to be opened under the National Civil Aviation Secretariat, and was thus state subsidised. On-site accommodation was free of charge; the only cost was for the jumps, inclusive of rig hire, which cost 17/6d (roughly 87p) for 2,500 metres, which was 8,200 feet. Bunkhouse and showers were spotlessly clean; there were offices, classrooms, a games room/bar and a packing room with twelve double tables. All student working areas were kept clean by us, the course students, YHA style. The Chief Instructor was Claude Bernard, a complete professional, who had three thousand jumps to his credit and who was also, as I was to discover, a quiet and effective disciplinarian. His instructional staff were Mingam, Rougebec and Kazmaryk. That evening we were both issued with EFA 650 assemblies(single blank gores) and shown how to pack; a far cry indeed from our own self-modified government surplus equipment. The following morning we boarded the Rapide, which was itself a revelation with an inflight door and bench seats, refinements unheard of in the 1963 UK. The aircraft was flown by Monsieur Distival, a taciturn and diminutive figure sporting a cloth cap, and wearing an ancient back type parachute. Jumpmaster Kazmaryk briefed the pilot: *"Monsieur Distival s'il vous plait; un passage à six cent, un passage à mille cinq et un à deux mille, parallèle à la route, direction Chagny; huit personnes à bord, on peut y aller"*. With eight jumpers on board we rolled and bumped along the grass strip parallel to the N6 and lifted off in a tight left hand turn, away from the river Saône glinting away to the east. We ran in at 2,000 feet over the airfield, north toward Chagny with the railway track on our left, for the Siki run. The French eschewed our familiar disposable paper streamers in favour of a permanent WDI – a massive red and white striped rectangular cloth strip weighted to the appropriate rate of descent by a broom handle type piece of wood (an idea which I copied when I went to back to Weston). Distival certainly knew his business as he banked left in a climbing turn and ran in precisely over the Siki on the first pass for Geordie and myself, a familiarisation descent from 5,000 feet. The next day we were given a spin test from 7,000 feet, then a second jump to demonstrate alternate turns and track. These jumps were observed on telemeters and we were debriefed in the classroom later. Having apparently satisfied M. Bernard that we were reasonably competent, we were issued with the most advanced canopies the Centre had to offer, EFA 656 low porosity TUs. Over the next three weeks we made a further twenty five jumps, learning barrel rolls, forward and backward loops, stable delay back down and instruction in relative work. One morning, halfway through the course, the jump brief was for alternate left and right barrel rolls. Once on the aircraft we were put at the end of the stick and instructed to remain in the aircraft for twenty seconds after the last man. This we did, leaving ourselves with a six hundred metre track to the opening point before completing the said manoeuvres. The staff did not miss a trick; three sets of telemeters were manned and every jump was observed either air-to-air or ground to air. No one was allowed to touch the telemeters except Centre staff. We would typically make two jumps before lunch followed by the classroom debrief; then repair down town to a restaurant for a couple of hours lunch. Two more jumps, repack, classroom debrief, sweep out the packing room and down town again for the evening meal.

Technical discipline at the Centre was strict, although the rules were unwritten. Stand up landings were forbidden as I discovered one day when walking back in to the packing shed with Geordie. It had been raining and I landed on a muddy patch of turf next to a large pool of water. To protect my immaculate white jumpsuit I made a PJI stand up landing, followed two seconds later by a belated hesitation side left PLF. As we walked past Bernard, standing with folded arms outside the packing shed, Geordie said: "I think he wants to see you". Too true he did. "I am sorry Monsieur Bernard" I apologised. "So am I", said the Chef. "Peacock will not jump the next day". The said next day dawned clear, bright and warm, perfect jumping weather. The rest of the course made three RW jumps each whilst I was busy with bucket and mop in the latrines.... No harm done, all forgiven and forgotten a day later. I returned to the UK shortly thereafter twenty-eight jumps the wiser, having learned more in three weeks than in the previous three years. For me, Chalon established the gold standard for contemporary sport parachute instruction, and Claude Bernard ranged alongside Stan McCabe at St Athan as the professional instructor to emulate.

Meanwhile, back at PTS, the Display season was under way. Peter Hearn had handed over to Peter McCumiskey as team leader and, as the team was still not established, jumpers continued to be drawn from Trials and Training flight. The Big Six had broken up and we sport jumpers were no longer automatic choices. Nonetheless on the eleventh of May I was in the team which took the Argosy out from Benson to Clermont Ferrand in the Auvergne region of central France. The venue was the airport of Aulnat, to the east of the city, situated amidst the hills in a huge natural amphitheatre, bounded to the west by the spectacular volcanic region of the Puy de Dôme. The occasion was a National Air Display and parachuting was one of the main attractions, all over town there were huge posters advertising the star jumpers, top billing going to Jean Claude Dubois who two months previously had established a high altitude record by parachuting from 22,000 feet on to the summit of Mount Kilimanjaro. The next day dawned with crystal clear blue skies, light winds and a one hundred thousand crowd. We opened the parachuting from the Argosy with our 12,000-foot track pattern, then relaxed on the grass to watch the rest of the show. The French Army team had brought their Nord Atlas and all the French jumpers, military and civilian alike, were aboard and awaiting their turn. First out was a heavy drop from the tailgate at 1,000 feet – a Simca convertible followed out by four static line jumpers who landed next to it, de-rigged it and drove it off in about ninety seconds flat. The second pass was from 9,000 feet, with a civilian team jump. The aircraft came round again at 12,000 feet with the star attraction, Jean Claude Dubois with all the sky to himself, the focus of a hundred thousand pairs of eyes, demonstrating a superb solo sweeping track pattern picked out in white smoke, complete with live running commentary from the jumper in freefall, via a throat mike hooked up to the public address system. The final item was the French military team from Pau, who included the current 1962 World Accuracy Champion, Gérard Treves. This was an airshow that lived long in the memory. It was also to be my last RAF demo appearance for three and a half years.

Jake and I continued jumping at Kidlington for the next few months and should have gone together to the European Championships in Leutkirch at the beginning of June. The British team was to be Norman, Geordie, Jake and myself; Jake had applied for the trip as expedition training, which meant we were on duty and entitled to Service transport. Two days before departure we were informed that the expedition had not been sanctioned and we were on our own; we had to take annual leave and pay our own way to the south of Germany. Jake had no leave left, so Norman, Geordie and I took the long train journey south across the continent. The team was made up by Les Howe, a civilian jumper who had been with us at the same venue in 1961. Leutkirch was as hospitable and picturesque as previously, but the competition had a much higher profile. Leutkirch had been selected by the International Parachuting Commission (CIP) as the venue for the 1964 World Parachuting Championships and this was effectively a dry run. The opposition was formidable, featuring in particular the US Army Golden Knights – Dick Fortenberry, Phil Vanderweg, Coy MacDonald, Gerry Borquin and current Style World number two Jim Arender. They were all jumping 7 gore 1.6 low porosity TUs – "Conquistadors" and a prototype 9 gore silk TU. CIP regulations deemed that the descent rate of a competition canopy must not exceed 5 metres per second. This immediately ruled out my C9 1.1 oz ripstop TU so I was restricted to jumping a double L with about 50 percent reduced capability.

In the event, wind speeds were particularly light for the eight days of the competition, which consisted of four team and four individual accuracy jumps. Top two teams after three rounds were the Golden Knights and ourselves; on round four we jumped first and were all inside the five metre scoring circle, sitting in first place. We were standing watching as the big H34 lifted off to 5,000 feet for the last round with the Golden Knights on board. Prior to take off the wind, although only about five knots, had switched 180 degrees. We watched with disbelief as the Yanks ran in downwind and exited some five hundred metres the wrong side of the target. As Fortenberry, the lead jumper, passed over the control tower at five hundred feet and one hundred metres short he took off his helmet and hurled it to the ground in sheer frustration... . I treasure my first gold medal to this day. For the record we also took silver as second overall in the combined events.

On our return to Abingdon, we were summoned to the OC's office, presumably to receive official congratulations. Wrong. In company with Jake and Snowy, we were summarily given to understand that we would all be posted off PTS at the first available opportunity, the reason given being that, in the opinion of the OC, we had been around the Parachute Training School for long enough. Wing Commander Bernard F. Stannard(see Chapter 1) was undeniably the boss and, by the end of the year, Norman had gone to Kenya, Geordie to Aldershot, Jake and Snowy to Singapore and I was on my way to Cyprus. With Peter Hearn also posted to Singapore, and Tommy commissioned into the RAF Regiment, the diaspora of the sport jumpers from the hangar was complete.

This all notwithstanding, the following month we participated in the British Nationals at Sywell and caught up with the Golden Knights again, still on their summer European tour. Highlight of the Meet, which was dogged by indifferent weather, was undoubtedly their final demo, which was a freefall stick of twelve jumpers from the Otter at 1,000 feet. At work, as the trials team, we were working on freefall equipment and were loading the Bergen up to sixty pounds and jumping regularly at Weston. Jake and I continued to be busy with the Club at Kidlington, taking the Dragon up to 10,000 feet along with some of our Hereford colleagues.

Meanwhile, *pace* the OC, at PTS all our sporting initiatives had not been in vain. Moves were underway to create an official RAF Abingdon Sport Parachute Club, presumably on the premise that if you can't beat them, join them. Under the chairmanship of Squadron Leader Mike Stamford this Club came into being in August at Weston on the Green. We had taken delivery of a de Havilland DH89 Dominie trainer from the Royal Naval Air Service, at a cost of £400. 00. This princely sum included numerous spares, including two extra engines. On 28th August 1963, with Mike Stamford running the programme we flew three inaugural lifts, two at 5,000 feet and a final lift to 7,000 feet. Jumpers were Norman Hoffman, Tommy Moloney, Jake McLoughlin, Geordie Charlton, Robbie Robertson ("Big Rab", not Snowy) Mike Stamford and myself. Our pilot for the day was 47 Squadron Beverley captain Flight Lieutenant Crawley. Although I did not know it at the time, I was not to parachute with Jake again for twenty years. The sorcerer and his apprentice had reached the parting of the ways. As Jake would have said: "When you reach a fork in the trail, you've got to take it". My Cyprus posting had come through, and in a couple of days I was on my way.

**Chapter 4** | # *Cyprus*
*1963-1966*

On the first of September 1963 I packed my kit, booked out of the Mess, and headed for Gatwick. The following day I flew out to Cyprus to report to the Physical Fitness Section at RAF Nicosia in my unaccustomed guise as a station PTI. My new boss, the PFO, was Flight Lieutenant Dave Wright, a Scottish international water polo player and I was quickly to find out that swimming was the prime function of the Physical Training section, which from the month of May onwards based itself at the Olympic standard fifty-metre station swimming pool. The staff comprised a flight sergeant, another sergeant besides myself, and two corporals. I was given a cordial enough welcome, although I sensed that my brevet seemed to be regarded in slightly ambivalent fashion by my new colleagues. RAF Nicosia was situated a few miles to the west of the capital itself and was the second base on the island, the larger RAF Akrotiri being on the coast near Limassol some seventy miles to the south. Nicosia was home to No 70 Hastings Squadron and 29 Squadron, which flew Gloster Javelin interceptors. I moved into the Mess and mentally assessed my priorities.

First I had to find accommodation for Helen and our two girls. They had flown out to stay with Helen's family in Germany pending my finding a hiring or Married Quarter. Second, I had to start parachuting as soon as possible. On posting, my terms of reference included giving support to the Near East Air Force Parachute Rescue Team and No. 3 (LAA) Wing RAF Regiment, both based at Akrotiri. The Officer in charge of the NEAF Rescue Team was Flight Lieutenant John Robinson with Flight Sergeant Hughie (Dinger) Bell as his number two. This rescue team comprised medical and mountain rescue personnel, with the RAF Regiment in support. Another friend was Flight Sergeant George Bruce, ex PTS, who was running the Mountain Rescue Team, at that time also based with me at Nicosia. This now made four qualified active PJIs on the island. Six days after arriving at Nicosia I excused myself from the PTIs and their Olympic swimming pool and flew down to Akrotiri to meet John Robinson, Dinger and the rest of the team who shared a headquarters and parachute training compound with 3 Wing. This was a most fruitful meeting indeed as it rapidly became apparent that John was massively keen to start freefall training on the island. All they needed was kit and an instructor, and it just so happened that I had brought out four B4 rigs with me to Cyprus, being my share of the now defunct Kidlington Skydivers Parachute School. My apprenticeship was over, and within two weeks we had a freefall programme up and running.

This opportunity arrived with my first day's work at Akrotiri on 27th September. Because of air traffic considerations all parachute programmes had to be completed by 08.00 hrs, and in consequence I flew out from Nicosia at 04.30 in a 70 Squadron Hastings on my first sortie as despatcher for RAF Regiment personnel, a static line programme on to the Ladies Mile DZ. I had previously asked Chris Eddy, the Hastings captain, if there was any chance we could do some freefall jumping once the troops had gone. He proved most enthusiastic and gave John Robinson and myself a perfect run in at 5,000 feet as a final pass. My next jump in Cyprus was on the same evening, a static line night jump followed by a fifteen-mile night march with the NEAF rescue team from Ladies Mile to the Kourion amphitheatre. I had indeed literally fallen amongst friends. Over the next three weeks John Robinson, Dinger Bell, George Bruce and myself made half a dozen freefall jumps from the Hastings after the static line troops had been despatched, before the Senior Air Staff Officer (SASO) at NEAF HQ heard about it and promptly banned the practice, deeming, quite correctly of course, that we were using non-Service equipment and had no authority whatsoever.... Nonetheless, an abiding memory remains of a solo jump from 10,000 feet at seven o'clock one morning over the Ladies Mile beach DZ. I had despatched Dinger on a five second delay and the Hastings went up to the top with only myself and the loadmaster left in the back. We ran in over Limassol bay, the green light came on just past the shoreline, and I left the starboard door with the whole sky to myself. The Akrotiri runway was over to the left, the base itself was fringed with dark green orange groves, the salt flats glittered ahead in the clear early morning sunlight and I went into a no-lift dive then tracked all the rest of the way down, just because I could. Fabulous experience. Opened at 2,000 feet, nil wind, and I hit the sand a half metre from the target centre. I had been on the island for five weeks and it was only going to get better.

Back at Nicosia I had found accommodation for the family in a small bungalow in the Ayios Demetrios district only three miles from base. Tangled grape vines covered the carport, lemon and orange trees grew around the front lawn. Helen and the girls flew in one evening in mid-October to be welcomed by a temperature of a balmy 22 degrees. This was to be the beginning of a three-year break for us all from the hectic PTS schedule and we intended to make the most of it.

November proved to be a very busy month for 70 Squadron in the parachuting role; we ran a pre-para selection course on the cliffs behind the base, followed by a basic course. Eighteen students qualified and after three days ground training we dropped them on their first descent on eighteen single passes. Yes, eighteen single passes in a Hastings… . One pass stands out in particular, John Purdie, RAF medic. As the red came on he moved into the door, seemingly removed the chewing gum from his mouth, and dropped it into my hand. I immediately threw it out of the door into the Mediterranean Sea and resumed my grip on his waistband. He turned to me with a look of mild horror, displaying a two-tooth gap where his upper plate had been half a second previously… . As Jake would have said "you're bound to lose a few"… . Later in the month we shifted our attention to the west of the island with training jumps for visiting 3 Para at the Morphou Drop Zone, culminating in a battalion night drop from the Hastings on Exercise Solinus II.

The intervention of the SASO meant we had to seek elsewhere to continue our freefall programmes, so naturally we looked to the Army. 16 Flight Army Air Corps were based at Kingsfield in the Dhekalia Sovereign Base Area, on the east coast about sixty miles from Nicosia, and two weeks after the RAF embargo we were operating again. The AAC already had much experience in dropping jumpers and the CO, Captain Pete Courtnay, had welcomed us with enthusiasm. They had a Guy Fawkes party scheduled and asked us to open their show with a parachute demonstration. As John, George and Dinger were not yet fully up to speed it had to be a solo by myself from 5,000 feet. I jumped at last light into their arena trailing smoke in a short track to land on target, they were delighted, and a subsequent over-hyped headline in the garrison Dhekalia News did us no harm at all. Now that we had access to aircraft and to an unrestricted DZ at Kingsfield airstrip in the Sovereign Base Area we were confident we could form ourselves into the Cyprus Combined Services Parachute Club. The founder members were George Bruce and myself from Nicosia and John Robinson from Akrotiri. Right from the beginning we were almost overwhelmed with volunteer student jumpers, the first of whom were members of George's mountain rescue team. In view of our limited resources we had decided from the outset that only parachute-trained personnel could be accepted for freefall instruction. In addition, the landing area was the end of the airstrip itself, and consisted of hard compressed gravel, demanding good proven landing technique. Our opening training programme took place on the 1200 metre Kingsfield strip on the 16th of November 1963, and, as we had no accommodation on the airstrip, all the parachutes were stored in the RAF Nicosia Safety Equipment Section. We had a good friend there in Jerry Hoyt, who gave us hanging space and the use of his packing tables. Every Saturday morning I would leave Nicosia at 06.00 and drive the sixty miles to Dhekalia with the gear. Meanwhile, John Robinson plus George Bruce and his team, now relocated to Akrotiri, would rendezvous at the airfield at 07.30. We would jump for about three hours until the sea breeze went above limits, then repack for the next session. George's mountain rescue team would often then proceed north for an exercise in the Kyrenia Mountains. In all we were to complete six sessions before Christmas… .

The situation was to turn dramatically on Saturday 21st December when violence broke out between the Greek and Turkish communities on the island. This rapidly escalated into a full scale conflict, and, by the 28th of December the Cyprus garrison had been reinforced by the 1st Battalion the Parachute Regiment and the 16th Independent Parachute Brigade Group. Deployed with the latter were 21 Recce Flight Army Air Corps, to be based at RAF Nicosia. The island was partitioned with the Turks to the north and the Greeks in the south and the so-called Green Line running through the centre of Nicosia. After four weeks the situation had stabilised sufficiently for the visiting Army sport jumpers to get together and consider jumping in any spare time they might have. Many of my old friends from the UK Army teams were now right on the doorstep – Captain Tom Ridgeway, Leo McArdle, Bob Reid, Jim Walmsley, Mike Turner, and Pete Paganelli among them. By March 1964 all visiting forces had been transferred to United Nations command (UNFICYP) and exchanged their red berets for UN blue, and Tom had organised a Beaver for jumping on the airfield. In April Tom's UN team gave a demo into the station sports arena for a 70 Squadron party, 7,000 feet from the Beaver with smoke, whilst I was given an honorary UN blue beret for the occasion.

The presence of 21 Recce Flight on the airfield was indeed a big bonus for all of us. One of their routine sorties was the mail run from Nicosia to Dhekalia to Episkopi and return. I had a good deal going with the CO which enabled me throughout the summer, twice a week before going to work, to hitch a ride on this detail, with an 05. 00 takeoff and the right hand door removed. We flew low level to Dhekalia, picked up the mail, on to Episkopi, drop and pick up mail and then back over the Troodos mountain range to Nicosia. The captain would clear with ATC, then run in at 7,000 feet over the airfield for me to hop out. We also resumed activities at Kingsfield and, as news of our activities spread, we were soon joined by Americans

Bill Ramey and Bob Muller from the Embassy staff, whilst Tony Dale came to us from Weston. Tony was an accomplished pentathlete and member of the Command swimming team who later remustered into the PT Branch on his return to the UK, thence to No 1 PTS and Boscombe Down. A further significant development occurred when, in February 1964, No. 2 Field Squadron (Para) RAF Regiment was deployed to Nicosia, under the command of Squadron Leader Gerry Wilson. Gerry was unique in the Service in that, along with the RAF Regiment shoulder badge he wore pilot's wings, parachute wings, and the ribbon of the Military Cross with which he was awarded for gallantry in the Yemen in 1958. http://www.telegraph.co.uk/news/obituaries/military-obituaries/air-force-obituaries/8832548/Wing-Commander-Gerry-Wilson.html.

Gerry proved to be a most useful ally indeed as he joined us at Kingsfield as a club member on our return there later in the summer, and the following year he was to be elected as Club Chairman. Meanwhile we had obtained funding for the Club to purchase Irvin Skydriver 9 TU canopies to replace our old C9s. These Irvin canopies were the UK version of the American Conquistador TU canopies, and were 1. 6oz low porosity nylon fabric with a 9-gore separation. At last we were all equipped with bespoke canopies to replace the government surplus 1. 1oz ripstop parachutes which had served us so well for the past three years. We took delivery of the Irvins at the end of September and George Bruce and I said farewell to the C9s on 22nd September with a jump onto the airfield at Nicosia from 10,800 feet, which was our highest so far. The Auster, flown by Mike Ashley, gained height by flying eastwards out to Larnaca then running back in parallel to the Kyrenia mountains. I remember using these landmarks out of the right hand door to check our inbound progress before eventually reaching the overhead at Nicosia some forty-five minutes later. Despite a bank of fog persisting down to about one hundred feet we found our way through and made the centre of the airfield with no dramas.

All this sport parachuting activity was, of course, being pursued in addition to my two main tasks as a Nicosia PTI and support PJI to John Robinson, 3 Wing and the NEAF Rescue team. Toward the end of 1964 it became increasingly apparent that this double commitment was putting a strain on everyone concerned and, on the premise that no man can serve two masters, a solution had to be found. The upshot was the creation of a new establishment of a Wing PJI on 70 Squadron to provide continuation training and screening for the Air Quartermasters in the parachuting role; I was posted internally from Admin to Flying Wing to fill that post whilst the station PTI vacancy was filled full time by Sergeant Gary Swan-Brown, an RAF basketball player. This new arrangement definitely came as a relief to all parties, particularly, I suspect to Dave Wright the PFO, and most certainly to me. My new boss was OC Flying Wing, Squadron Leader Jim Rhind, and the adjutant was Flight Lieutenant Bob Maltby. I was given a desk in Flying Wing HQ adjacent to 70 Squadron, and I persuaded the OC to allocate some hangar space for a Hastings mock fuselage for continuation training of the 70 Squadron AQMs. I organised a Queen Mary flatbed transport for the mockup fuselage, which was surplus to requirements at the Akrotiri training area, laid down a matted area and was ready to go. The Wing PJI was up and running. Early in 1965 we were kept very busy with basic courses for Rescue Team personnel, and continuation jumping for the RAF Regiment both of 3 Wing and 2 Field Squadron. We found a new dropping zone at Evdhimou, inland from Episkopi in the southern Sovereign Base Area, and used this extensively for day and night descents as an alternative to Ladies Mile, where the salt flats were prone to flooding in winter. We also ran a couple of exercises in the Libyan Desert just outside RAF El Adem airbase. The final trip was to be repeated the following year, with potentially catastrophic consequences.

On the sport side we continued with student training programmes at Kingsfield and advanced training at Nicosia. I also made a solo demonstration descent into the station sports stadium on the occasion of 70 Squadron birthday party to be given an enthusiastic welcome by the (female) DZ party. This featured in a short article I penned at the time and which appeared in the Spring 1966 edition of

Sport Parachutist (page 9) under the heading "Cyprus Scrapebook" (*sic*). http://www.bpa-archive.org.uk/mag_archive/magazines/008-1966-1.pdf. Tony Dale had by now progressed and joined me on several local sorties on the airfield, the most successful being his first sixty-second delay, courtesy, as ever, of 21 Flight. We had obtained permission from Nicosia Air Traffic Control to excavate a 20-metre diameter sand pit on the airfield, so now we had a soft target to go for. In May George Bruce and I made a demo into the sports arena at Dhekalia, which was about three hundred metres inland from Larnaca Bay. George was enjoying his jumping, and his tracking ability was improved beyond measure on this particular occasion. The WDI went about six hundred metres and the run in was out to sea. I spotted the aircraft, exited and tracked back for effect. George opened a little high and came in about thirty seconds later. On the debrief George reported having difficulty with his smokes prior to exit which delayed him a good five seconds. He told me that, as a non-swimmer, the sight of the expanse of water separating him from the shore provided him with an incentive like no other, and his consequent inbound track reached an efficiency quotient hitherto unachieved...

In September we heard that the Parachute Regiment Display Team – Red Devils (alias Red Freds) http://www.red-devils-fft.com – were due to visit Bahrain to give a series of demonstration jumps. 1 Para were at the time serving with the Bahrain garrison, and John Robinson organised a short detachment over there for himself, George and me, ostensibly for a triangular competition against the two Army teams. We flew over early in October to meet up with Geordie Charlton, on detachment from Pitts Road with 1 Para, and Leo McArdle, a very good friend from the previous year. The Red Devils' own DH Rapide G-AGTM, was flown out from Farnborough to Bahrain, via Lebanon and all points east, a flight which took seven days. The aircraft was heavily laden with a complete public address system for the shows, also as passenger on board was the pilot's wife, who was reportedly eight months pregnant. The couple settled in a local hotel to recuperate, and handed over the Rapide for team training at the Zallaq airstrip on the west coast of the island, about fifteen miles from the capital Al Manamah. Jim Walmsley was on his first year with the team, and was jumping with a Bergen rucksack. On the first demo he made a dive exit and caught his top pin on the top of the door, bending, and thus jamming, his top pin. This of course gave him a total malfunction which resulted in a reserve ride from 1500 feet and caused him to land outside the stadium. This was the only out landing of all the shows, a tribute to the high standard which the Red Devils had already achieved in this, their second season since formation. The team had already established close links with the US Army Golden Knights and had visited Fort Bragg earlier that year on a training detachment.

During that visit they had re-equipped themselves with new Para Commander canopies, the first time we had had the chance to see them. These parachutes had first been used in competition by the American team at the previous year's World Championships in Leutkirch, and were now the hottest canopies on the market. The Mk 1 Para Commander was a derivation of the French Lemoigne ascending parachute, which had now been modified and developed by the Pioneer Parachute Company as a freefall canopy. It had a vastly superior performance to the hitherto ubiquitous TU, being constructed of 2.2oz taffeta nylon and combining increased lift, drive, and manoeuvrability with a low rate of descent. This design was rapidly adopted with various modifications by all the parachuting nations and was to remain the main high performance canopy for the next eight years, before being superseded by the first generation ram-air parachutes in the early nineteen seventies. I made my first PC descent of many that September, before converting fully twelve months later. John and George were recalled to Cyprus a week early, and I carried on assisting Geordie and Leo McArdle in the running of a basic course. The Zallaq detachment was a most useful interlude indeed, I managed nineteen jumps in the ten day period and, as well as progressing many Army students, I managed some intensive style training. Although Cyprus was a valuable and greatly enjoyed posting, which I would not have missed for anything, I was conscious of being away from mainstream jumping and the injection of fresh ideas and techniques provided by the Red Devils was a most welcome fillip.

We returned to Cyprus at the end of October, to be greeted with the news that Gerry Wilson, as commander of the NEAF rescue team, had obtained authorisation for us to use a Service aircraft – a Pembroke – for a freefall demonstration using our own kit. John Robinson, George and I jumped from 5,000 feet on a rehearsal at Akrotiri, and the following day we took it up to 9,000 feet for a demonstration for NEAF Staff officers. This was however, to be our last Service freefall jump for another six months and normal service was resumed at Kingsfield and Nicosia using the Austers. In November George and I made a demo for a military tattoo into the Dhekalia garrison sports arena, scene of our jump the previous May. It was evening; we got out at 8,000 feet and completed a baton pass before opening, then coming in for a virtually simultaneous side-by-side landing. Early in 1966, John Robinson was tour expired, and was replaced by Flight Lieutenant Ted Allen from PTS. Dinger Bell had also gone back to the UK, and Paul Hewitt came over as Flight Sergeant in his place. Ted, who was freefall trained, was then instrumental in obtaining Service freefall parachutes for use in NEAF and in April Ted Allen, Paul Hewitt and myself made two Hastings descents from 12,000 feet using Irvin PB4s. Two days later, we three jumped again for the 70 Squadron 50th Anniversary party, a track pattern with smoke landing right in front of the Squadron dispersal.

The following month, Ted had organised Exercise Sandfly, a training sortie out of Akrotiri for a DZ out in the Libyan Desert at Ras al Ilbah, some seventy miles west of Tobruk. We took off in Hastings 575 from RAF Nicosia at 02.40 with twenty team members on board, all with PWCs, plus Paul Hewitt as drifter. The loadmaster was Ivan Richardson of 70 Squadron and the pilot was Flight Lieutenant Chris Eddy. We arrived overhead the DZ at about 06.00, to see the smoke from the sodium DZ marker blowing horizontally across the rocky desert. Ted radioed up, surface wind 12 knots, clear drop. Round we went, and out went Paul on the green. A couple more dummy circuits, then, from the DZ: "Negative Drop, return to base". The wind had gone above limits; Paul had landed in a rock-strewn wadi downwind and had sustained a broken leg. We returned to RAF El Adem intending to disembark and await the return of the DZ party and Paul. We came in to land and the touchdown was extremely heavy, the aircraft with twenty troops with full kit on board bounced an estimated thirty feet into the air and hit the runway again with the starboard undercarriage taking the impact. The oleo collapsed and we careered along the strip at an extreme angle, waiting for the starboard wingtip to dig in and send us into a giant cartwheel. At this stage, the port undercarriage collapsed also and the Hastings dropped level and carried along sliding on its belly, with the fuselage rapidly filling with a choking dust coming up through the floor. The aircraft skidded violently through a one hundred and eighty degree turn and finished up at rest on the rock-strewn earth parallel to the runway facing the way it had come. Seatbelts unfastened, we opened the port door and the troops started to clear the aircraft in short order. In an attempt to speed up the evacuation, I removed the starboard door, only to be confronted with a fireball from the starboard wing. I replaced the door with alacrity, and turned around to find myself on my own in the now deserted aircraft. I exited the port door at some speed and sprinted to join the rest of the troops and the crew a hundred metres away. By this time the fire crew had arrived and covered the starboard side with foam. Full credit for this most rapid response must go to the Corporal in charge of the Fire Section Duty Crew, who hit the alarm button the instant he saw the Hastings make first contact with the runway threshold. We flew back home the following day on a Britannia, leaving the Board of Inquiry to pick over the pieces.

My three years in Cyprus were coming to a close, although we returned with the Rescue Team to the Libyan Desert in July to re-run Exercise Sandfly, this time totally without incident. We continued to use the 21 Flight Austers on the airfield, with our new

Station Commander, Group Captain David B. Fitzpatrick taking a most active interest and running the DZ for us on several occasions. Sadly, the Club at Kingsfield now had to be wound up as the Auster 9's of 16 Flight were replaced by Westland Sioux helicopters, which were not cleared in the parachuting role. My last jump on the island was, fittingly enough, from a 70 Squadron Hastings, this time totally legal and authorised, using an Irvin PB4 on to the Ladies Mile DZ. During my three years at Nicosia I had completed three hundred parachute descents on the island, and, considering this was officially a PTI duty tour, I had no complaints at all. My family, too, had benefited enormously; despite the travel restrictions imposed by the Emergency we had travelled the length and breadth of this beautiful island, sunned ourselves on its beaches north, east and south, from the panhandle to Paphos. We had explored the Troodos and Kyrenia mountains in winter and in summer, and returned to the UK after three happy years in the sunshine. All in all, a tour to remember, but it was time to return to the Parachute School and to mainstream jumping.

**19.** *With Jake McLoughlin in the Beverley freight bay, 1961.*

**20.** *Daily Express 1st February 1962. SAS Trooper Keith Norry pictured before the fatal descent.*

21. *Royal Air Force Parachute Display Team Abingdon 1962. Paul Hewitt, Self, Jake, Peter Hearn, Snowy, Tommy.*

**Dans le ciel, sur la piste minute après minute...**

Gil Delamare (à droite) a tenu à féliciter les paras de la R.A.F. pour leur magnifique saut groupé

22. *Rouen Air Show 24th June 1962. Self, Paul Hewitt, Peter Hearn, Snowy, Jake, Tommy and Gil Delamare.* *Photo Paris Normandie*

69

**23.** *Peter Hearn with trophy at the City Hall reception in Rouen.* From left are *Tommy, Jake, Paul Hewitt, and myself, with Beverley aircrew. Snowy is half in shot on left.*

**24.** *The Parachute Centre at Chalon-sur-Saône, April 1963.*

**25.** *My C9 five gore TU canopy. Cork Air Rally at the Farmer's Cross
Airfield, July 1962. Note crowd invasion of the target area.*
*Photo courtesy of the Irish Examiner*

**26.** *EFA 656 canopy 1963. This was standard issue at French centres; we would still be using American surplus equipment for our students for the next ten years.*

**27.** *Nice exit from the Chalon Rapide in April 1963.*

**28.** *Flight Sergeant Hughie (Dinger) Bell at the training area behind 3 Wing HQ. RAF Akrotiri 1963.*

**29.** *RAF Nicosia Sports Arena demo with the United Nations Team April 1964. Tom Ridgeway, Pete Paganelli, Leo McArdle, Bob Reid and the author.*

30. *Helen and the girls at RAF Nicosia in 1964.*

**31.** *My Irvin Skydriver 9 gore low porosity TU canopy, Dhekalia Kingsfield airfield 1964. This landing area was rock solid and took no prisoners.*

75

**32.** *With 70 Squadron Air Quartermasters. Nicosia 1964.*

**33.** *On the Day Job. Despatching No. 2 Field Squadron RAF Regiment from the Hastings.*

76

**34.** *With Tony Dale, RAF Nicosia 1965. Our pilot is Gordon Emerson from 21 Flight Army Air Corps, and the aircraft is an Auster 9.*

**35.** *RAF Akrotiri 1965. With Sqn. Ldr. Gerry Wilson, George Bruce, John Robinson, and Pembroke pilot Flt. Lt. Chris Yates before a NEAF Staff demo.*

77

**36.** *Red Devils in front of their Rapide at Bahrain Zallaq airstrip October 1965: Jim Walmsley with Bergen rucksack, Brian David, Ernie Rowberry, Charlie Gowans, Gus Martin, Keith Jones, Jack Fowler.*

**37.** *Hastings crashed on landing, 4th May 1966 at RAF El Adem. The Airfield Fire Section were certainly on the ball for this one.*

78

**Chapter 5** | *Falcons*

*1967–1968*

We bade farewell to Cyprus and flew back to the UK on 5th September, and settled into our new Married Quarter in the middle of October. We had enjoyed a short break in Germany and I took the opportunity to visit the Rhine Army Parachute Centre in Bad Lippspringe, where Mike Turner was Chief Instructor, and made a couple of jumps with the Mk 1 Para Commander (hence PC). This was by now the standard canopy used by the Falcons Display Team and was to be virtually the only canopy I used for the next twelve hundred descents. I reported back to work on Basic Training Squadron and was initially assigned as a "spare" instructor. In this capacity, my first jump back at PTS was 12,000 feet from an Argosy, making a five-way over Weston. The next jump was a night drifter, then another with PWC. The following week I was given a section on Regular Basic Course 652, making a couple of balloon descents and seeing this course pass out in mid December. Having eased my way unobtrusively back into the system I was then moved to Freefall Training Flight/Display Team and there I was to remain for two full years.

Things had certainly moved on in the three years I had been away, most important of course was the fact that the team was now fully established for Display duties, and had already in 1965 been designated as the Falcons. The definitive history of this Team appears in Peter Hearn's seminal work of the same name http://www.amazon.co.uk/Falcons-Peter-Hearn/dp/1898697191. The Team Leader was now Flight Lieutenant Stuart Cameron; deputy was Flying Officer Geoff Greenland, with Terry Allen as team Flight Sergeant. In addition, Terry doubled up as team cameraman, and in this role did much to publicise the Falcons with his air-to-air photography, using a motorised 35mm Nikon. This work was augmented by Tim Tasker, who jumped a helmet-mounted 16mm Beaulieu cine camera. The team was equipped with Mk 1 PCs, in a 4-pin Pioneer container and a front-mount I. 24 reserve. A further innovation was now that all team members were, of necessity, qualified to pack their own parachutes. The aircraft in use was the Argosy, jumping from the side doors, although we could use the tailgate if circumstances demanded. Training started at Weston at the end of January with the high display format consisting of two six-man tracking groups. One group would exit slightly shallow and track upwind along the line of flight; after a 10-second gap the second group would leave and track back along the windline, the idea being that an enormous V shape would be etched on the sky by the trailing smoke. It was my opinion that this pattern was not particularly effective, as it was two-dimensional and lacked any transverse movement; it was also technically suspect in that jumpers were potentially placing their canopies below freefalling colleagues. It was, however, persisted with for another three seasons. After seven jumps in five weeks at Weston, we decided to fly out to El Adem for some supposedly fine weather training. We stayed there for one week bedevilled by low cloud, made two jumps only, and then came back to an early British springtime where we managed a dozen demo practices from 12,000 feet with no problems at all. The season was underway.

Running parallel with this jumping was the Royal Air Force Sport Parachute Club, which I had left over three years previously, and I signed in again with two jumps in November. Our original Navy Dominie, G-ASFG bought for £400.00 in 1963 (Chapter 3), had been replaced in 1965 by the de Havilland Rapide G-AGSH, which had seen previous service with British European Airways. The aircraft was kept in F (Belfast) hangar at Abingdon and our primary pilots were Chief Tech Con Greaves, who was also Chief Gliding Instructor at the RAF Bicester Club, and Gerry Schellong, who had been with the Club from its founding days in 1957 with the Tiger

Moth(Chapter 1). Both were truly dedicated individuals, equally as keen as, sometimes even keener than, the jumpers to get into the air. Equally supportive were the ground engineers who kept the machine flying, often being called out in the middle of their weekend without complaint. The Club Chief Instructor was now Geordie Charlton, accompanied by Ken Mapplebeck who had been making a name for himself as a jumper over the last couple of years. Geordie buttonholed me on arrival at PTS and enlisted me on the Club Committee. Geordie, Ken and I were to form a most fruitful two-year relationship both as display jumpers and as a competition team. I had by now qualified as a BPA Advanced Instructor, had achieved Examiner rating, and immediately became totally involved. We took the Rapide out of the hangar again in February and by mid April I had completed twenty Club jumps.

A big bonus was the fact that we were allowed to use our RAF PCs for Club jumping. This privilege was generously extended to me by Stu Cameron who gave permission for me to take one of these rigs to Chalon in April, where I made thirty competition training jumps in a couple of weeks under the guidance of Claude Bernard, still in charge at the Centre, which was now re-equipped with the Broussard in place of the Rapide. This interlude gave me more canopy time with the PC and some expert style coaching. Back home at Weston we had had the old sand pit in the middle of the airfield extended from its ten-metre diameter to a full fifty-metre target area. This extension was necessitated by a change in accuracy technique following the introduction of the Para Commander. Accuracy approaches were now made downwind, aiming at a 15cm dead centre disc. Given competition wind limits of 7m/sec (15mph) and a 12mph PC airspeed it can be seen that downwind accuracy touchdown speed could potentially be in the order of 25mph. Hence the need for a sufficiently large sand pit, which was subsequently upgraded to competition standard and filled with washed pea gravel to a depth of twelve inches. Ken, Geordie and I made the most of our opportunities and of the some three hundred jumps I made that year, fifty percent were competition training jumps out at Weston from the Rapide.

On the civilian sport parachuting scene, the BPA secretariat were still based in London, at 75 Artillery Mansions in Victoria Street; Brigadier Wilson had stepped down as Chairman at the end of 1966 and the new Chairman was Wing Commander Gerry Turnbull, the former OC PTS. The first honorary Secretary General, Group Captain Caster RAF, had also retired and had been replaced by ex Naval Commander Robin Letts, on a full time salaried basis. At this time, in 1967, the sport was pretty much military dominated; of twenty BPA Council members, thirteen were servicemen, with seven civilians. There were eighteen Advanced Instructors, including only two civilians – John Meacock was one. Two-thirds of Approved Instructors were also military. It was inevitable that this should be so, in that all the impetus for freefall sport parachuting had originated in the Armed Forces; parachuting being primarily a military activity, which had branched out into display jumping and thence into competition by military teams. This was an historical imbalance and was addressed in most diplomatic fashion by Brigadier Wilson in his outgoing address to the 1966 Annual General Meeting. For our part, jumpers were jumpers, and I personally never encountered any animosity from any faction, although this was undeniably an issue in some contemporary civilian circles.

Back to the day job in early May, and the Falcons were quickly into the demo season with a high show at the RAF Scampton Sports Day, where we met up with Ron Mitchell, recently commissioned and on his first tour as Station PFO. The DZ was naturally the sports field, with an immaculately laid cricket square in the centre. The target crosses were well clear but a couple of jumpers landed, either by accident or design, right on the wicket itself much to Ron's justified annoyance. We followed up at the Biggin Hill Air Fair, RAF Gütersloh, and at Hucknall. On the 9th of June we took the Beverley over to Karup in Denmark, before reverting to the Argosy for four shows in a seven-day period at the end of June, which saw us fly to Toulouse, to Brüggen and Wildenrath and thence to Lyon. Wildenrath on the Friday was a huge show, attended by the Chief of Air Staff and over fifty thousand spectators. I remember we had to fly around for an hour and a half before jumping, then repack in haste on a swelteringly hot evening before loading up the Argosy with several crates of champagne, donated by the organiser as our schedule left us with no time to attend the reception. We took off for Lyon ninety minutes later and rehydrated with the bubbly en route. We only managed the rehearsal at Lyon on the Saturday, the main show on the Sunday was weathered out. Back to base until the following Friday, then it was away again airborne for Pescara on the Italian Adriatic. We touched down just after lunch in Nice and the Argosy unaccountably became unserviceable for twenty-four hours. The aircrew obviously had previous local knowledge, and we took advantage of the free Saturday to enjoy the sunshine on the beach and extend the *entente cordiale* to the local populace. Off again the following afternoon, we arrived in Pescara too late for our rehearsal, having to settle for an 08.00 takeoff on the morning of the show to go through our paces from 12,000 feet. By the late afternoon the weather had deteriorated to such an extent that, although we flew for over an hour, we were unable to jump. We arrived home on the Monday evening; next day Geordie, Ken and I were out at Weston for three more training jumps. By early August we had completed forty in the next three weeks whilst the Falcons were on summer stand-down.

On the 5th of August we were off again, this time to Canada where we were scheduled to appear at the Abbotsford International Air Show in Vancouver. http://www.abbotsfordairshow.com/index. php?p=1_9_history. The Falcons did not travel light; we always took our own DZ Landrover lashed down in the Argosy. Team personnel and support staff invariably brought our numbers up to about twenty per trip; kit included all parachutes and spares, smokes etc. The Benson loadmasters did their sums and realised that the aircraft simply could not clear the 12,000-foot Canadian Rockies with all this on board and said they'd see us out there. Accordingly we turned to 53 Squadron at Brize Norton for use of a Short Belfast. This machine of gargantuan proportions was fully capable of lifting us all there and back, as long as we weren't in a hurry. Having been issued with vitamin C tablets against scurvy (standing joke), we left Brize at 10.00hrs on the 5th of August and, with a cruising speed of 270 knots across the Atlantic, night stopped at Gander (Newfoundland) some nine hours later. The next day we flew west for fourteen hours and three thousand miles to reach Vancouver, having re-fuelled at Winnipeg. The landscape which unrolled beneath us for hour after hour from cruising altitude consisted of seemingly endless evergreen forest and lakes. We lashed hammocks in the back and had at least three card schools going atop the boxes containing the rigs. No iPods in those days.

This year the Air Show was to be a special event, forming part of the Canadian Centennial celebrations and we were to represent the Royal Air Force along with the Avro Vulcan bomber. In addition to military aerobatic teams from Canada and the United States, there was a considerable incursion of many private light aircraft, both modern and historic, from over the border, and the whole weekend took on the complexion of a three-day mass aeronautical rally. We arrived in Vancouver on the Sunday evening, and were booked into the Towers Hotel, just off Royal Avenue next to New Westminster City Hall. The next day Ken and I drove out to the Abbotsford sport parachute club, where the owner, Bill Hardman, made us most welcome, while in turn we made ourselves useful as we put out one Club member on his C licence qualifier from the local Cessna 180. We returned the next day to jump again; for transport, Ken and I had the use of a Lincoln Mercury Monarch sedan, and thereby hangs a tale. Over breakfast at the Towers on the first morning we had met perchance a local realtor, Fred Filbert, and his lady wife. We got on so well that this gentleman loaned us his car for the duration of the stay. We asked if we could do anything in return; it was agreed that he give us both five hundred of his business cards for future use... .

We reported at the airfield for rehearsals on the Thursday morning: our first lift was for the benefit of the local press and we carried photographers and reporters on board as we made the first of our three training jumps. It was mid August with nil wind conditions and a baked hard surface, which combination proved a bit too tasty for Stu Cameron who suffered a fractured fibula on landing one of his early jumps. This precluded his further active participation and he handed over to Geoff Greenland for the rest of the trip. Friday was the first Open Day, and Ken and I were able to provide Fred Filbert with some publicity, as we packed the business cards into our PCs. On opening, these fluttered down among the spectators from two thousand feet, much to Fred's delight and hopefully to good effect. This confetti cloud was noted by Tim Tasker, above us when we opened, much to his puzzlement. Nothing was said about our private enterprise, sure Tim and Terry Allen would have done the same, given the opportunity.... We put on the high show to capacity crowds the next three days. After each day the local hospitality was nonstop and we had more private invitations than we could cope with. We also found time to visit Stanley Park, a thousand acre area to the north of the city, which was the original territory of indigenous Indian tribes and dedicated to their heritage. This was one of our more memorable trips, and Sunday was the final day with the inevitable party; on Monday morning we poured Pete George onto the Belfast, lashed down the Landrover, and flew twelve hours to Gander, arriving just after midnight. Next evening we took off for the overnight to Brize, arriving for a late breakfast the following morning. This was a pretty concentrated ten days, involving forty-four flying hours in transit across nine time zones and return, eight hours jump flying, six high shows, and (for Ken and me) two civilian sport jumps. Next weekend, Ken and I made eight jumps at Weston on the Sunday (still all for an extra six shillings and ninepence per day).

The following weekend we were off to Italy again, to Ravenna on the northern Adriatic coast. In my time on the Falcons, there were major Air Shows at many European cities, with aerobatic teams from France (Patrouille de France), Italy (Frecce Tricolori) and of course the Royal Air Force Red Arrows, flying the Folland Gnat. We got to know the Arrows team quite well, through meetings at briefings and post-display banquets. That weekend both our teams were out on the airfield before the morning dress rehearsal, and a couple of our members wandered some twenty metres upwind of the Arrows team relaxing on the grass, and set off a couple of Wessex canisters, which enshrouded the red-clad flying aces in pungent orange smoke, much to their voluble discomfort. Retribution was not too far away; we were sitting under the shade of our Argosy's wing awaiting our turn to go when a couple of the scarlet Gnats beat up our group at about two hundred knots. These people flew at us BELOW the Argosy wingtip. Respect indeed. This was of course 1967, the Ramstein disaster was some twenty years in the future, and in those days the rules regarding horizontal separation from the crowd line were a little more flexible. We then took a couple of weeks off before another demo at the Belgian Parachute School at Schaffen. In October we had the use of a C130 Hercules for the first time, making a couple of jumps, and the year ended with a further training detachment to El Adem, where we made a dozen jumps in ten days, most from 16,000 feet pre-breathing oxygen from the on-board console.

The 1968 season opened for us in late January, with competition training at Weston. In February Geordie and I were engaged in filming a commercial for the Milk Marketing Board. Tim Tasker, somewhat reluctantly it must be said, handed over the Beaulieu cine camera to me and we flew the Rapide five lifts in one day with Gerry Schellong hauling the Rapide up to eleven thousand feet above Weston, earning some valuable revenue for the Club as well as giving me equally valuable camera experience in the process. This assignment had been secured by our new OC PTS, Wing Commander Dick Mullins, who took a keen interest in the Club and who gave us a lot of support, particularly important as this year was a World Championship year, and Geordie, Ken and I were going all out for a place on the British team. We were fortunate in this respect, in that the Falcons had a total of sixteen instructors to select from, which gave OC PTS a bit of leeway in terms of giving us time off team duties for competition training. The Falcons leadership had now passed to Flying Officer Geoff Greenland, with Terry Allen starting his fourth season as team Flight Sergeant and cameraman. We had also acquired a team mascot in the shape of a real live Indian Lagger Falcon christened Quinquaginta by our Advanced Training Squadron Commander, Brian White, in recognition of the fact that this was the 50th Anniversary of the Royal Air Force. This being rather too much of a mouthful for the majority lacking a classical education, we all called him Fred, and despatched Alan Rhind up to RAF Lossiemouth for a five-day Falcon handling course, built a cage behind the section, acquired a bird tray and henceforth took him wherever we went.

Early in March we were out to El Adem again for a couple of weeks, this time I spent most of my jumps following out from the Argosy tailgate working with, and critiquing, student jumpers. Our first show back in the UK was at RAF Thorney Island; my logbook shows a surface wind of 25 knots. I remember backing in, standing up, then taking off again backwards at speed under an inflated canopy (shades of Everleigh eight years earlier). My smoke brackets snagged and tripped me up, and I succeeded in breaking my elbow on the second landing. This accident put me out for three weeks. On the 29th of March we flew out to Milan Malpensa via Nice, this time with no stopover. Our final destination was Vergiate, some five miles north of the airport. The next morning, I took advantage of a couple of free hours to explore the beautiful Lombardy countryside on the doorstep of our hotel and take a few photographs. We were in Vergiate for the International Air Show where we received top billing alongside the Frecce Tricolori and the Patrouille de France. The airfield was only a few miles south of the Italian Lakes, and the visuals as we flew a low-level holding pattern for over an hour were absolutely stunning. Cloud eventually restricted the show to 3,000 feet, the following morning we were on our way back to the UK for ten more training days before our next excursion into the demo arena.

This was the Biggin Hill Air Fair, and took place on the Sunday afternoon, the 12th of May. The weather was cold, low cloud and rain, with the smoke from the sodium flare horizontal across the airfield. The Argosy ran in and out of the cloud base, and we all left at four thousand feet in a sim. six over eight hundred metres to the southwest of the field. I was about number four, once out of the aircraft I dipped a shoulder, turned outwards and pulled on the number three's extractor at around two and a half thousand feet. As I ran toward the twin marker crosses I could see the red and white roundels of our Para Commanders widely scattered and disappearing over the dispersals towards the wooded areas behind. The smoke was hugging the ground and from about eight hundred feet I saw one canopy touch down between the markers, remain inflated, and drag the helpless jumper across the runway towards the flight line where several of the display aircraft were running up their engines. The canopy hit the live prop of a Mustang, and instantly imploded into a whirling blue ball. From eight hundred feet I heard the bang as the engine seized and stopped. I was then carried by the squall over the runway, over the Mustang, over the dispersals and managed to find a few clear square metres behind the fire section to land in. As I returned to the tea tent I came upon Geoff Greenland wandering around looking pretty bemused with his finger strapped up. He had a small remnant of blue taffeta nylon in his hand, a section of his canopy, given to him by a young spectator. He was still in shock, only later understanding that it was he who had been dragged into the prop, which wound up his canopy and lines and pulled him in a couple of feet under the nacelle before the engine stalled. His container was shredded and the ripcord housing was completely severed by the propeller. It was that close. Once again, SOPs for Falcons Air Shows were amended accordingly… . Two weeks later, we flew out to Bari, on the heel of Italy, for what was to be my final Falcons demo of the year. From the end of May Geordie, Ken and I were excused duty to train for the upcoming British Nationals; in the event we made ninety-five jumps in the following five weeks. Not even the visit to Abingdon by Her Majesty Queen Elizabeth the Second for the Royal Review warranted our recall. We were out at Weston working on our style training.

The British Nationals that year were held at the APA Centre Netheravon on the weekend of the 5th, 6th and 7th July. On the morning of the fifth, we each made five practice style jumps at Weston, then drove the fifty miles down to Netheravon where the Meet Director decided to crack on straight away with the Style event. By nine that evening we had completed the three style rounds and secured the top three places. Over the weekend we finished off the accuracy event, coming second in the team event to the Red Devils, but our style times gave us the edge to take the Team Overall title. The top five competitors were selected to represent Great Britain at the 9th World Parachuting Championships in Graz, Austria. Geordie Charlton, Ken Mapplebeck and myself from the RAF, Brian David from the Red Devils and Dave Savage as the lone civilian. Team coach was Mike Turner and Head of Delegation was Major Peter Schofield, Team Commander of the Red Devils. Because of the continental weather conditions prevailing, the Rhine Army Parachute Centre at Bad Lippspringe was selected as the training venue. Mike had organised a Cessna 175 from Biggin Hill for three weeks, which was to leave on Monday the 15th with Geordie and myself on board, whilst Mike, Brian David and Ken left Aldershot on the Sunday in a van loaned to us by British Leyland. Geordie and I were weathered in at Biggin on the Monday, eventually arriving at Lippspringe early Tuesday evening. Mike was waiting for us with pliers in one hand and a coffee for the pilot in the other. He removed the split pins, took the door off, and put Brian and Ken on board for an accuracy load before dark. Geordie and I smiled at each other, looking forward to a meal. No chance; Mike had our own rigs ready so we jumped accuracy ourselves in the semi-gloom. This was to set the tempo for the next twenty days.

We jumped continuously from 16th July to 7th August; I personally made 137 jumps, 40 style and 97 accuracy. First take-off was 05.00 daily, and most of the accuracy jumps were from two thousand feet; occasionally when we had low cloud early morning, we took what we could get although we never jumped from lower than twelve hundred. One Saturday we had been weathered out, it cleared later on and Ken and I were up for a style jump. Passing six thousand cross wind, we noticed smoke coming from the heater, and flames appeared from underneath the engine housing. I was kneeling next the pilot with Ken in the back. John, the pilot, said "I think you had better…" but Ken was already gone. I was out on his back and we both turned a set from six thousand. The aircraft passed us in freefall and John made the airstrip and landed dead stick, while Ken and I landed several fields and woods away. The Cessna was fixed that evening and we carried on. The most jumping we did was fourteen in one day, and were completely weathered out on only three occasions, when Mike relented and took us to the Moehne Dam for a day out, an awe-inspiring structure indeed, with a special significance for the three of us from the Air Force. The Cessna eventually went unserviceable on the last two days so we finished up using an Army Beaver and the Centre's Rapide. All in all it was a most worthwhile training camp, with variable and varying wind conditions such as we might expect down in southern Austria. Our final day was Wednesday 7th August; we made eight team jumps and were as ready as we ever would be. The following afternoon we packed our kit into the van, and headed south. Graz was some nine hundred kilometres away, and Mike was impatient to get down there nonstop. After a midnight transit of the Austrian Alps, round first-gear hairpin bends, brushing towering limestone cliffs with dimly-glimpsed lakes lurking in steeply-wooded valleys, we arrived about five in the morning on the Friday and looked for coffee in the market place under the shadow of the famous clock tower. We contacted the Organisers and headed off to the competition site at the Graz Thalerhof airport, left our parachutes in store, and then moved on to our accommodation in the University hostel.

The competition area was in a clearing some five hundred metres to the west of the main runway, backing on to a wooded area. The target area is still there to be seen today, forty-five years later. The team tents of the twenty-six competing nations were ranged in a semi circle one hundred metres from the target centre. The aircraft in use were Antonov AN2s from the USSR, the DDR, and Czechoslovakia. We made one practice jump on the Saturday; then we had a three-day hold until the organisers and judges finally got their act together, and finalised the rules and conditions. International competition was still in its relative infancy, rules were still being updated and developed year on year. The points-based scoring system remained unnecessarily complicated; in accuracy for example, 250 points were awarded for a dead centre and points deducted for each centimetre off the disc. The dead centre disc was 15cm in diameter and everything was measured manually, a fichet being placed at the first point of contact. The electronic pad was still six years in the future. The Style event was similarly points based. A further anachronism was in competition management, in that the individual accuracy event was just that – each competitor jumped on his or her own individual pass for four rounds. Team Accuracy was a separate event, comprising three rounds, four jumpers per team. It was not until several years later that the International Parachuting Commission (CIP) adopted the International Military Sports Council(CISM) rules in that Team Accuracy and Individual were combined, individual results being extrapolated from the team scores. With 26 nations competing, comprising 129 male and 53 female competitors that made for a lot of go-arounds for the Antonovs to finish the four-round Individual Event. Under these conditions it was not surprising that the competition took two weeks to complete.

At the end, the Meet was dominated by the USA and the Soviets, who took first and second places overall respectively, with the DDR in third place. Canada was fourth and Czechoslovakia was fifth, whilst the Brits achieved their best result so far with sixth position out of 26 teams in the World Overall standings. Whilst the Soviets dominated the Style event, the USA had marginally superior accuracy jumpers. This notwithstanding, the latter were comprehensively outjumped by the Czechs, using the KRAS PTCH-7. Czech jumper Jaroslav Kalous won the male Individual Accuracy with four DCs, after a dramatic three round jump-off with Australian Colin King; Helena Tomsikova won the female Accuracy, and the Czech female team took the Team Accuracy event. Only a disastrous first round jump pushed the Czech male team into 15th place in Team Accuracy. This certainly worked to our advantage as we achieved the first-ever British medal at a World Meet, coming in bronze position behind the DDR and the USA. Geordie scored two dead centres and a 17cm in this event. The camaraderie between competitors was exceptional, although there was a poignant interlude at dinner one evening, when the Czech team appeared as a group in silent protest as Soviet armour rolled into Prague on the night of 20th–21st August. We Brits made friendships, in particular with the Czech competitors, which endure to the present day; and Ivo Skotak loaned me a PTCH 7 to jump on the closing ceremony. Following the medal presentation Mike collected in our jumpsuits to return to the BPA office, and we headed for home the following morning with abiding memories of a great competition experience in the most beautiful Styrian landscape, of many new friends, and of the outstanding hospitality of our hosts.

We returned to the crew room after a few days off, with a sense of *déjà vu*. Life continued at PTS and, medals or no medals, the main task remained. The team split up, Geordie was scheduled for Hereford, and Ken went to Cyprus; whilst I, having been promoted at the beginning of July, was back on the floor as a Syndicate Flight Sergeant. I would rate 1967–68 as the most intensive period of jumping of my career; in all I made over six hundred descents, a respectable number for that era. I would also rate Geordie and Ken as the best two individual competitors the School has ever produced. Geordie represented Great Britain at four World Championships, Ken at three. Both possessed a fiercely competitive instinct and it would be invidious to separate them in terms of ability. Suffice it to say we enjoyed an unforgettable two years together, and that Ken and I would continue to work together in the international arena for many more.

38. *RAF Falcons Mk 1 Para Commander canopy 1967.*

**39.** *Falcons Abingdon 1967. Dave Jones, George Muir, Self, Stuart Cameron, Les Evans, Andy Sweeney with shades, Ken Mapplebeck, Pete George. Back to camera, Geordie Charlton plus one unidentified jumper with his pack elastics unfastened... .*

**40.** *Geordie Charlton and our Rapide G-AGSH. RAF Weston on the Green 1967. The equipment is a Pioneer 4-pin main with 2-shot Capewells.*

94

**41.** *RAF Falcons at Nice Airport in July 1967, en route for Pescara. George Muir, Brian White, Alan Rhind, Brian Hedley, Mervyn Green.*

**42.** *Loading the Belfast at RAF Brize Norton en route for Vancouver. August 1967.*

**43.** *Royal Towers Hotel New Westminster, Vancouver, August 1967. Ray Brettel, Ken Mapplebeck and Les Evans. Note the event board for the Centennial Air Show.*

**44.** *Team repack at the Abbotsford Air Show behind the Argosy tailplane. Note tension devices for packing. Note also Stuart Cameron injured and on crutches.*

**45.** *British Team training camp at RAPA, Bad Lippspringe, July 1968. Self, Geordie Charlton, Peter Schofield, Mike Turner, Dave Savage.* Kneeling: *Ken Mapplebeck and Brian David.*

**46.** *9th World Parachute Championships, Graz, southern Austria, August 1968. This is the 50-metre target area with a Czech PTCH 7 canopy on finals.*

**47.** *Antonov AN2 jump aircraft. We had a total of nine available; these three are from the USSR, Czechoslovakia and the DDR.*

**48.** *Australian Colin King with first placed Jaroslav Kalous from Czechoslovakia. Note the 15cm dead centre disc.*

98

**49.** *British Team Bronze medal winners in Team Accuracy at the 9th WPC 1968. Brian David, Geordie Charlton, Ken Mapplebeck and the author.*

**50.** *Long Service Medal 1969. Presented by RAF Abingdon Station Commander, Group Captain R. C. P. Thompson.*

**51.** *RAFSPA Team, British National Championships Netheravon 1969. Winners Overall Team and Team Accuracy. Bob Swainson, Tony Born, Tony Dale, John Robinson, Gp. Capt. Thompson, Mike Deakin, and the author.*

**52.** *RAF Falcons Team 1970.* Back row: *Bill Cook, Dave Ross, Sid Garrard, Joe Featherstone, Les Allworthy, George Long.* Front row: *Barry Furness, Alan Rhind, Alan Jones, Dave Cobb, Self, Pete George, Doug Dewar.*

53. *With 16mm Beaulieu cine camera at RAF Sharjah in October 1969.*

54. *RAF Outdoor Activity Centre Llanwrst in the Conwy Valley, January 1970. Doug Dewar, Pete George, Pete Davis, Sid Garrard, Smokey Furness, Al Jones, Dave Cobb, Dave Ross, Alan Rhind, Les Allworthy, George Long kneeling.*

**55.** *Pete George, Sid Garrard, Pete Davis, George Long, local guide, Doug Dewar. Above the Llyn Cowlyd Reservoir, January 1970.*

**56.** *US 8th Infantry Division Airborne School Wiesbaden. Team kitting up for wings jump. Joe Featherstone, John Grimes, Commandant "Dutch" Passalaigue, Dave Cobb, Dave Ross, Roy McCluskey, Harry Appleby, back to camera. Bill Cook is on the right.*

102

**57.** *Joe Featherstone and Smokey Furness over the Juweiza Drop Zone Sharjah 1970.*

*Photo Alan Rhind*

**58.** *Juweiza DZ Control 1970. Brian White, Ray Willis, Roy McCluskey, Joe Featherstone, Snowy, Henry MacDonald, Al Jones.*

103

*59.  Drop Zone neighbours at Juweiza, Sharjah 1970.*

| Chapter 6 | *Coach* |
|---|---|
| | *1969-1970* |

We returned from the World Parachute Championships in time for what was left of the PTS stand down, and for the next twelve months I was fully employed on Basic Training Squadron as a syndicate Flight Sergeant. The C130 Hercules was now coming in to replace the Argosy, and from September 1968 until April the next year most of my jumps were military static line, working on balloon programmes, Hercules aircraft drills and jumping the Mk 4 PX canopy with the net skirt. In April, the club opened at Weston again for business, we had quite a few promising young competitors, not only from the PJI ranks but also airmen from Abingdon and other neighbouring units. From the middle of July Geordie and I ran a training camp at Weston as a lead up to the Nationals; this was to pay off handsomely, as the RAF team swept the board at Netheravon in August, winning both the Team Accuracy and Team Overall event. The team was John Robinson and Tony Dale (PJIs), plus Mike Deakin, Tony Born, Dave Brewin and Bob Swainson, with myself as coach. Our best jumper was Tony Born, placed 4th in Style and 4th overall. Tony continued to work hard at his jumping, and next year was to earn his place along with Geordie on the National team at the 1970 WPC in Bled.

Come September and the PTS management decided I could be spared from Basic training, and moved me on to the Falcons under the new title of Team Coach. This job description suited me fine, and, as the first current competition jumper to be so appointed, I felt I had some experience to offer. My immediate boss was Team Leader Flight Lieutenant Dave Cobb, who had been number two to Mervyn Green the previous year. Our own number two was Flying

Officer Alan Jones (ADG), and I considered myself exceptionally lucky and privileged to be able to work with these two Team Leaders over the next two years. As well as coach, I decided to take on the job of cine cameraman, with Allan Rhind looking after the still photography on the Nikon. The rest of the team were Pete George, Joe Featherstone, Sid Garrard, Les Allworthy, Doug Dewar, and Dave Ross from the 1969 team, plus newcomers Barry (Smokey) Furness and George Long. Making a comeback was Bill Cook, a member of the 1967 team. Harry Appleby was our permanent DZ man.

For this season we would be using the C130 most of the time as the Argosy was being phased out. At our first briefing, Dave and I felt that one of the first issues to address was the high show – the track pattern. I voiced my reservations regarding the visual impact of the pattern, and also my misgivings over safety issues. Dave was with me all the way on both points, having been dropped way deep over the Irish Sea on a previous season's demo at Jurby, Isle of Man. We decided to return to an extended variation of the original pattern at Farnborough 1961; the whole team were to form a thick smoke column; then six trackers would radiate out for twenty seconds, then track turn back for the opening point. We now had twice the number of jumpers as at Farnborough, and decided on a simultaneous six exit from port and starboard doors. First three on either side would form and hold a six-way, the next six would fall in their smoke column for twenty seconds, then split six ways for a forty second out and back track. The visual effect was most spectacular in light wind conditions when the exit was nearly overhead. This was discussed with the team, and all were in full agreement that this was the way forward. My only other concern was to tighten up the accuracy; jumpers were reminded that the team would be judged not only on the air work but also on the precision of landing. We put out two crosses ten metres apart, and I wanted all canopies overlapping these two targets every time.

Our first winter training session was organised for Sharjah in the Persian Gulf. In 1969 the RAF still had a base there, and we flew out in the C130, via Malta, at the end of October. We recced a Drop Zone at Juweiza, some ten miles to the east of the Sharjah main runway and started work on practising the high pattern. Dave Cobb had very limited spotting experience, and the featureless desert made this an even more difficult exercise. Day one did not go particularly well; groups were widely scattered among the dunes, giving rise to some mutterings from the troops, and we therefore decided to give Dave some concentrated practice in the door. On our second session we flew two consecutive sixty-minute sorties making ten passes each time, dropping jumpers in pairs from 12,000 feet so Dave could have some continuity. At the end of the day Dave, albeit slightly hypoxic, was controlling the spot with the confidence of a veteran. Spotting an aeroplane of this size gives one quite a sense of power when compared with a light aircraft; give five left and the machine banks into a massive turn then settles on the new heading, call the green, pull the smokes, and away go the whole team clearing the doors inside six seconds. For present day jumpers, the advent of GPS and square canopies has rendered the art of spotting much less critical; current canopies can make up an error well in excess of one thousand metres, whereas with a Para Commander it was five hundred at best, and half that in the days of the round canopy TUs of the early 1960s. For myself at least, one of the most rewarding experiences parachuting had to offer was the accurate spotting of an aircraft load of jumpers from altitude into a tight DZ under marginal conditions. I contented myself with follow-outs for the first four days; then put on the Beaulieu camera to film some of the air work. I look at the miniature Go-Pros today with a wry smile; I had a 16mm film camera powered by two dry batteries stuffed inside the jumpsuit. There were two minutes of film per magazine, enough for two sorties, running at 32 frames per second. I soon got the hang of the job, but always had to support the head on opening, as the camera weighed ten pounds. RAF Sharjah was a popular venue, with guaranteed parachuting weather, and no airspace problems. It also provided a great winter break with temperatures in the mid to high twenties. We cemented good relations with the local Sheik, giving him an airfield demo on the 5th of November, and we always found ourselves welcome in the Sergeants' Mess.

We returned to the UK in mid-November after twenty jumps apiece, then made another dozen or so before the Christmas stand down. In the middle of January, as there was not much parachuting weather, Dave and Al Jones decided the team should have a change of scene and organised a short detachment to the RAF Outdoor Activities Centre at Llanwrst in North Wales. This proved to be a most popular idea and a most successful break. After a couple of days acclimatisation we took the bus to Madryn on the Conwy Bay coast, up a single track road to the drop-off point then trekked back the twenty or so miles over the top of the Drum (*Carnedd Penyborth-goch*) back to Llanwrst. I remember at the summit at two and a half thousand feet we were thigh deep in snow and walking a compass bearing to avoid the vertical crags in a white-out with less than fifty metres visibility, drawing heavily on our rusty basic map reading skills. The change of scene did us all a power of good as we camped overnight on the hill west of Dolgarrog, and walked home down the valley via Trefriw the next morning.

Back at PTS we were weathered in most of the month, and at the beginning of March we were once again out in Sharjah for another twenty high jumps in a couple of weeks. There were no particular dramas, and both Dave and I were happy with the progress the team were making.

In April the first two demos, Gaydon and Southend were blown out, and we reverted to the Argosy at the end of the month for our return to Vergiate where we gave a couple of high shows. In early May we flew out to Wiesbaden in Germany as guests of the US Army 8th Infantry Division Airborne School. The CO was Major "Dutch" Passalaigue who I had met in Leutkirch back in 1963. We jumped a rehearsal on the Saturday, followed by an American static line wings jump from the H34 using their T10 parachutes. I remember (strange, which inconsequential events one does remember) doing a standup under this huge docile canopy and judging my landing height by watching my shadow approach the ground; the reserve was positioned so high I could not see over it. The next day we performed a high show from 9,000 feet then enjoyed (as I definitely recall) a particularly memorable evening downtown Wiesbaden then back home on the Monday morning.

On Thursday the 14th of May we used the Argosy for a demo rehearsal at the Abingdon Town Cricket Club ground by the river. The following Saturday we flew down to Bentwaters in the C130 for an Open Day demo at the USAF base. This occasion proved to be a crunch point in the team's professional performance; things did not go well. It was a hot day, with light winds, the exit point was virtually overhead, and for some reason the exits were slow beyond belief. Coupled with this was a lack of awareness, and out of twelve jumpers only four of us made the target area; Dave Cobb, a couple more, and myself. The rest were strung out over about five hundred metres short. Agreed the winds were light, but that was no excuse. After everyone had reported back, Dave gave a short debrief and handed over to me. What angered me most was that some of the errant jumpers treated it as a joke; I swiftly and forcibly corrected this attitude, and from that point on we understood each other much better. At the end of the month we used the C130 for the Abingdon Town demo; strange indeed it was to fly low level over a familiar built-up area in such a large airframe. On the 5th of June we flew out to Tirstrup in northeastern Denmark, we jumped twice over the airfield on the Saturday. I took advantage of the second jump to do some filming. My logbook for that particular weekend records 12,000 feet, track pattern demo, excellent all round; the Bentwaters debacle was behind us and we were back in business. Over June, July, August and September we made over fifty demo jumps, including rehearsals, at twenty-five venues, from Norwich to Newcastle, Tirstrup to Tollerton, and Wiesbaden to Waddington. In July we jumped at RAF Patrington (where??), a radar station in an East Yorkshire village just north of the Humber Estuary. This was my boyhood home territory and, by coincidence, the jump run took us right over the old Hedon aerodrome where, back in 1938, I had been taken to a prewar airshow. I can distinctly recall parachutists on the programme making low level demo jumps; the picture of the oscillating white canopies remained in my memory over the intervening years; now I was in the same business, turning in over the Humber three miles to the south and exiting the C130 at nine thousand feet in a hailstorm at the back of the tracking group over the village, before turning and hammering back to the opening point. Home territory indeed. Standups all round, tea and sandwiches, kit on the bus then a couple of hours back on the road to Waddington to pick up the Herc for home.

Interspersed with this for me was also work at Weston, as the British National team ran a training camp for the upcoming World Meet in Yugoslavia. I was helping judge the accuracy, and also doing camera runs on the style jumpers, John Meacock, Geordie, and Dave Savage. The Royal Air Force maintained a strong influence in the BPA at the time; Gerry Turnbull was still Chairman of the Association, and by this time Bill Paul, who had retired from PTS as a Squadron Leader, had been appointed as Secretary General. Squadron Leader Alan (Doc) Johnson, erstwhile Senior Medical Officer at Abingdon, freefall jumper, and now at the School of Aviation Medicine at Farnborough, was Chairman of the Safety Committee, while Geordie and Tony Dale were members of Council. Doc Johnson was British Team Head of Delegation at the aforementioned 10th WPC in Bled with both Geordie and Tony Born on the team. For the record, Bob King and Bob Hiatt made their first appearance here on the British team, names which will feature prominently in future pages as international jumpers.

Saturday the 19th of September was Battle of Britain day and we flew three demos at St Mawgan (abortive), St Athan, and Benson, where we jumped the high show in perfect nil wind conditions. At the lineup the team had the honour of being presented to the reviewing officer, Marshal of the Royal Air Force Sir Arthur Harris, the wartime AOC-in-C of Bomber Command who had retired to the neighbouring town of Goring-on-Thames after the war. Dave Cobb's final demos were at RAF Waddington at the end of September, where we jumped on two successive days for the RAF

Staff College and the Joint Services Staff College. At the beginning of October we flew up to Teeside and back, an abortive round trip of two hours and that was it. It had been a genuine pleasure to work with Dave, we remain good friends and keep in touch to this day. Nonetheless, the show had to go on, and in October Dave handed over to Flight Lieutenant Alan Jones as the new Team Leader, with Flight Lieutenant Gwynne Morgan as deputy. Flying Officer John Parry was assigned as DZ Officer and commentator, with Harry Appleby as DZNCO.

Under this new regime we flew out to Sharjah early in November from Lyneham, on what was probably our most intensive and successful training and selection detachment so far. We had all the team from last year, and brought along triallists Ray Willis, Bob Souter, Henry MacDonald, Ty Barraclough, Tony Dale, Joe France, Joe McCready, Chris Buchan and Denis Wreford, plus Flight Lieutenants Roy McCluskey and John Grimes. Squadron Leader Brian White, OC Advanced Training Squadron was the Detachment Commander. We used the same Juweiza DZ, and settled in to a five jump per day routine: I decided to concentrate on the movie camera work, with Alan Rhind doing the stills with his Nikon. We were aiming for publicity shots; one we were particularly working on was a flag jump with Joe and Smokey on the flag with Alan and myself filming alongside. We had been there for ten days when, on the first jump one morning the RAF Ensign tore away from the handles, so I concentrated on filming Joe and Smokey on the two-way. Joe came in for the pull at 2,500 feet as briefed and he had an extremely sticky pull, which needed two hands before the handle came out. I filmed all this and dropped clear, smiling away to myself; came in to pull and my own handle locked absolutely solid. I speedily stopped grinning, gave it two hands without success, then turned on to my back as gracefully as I could, and operated the reserve. The container opened, and the canopy remained neatly folded in the pack tray, trapped in the burble (no pilot chutes on reserves in those days). I took hold of the canopy and hurled it clear, then grabbed my helmet with the ten-pound Beaulieu and winced in anticipation of the canopy-first opening shock. This duly occurred and I found myself open at one thousand feet drifting backwards on an un-modified non-steerable I.24 in an eighteen-knot wind. Landed backwards on the slope of a sand dune at speed but unscathed, to be collected by an inquisitive DZ party some five minutes later. Being well aware where sympathy comes in the dictionary, I neither expected nor received any. The camera survived also. What we did find out, however, was that, in the desert environment, the ripcord pins in the 4-pin container were jamming because of a buildup of salt deposits on the pins themselves. We grounded all the rigs, and had all the pins cleaned and lightly greased with candle wax. In future, all pins were wiped and treated on each repack. As ever, we learned about parachuting from that.

Next jump we took the Herc up to sixteen thousand and put together the first Falcons eight-way, three weeks after the Royal Green Jackets Team completed the first ever British eight-way on the 17th of October at Dunkeswell. Once again, Sharjah proved a most successful training and selection detachment, as well as giving us all a welcome break in the sunshine, and a chance to experience new cultures. We visited the Dubai Creek and the Souk (market) in Sharjah. The dusty souk had an almost Biblical aura; it literally appeared as if unchanged for two thousand years; the next twenty were to see unprecedented modernization. Following this detachment, we took four newcomers on board for the Falcons 1971 Team; Bob Souter, Ray Willis, Henry MacDonald and Ron Bullen. Falcons 1971 was, for me at least, the only place to be.

**60.** *Four of the Boscombe Down Trials Team pictured after breaking the British Altitude Record in July 1967. Ken Kidd, Peter Keane, Keith Teesdale, Les Hick. The Team leader was John Thirtle (not in shot).*

**61.** *Falcons lineup in front of the RAAF C130 at Williamtown in March 1971. Gwynne Morgan, Bob Souter, Barry Furness, Joe Featherstone, Snowy, Doug Dewar, Henry MacDonald, Alan Jones, Sid Garrard, Alan Rhind, Ray Willis, Ron Bullen.*

113

**62.** *The Falcons arrive in Hong Kong, November 1971. John Parry, Dave Ross, Bob Souter, Harry Parkinson, Ray Willis and our Safety Equipment Fitter.*

**63.** *Hong Kong Government Stadium ground recce. From left: Jim Hurford, Peter Hearn, Gwynne Morgan, George Sizeland, Alan Rhind, Al Jones half hidden, John Parry, Bob Souter, with Ron Ellerbeck and Ray Willis back to camera. Snowy is in the foreground, with our SE Fitter apart on extreme left, and Harry Parkinson extreme right.*

114

**64.** *Government Stadium from 2,000 feet (foreground). Victoria Park DZ on the waterfront is at top centre.*

**65.** *Demo at the Racecourse on 4th December 1971. With Jim Hurford (left) and Alan Jones.*

115

**66.** *Repulse Bay on the south side of Hong Kong Island.*

**67.** *Tourist for the day. The author on the Governor's yacht off Hong Kong harbour.*

116

**68.** *The nine survivors on the final demo at Yuen Long on 6th December 1971. Peter Hearn, Alan Jones, Harry Parkinson, Self, Gwynne Morgan, Sid Garrard, Bob Souter, Doug Dewar, Henry MacDonald.*

**69.** *RAFSPA DH Rapide at Weston on the Green 1972.*

*Photo Mike Hand*

117

**70.** *Gerry Schellong, right, with Air Vice Marshal Fred Sowery at the British National Championships, Weston on the Green, May 1972.*

**71.** *Heathrow 15th July 1972. Ken Mapplebeck, John Kemley, Bill Paul, Bob King, John and Sue Meacock. Brian Standring and Dave Savage in the rear.*

118

**72.** *Ken Mapplebeck exits the Cessna 182 during team training at Raeford, July 1972.*

**73.** *Cherokee warrior chiefs at the Opening Ceremony of the 11th World Parachute Championships in Talequah, Oklahoma July 1972.*

119

74. *British Team at Talequah in July 1972. Self, Dave Savage, Ken Mapplebeck, John Meacock, Bob King.* Kneeling: *Brian Standring, Sheila Luker (guest jumper), John Kemley.*

75. *The Target area at Talequah. The canopy is a Czech PTCH 8.*

**76.** *Air Force Medal, Buckingham Palace February 1973. With Mary, Helen and Heidi.*

**77.** *RAFSPA Robins Demo Team, Abingdon March 1973: Self, Ken Mapplebeck, Harry Parkinson, Peter Hearn, Peter Smout, Graham Pierce.*
*Photo Ray Willis*

**78.** *The author on Mk 1 Paraplane, February 1973. Note no stabiliser panels, no slider.*

79. *With Peter Hearn over RAF Abingdon in March 1973.*

*Photo Ray Willis*

# Chapter 7

# Oz to Hong Kong

*1971*

We returned from Christmas stand down to the bad news of a PJI parachuting fatality at Boscombe. Les Hick had died shortly before Christmas Eve as a result of a malfunction whilst testing a stabilised fall rig from 12,000 feet on the Fox Covert DZ. Les and I were old friends; we had served together for a couple of years as PTIs in Germany; he had previously seen service in the Royal Navy in WW2, had been decorated with the Atlantic Star, and then played professional football after the war. We both played in the RAF Geilenkirchen station team and he had been a witness at our wedding. He joined us at PTS in 1957 where we again played Station and Command football together. Les then went to Boscombe, where, in July 1967, he was a member of the five-man team which established a British parachute height record of 41,393 feet at the Larkhill DZ. Les was a true Yorkshireman and a staunch friend; he left us far too early.

This all notwithstanding, life had to continue, and the 1971 Falcons team reported for duty in January. We were blessed with good jumping weather for the next six weeks, making some two dozen high jumps both on the airfield at Abingdon and at Weston. In mid-January Alan Jones called me into his office with the news that we had been invited to Australia to participate in the Jubilee commemorating the fiftieth anniversary of the formation of the Royal Australian Air Force. This was a most prestigious invitation beyond doubt, and it was arranged that for the first three weeks we should train with the Parachute Training Flight based at RAAF

Williamtown, in New South Wales. The detachment commander was OC PTS, Wing Commander Norman Johnstone, with Ron Ellerbeck, Frank Weatherley and Geordie Maguire assisting John Parry and Harry Appleby on the DZ. An MOD film unit was concurrently shadowing the Falcons, and Ron was given a 16mm cine camera to take exit shots and also shoot ground footage on the detachment. The BPA have archived a film of the whole year's jumping at Home British Parachute Association.

We flew out from Lyneham on Monday the 8th of March in a C130 on our six-day trip down under. The freight bay was packed with kit and piled high with cardboard boxes containing the parachutes. Some of the guys rigged hammocks, and there were the inevitable card schools atop the boxes. The first leg was six hours to Akrotiri to refuel, then a further five to night-stop in Muharraq (Bahrain). Next day was seven hours to Gan in the Indian Ocean where we enjoyed a morning swimming and snorkelling. From Gan we went on to Changi (Singapore), thence the next day another six-hour leg to RAAF Darwin in the Australian Northern territories. Once disembarked, we enjoyed the hospitality of the Sergeants' Mess at their monthly Guest night, (over which event it is deemed prudent to draw a discreet veil), before embarking on our final two thousand mile leg across the barren Northern Territories, flying over Ayres Rock, into New South Wales and our final destination of Williamtown.

We settled into the Mess and reported in on the Monday morning for work. At that time, the Australian Parachute Training Wing was a joint Army/Air Force establishment, with parachute instructors drawn from both Services. The School Warrant Officer and Chief Instructor was Air Force WO Fred Huntley, and we had a great reception from all the staff. Our own Herc left us at this point and for the rest of the tour we were flown by Australian crews in RAAF C130s. Our prime pilot was Vietnam veteran Flight Lieutenant Al Adamson, who flew us on all our demos, and on most of the training jumps onto the Saltash ranges behind the base. One thing we noticed immediately was that the size and lack of features on these ranges made it difficult accurately to judge height in freefall; it was like jumping over open water. We alternated our programmes between filming RW exercises and demo practises, and our OC PTS, Norman Johnstone, ostensibly there to run the DZ, was determined to be fully involved. He surprised us one morning by appearing kitted up, with Fred Huntley and another Australian instructor, ready to jump. Unbeknown to us he had approached the Australian staff and undergone a day's AFF-type training before going off the ramp at 12,000 feet with his two Australian instructors. The good Wing Commander would have agreed that he was not a particularly prolific jumper, but he gained much street cred by making his first freefall on this occasion. Between 15th and 20th March, we flew fifteen sorties at Saltash: I obtained some useful cine footage over the Pacific seabord with Ray Willis, Bob Souter and Sid Garrard, flying an arrowhead formation and track, early attempts at what today is routine formation skydiving.

It was now time to get serious; we were scheduled to give demonstrations at seven major cities on four consecutive weekends as part of the RAAF Anniversary celebrations. The programme was Perth; Canberra, Sydney; Adelaide, Melbourne; Brisbane and Townsville. Sydney was the closest, and we jumped a rehearsal from 12,000 feet on the 23rd of March at RAAF Richmond before flying seven hours to Perth for another rehearsal at RAAF Pearce three days later on the Friday. The ground was absolutely parched and the DZ party set half the airfield alight with the sodium flares. We had to take drastic action to avoid the flames; otherwise we would have had no rigs left at all. The demo was scheduled for the Sunday, we were unfortunately restricted to 3,000 feet by cloud and rain but the accuracy was spot on as at least we had no distracting conflagrations on the waterlogged DZ to deal with. Monday morning back east across the continent seven hours to Williamtown, then a couple more training jumps before a low-level rehearsal at Richmond again. The surface winds were twenty knots plus, a few of the guys were dragged, and we were distinctly not amused; I recall that a full and frank exchange of professional opinion ensued between the jumpers and the hapless DZSO.

On Saturday 3rd of April, we jumped from 12,000 feet at RAAF Fairbairn (Canberra) before a full house of one hundred thousand spectators. I jumped camera, recording some close contact work with the base and even closer contact with several pairs of boots on the split. We followed this up on the Sunday with a similar show at Richmond; my logbook records another full house with a great aerial pattern and everybody on target. Two days later we did a full demo pattern at our home base Williamtown; logbook indicating a highly satisfactory exercise. We repeated this the next evening with a high show, this time landing on the sports field specifically for the families, who had extended superb hospitality to us all during the whole trip. We then had four days off over Easter, enjoying barbecues and a leisurely boat trip up the Hunter River. Back to work on the Wednesday when we flew south to Adelaide, capital city of South Australia. I remember Adelaide as being a truly beautiful city, built on a grid pattern, with elegant tree-lined boulevards and red brick villas in the suburbs. The demo DZ was RAAF Edinburgh to the north of the city. Once again, we had clear blue skies for the Friday rehearsal, but had to settle for a four thousand foot cloudbase and fifteen-knot winds on the Saturday demo. Repack, then airborne the same evening for the four hundred miles east to Melbourne for a demo at RAAF Laverton on the Sunday. We returned to Williamtown the next day, transiting between Point Cook and Tullamarine International. The pace was hectic; travelling showmen we undoubtedly were.

After seven nonstop weeks in Australia, our stay was drawing to a close; we spent the last two days at Williamtown packing up and saying farewells, before embarking on the ninety minute flight north to Brisbane, where we were scheduled for our final weekend double header. We jumped two camera sorties at the RAAF Amberley base on the Friday by way of rehearsal, before completing a high show on the Saturday, reprising Peter Hearn's first PTS team who jumped there back in 1959. After a swift repack, Al Adamson flew us the seven hundred miles north to Townsville where we completed our final show from 6,000 feet on Sunday 25th of April. Next day we

127

were reunited with our own C130, and left the 80-degree sunshine for a seven-hour westwards leg back to Perth. The following day we flew a further eleven hours back to Gan before transferring to a chartered Britannia for a twenty-hour final journey to Brize via Muharraq and Akrotiri. All in all, we had been out of country for the best part of two months, travelled thirty thousand miles, had completed major demonstrations at seven Australian cities and logged some one thousand jumps in total. We had had no injuries to speak of, and after this intensive pre-season workout, team morale was sky high.

Once back home we were straight back to work. Having arrived back early on Thursday we reported in the next day to prepare for a Saturday show at Speke Airport on Merseyside, six days after the Townsville show. Bob Souter had by now assumed duties as Falcon handler and we jumped the Argosy on a low level demo. The following Saturday I was at Netheravon, filming from the APA Rapide, then next day Sunday off to a high show at Doncaster on to the old airport by the Racecourse. Two days later we jumped low level at Weston for the Air Officer Commanding 38 Group, Battle of Britain ace Air Vice Marshal Denis Crowley-Milling, before flying out to Sweden in the Herc for a low show at Gothenberg. My next ten jumps were spread over three days at Weston filming team members for the BBC. The BBC followed us to Mildenhall for a demo where I also jumped camera but we were restricted by cloud to three thousand feet.

During this crowded schedule we had been working closely with the Joint Services Freefall Team and had all undergone High Altitude Low Opening (HALO) training including two sessions in the altitude chamber, experiencing the symptoms of hypoxia at first hand. We first jumped at Larkhill using the GQ Tactical Approach Parachute assembly (TAP), and I filmed the bundle from 12,000 feet. Next day we took the Argosy up to 22,000 over Fox Covert, jumping full combat gear. We left the tailgate and built a three-way, silent under a pale blue hemisphere; the base of which, two miles below us, was a dazzling white carpet of cloud stretching unbroken in all directions. There was a unique sense of detachment as we fell for a full sixty seconds before plunging into the ice cloud at 10,000 feet. We came out of the bottom at 4,000, and opened at 3,000 without any problems, (shades of Keith Norry, nine years earlier – Chapter 3). Two days later, on Sunday, I was back at Weston with the Rapide down at 2,000 feet for accuracy practise; we then took the Argosy north to Church Fenton for a Bank Holiday demo. From Church Fenton we flew direct to North Weald for our final demo of a nonstop and varied May schedule, encompassing twenty-six jumps in eleven locations, highest 22,000 feet, lowest 800 from the balloon at Weston.

The month of June opened with six days at the Paris Le Bourget Air Show, where we were restricted to one rehearsal from the Argosy on the Thursday before being weathered out for the remaining three days. A high point of the show was the arrival of the Soviet TU 144 supersonic transport (SST) http://www.military.com/video/aircraft/ military-aircraft/rare-1971-paris-air-show-tu144/2344147500001/ – the atrocious weather conditions can be seen in this particular video clip. Returning to Abingdon, we immediately flew out to Italy for a midweek show in Carpi, in Northern Italy. We jumped twice, including a successful demo at the Air Show on the Thursday, which was followed by a banquet for all participating teams. The team were quartered in Brescia, some sixty miles away, hence had to return by coach at the conclusion of the evening. Also returning to Brescia on the coach were the Red Arrows team who had been participating, and with whom we had always maintained an excellent relationship. This genial state of affairs regrettably became somewhat strained when our falcon mascot slipped his leash from the back of the bus and flew forward to perch his claws on the scalp of the Red Arrows team leader. Terse words were exchanged between the respective team bosses, and Fred and his chastened handler retreated to the rear of the coach for the remaining miles back to the hotel. Back home, the ensuing contretemps was swiftly resolved without resource to disciplinary proceedings and we jumped in quick succession again with two demos at Coningsby, followed by shows at Wiesbaden, Exeter and Toulouse Francazal to complete the month.

July was equally busy; we flew twenty-six sorties, (including, for some reason, a static line water jump into Studland Bay) with demos at Topcliffe, Cranwell, Hullavington, Wyton, Cottesmore, Thorney Island, Shobdon and Culdrose. As part of our HALO commitment we again fitted in a 21,000 feet sortie at Fox Covert where I jumped camera, filming a two way in full combat equipment. After the shows at Wyton and Cottesmore, Sunday the 11th of July was a day off, and I was invited to join the Royal Greenjackets Display Team, under the leadership of my old friend Jim Crocker, for their demo onto the lawn at Blenheim Palace, taking off from Weston; (a probable deciding factor was that I was able to supply free Wessex smoke grenades). I always enjoyed demo jumping, and this one was particularly relaxing, sitting at the back, someone else doing the spotting; eight thousand feet and forty seconds freefall from the Islander, cloudless skies and nil wind, four-man star and bomb-burst, with all canopies overlapping on the elegant cricket square in front of an appreciative audience at this most distinguished of stately homes.

August was a quiet month, the most significant occurrence by far being the return to PTS of Wing Commander Peter Hearn as the new OC. Peter slipped in quietly as the School went on a two-week stand down and we made one single demo jump at Chivenor. As already related in Chapter 2, Peter had been the first Team Leader on the 1961 team and we were happy indeed to have a jumper back in charge. Next month, on the 3rd of September, we flew out from Benson in the Argosy to RAF Gütersloh. The following day, Saturday, we jumped a rehearsal into the small airfield of Marl-Loehmühle, a small township on the northern fringe of Germany's industrial Ruhrgebiet. This was a glorious late summer weekend; next day we performed an afternoon high show at Gütersloh, repacked, then jumped early evening another high show for the Marl Aero Club before a sizeable crowd of local enthusiasts. Winds were less than five knots and the precision landings of the team were a credit to all concerned, not a man of the twelve outside ten metres. There followed a mass balloon festival and a generous reception in the clubhouse before we took the coach back along the autobahn to Gütersloh for the Monday return to Benson.

The rest of September was relatively quiet, with demos at Abingdon, Rissington and Leuchars. On the 21st we took the C130 up to 25,000 feet for a night descent at Fox Covert with full HALO kit. It was a totally moonless night, but clear; we were blessed with outstanding visibility, the southern English coastline was highly defined by streetlights for miles, the landmass of Sussex, Hampshire, and Dorset contrasting with the blackness of the English Channel. Exit was standard, settle down in your own airspace, observe for other jumpers and enjoy the ride down. The briefing was to allow the Hitefinder to operate the main and my attention was certainly closely focused on the twin altimeters from four thousand feet; at three the TAP rustled silently off my back, I located the DZ markers below and headed for home. Released the Bergen onto my feet, and lowered it at about two hundred, descending by then into pitch darkness. I heard the Bergen hit the ground a half second before I did, landing right alongside the only water trough within miles, avoiding bifurcation by inches. Could have been nasty… .

The following month it was decided that team training and selection would be carried out in Cyprus; we flew out from Lyneham to Akrotiri with the C130 on the 16th of October. We started jumping on the Monday and completed three high lifts without incident on to my old DZ, the Ladies Mile beach (Chapter 4). The next day we emplaned as normal to continue the programme; we had brought several new jumpers along to try out for the team, among them was Flying Officer Ralph Ramshaw, in his first year at PTS, and recently returned from a freefall course at Fort Bragg with the US Army. In common with the rest of the trainees, Ralph was jumping a TU in an Irvin PB5 harness. On the first lift of the day we ran in at 12,000 feet towards the salt flats, got out and opened as normal at 2,000. Facing into wind, I immediately noticed two or three high canopies behind me backing up towards the sea. Wrong. As I landed at Drop Zone

Control, Ron Ellerbeck took off at speed in the Landrover towards the waterline some eight hundred metres away. Two canopies, one PC and one TU were in the sea. Ron Bullen was on the PC, about thirty metres in the water and made it back to the beach unaided. Tragically, Ralph was further out in deeper water and was unable to free himself from the harness. The first person to reach Ralph was ex-Falcon Team member Mick Geelan, now based at Akrotiri, who was up early watching the programme. Mick swam out and Ralph was brought back to land, sadly too late for any resuscitation. Jumping was suspended for a week; on the day of Ralph's funeral we jumped on to the Akrotiri sports field and observed a one-minute silence in tribute. Ralph was a family man, an outstanding soccer player and had been a great prospect for the team: like Les Hick the previous December, he left us far too early. We returned home three days later, pretty subdued, and not to jump for a further three weeks.

The final act of Falcons '71 was played out, as had been the first, many leagues from home. We had been invited to Hong Kong to participate in the 1971 Festival, a ten-day trade and cultural pageant which engendered massive local publicity. We flew out from Brize on the 16th of November in a VC10 for the six thousand mile trip via Akrotiri, Gan and Changi, finally touching down at RAF Kai Tak on the Kowloon peninsula after nineteen hours airborne. The Falcons had some high-level support on board; with the team were the Abingdon Station Commander, Group Captain Bill Green, and OC PTS, Peter Hearn who, naturally, had brought his jumping boots with him. The MOD Film Unit were also there in force, as were the Royal Air Force Central Band. Barry Furness had left the team mid-season, having re-mustered to loadmaster; Harry Parkinson had taken his place and had slotted in effortlessly.

We settled once more into the Sergeants' Mess at Kai Tak; the first few days were taken up with introductions, TV interviews and publicity shots both for the local press and for our own MOD cameramen, with falcon Fred prominently on show. We were scheduled to jump at various venues on the island, as well as several up-country in the New Territories. The centrepiece of these demos was the Government Stadium, set in a natural bowl with steep cliffs on three sides and a main highway on the fourth. Six times we were to jump there and P hour was to be 22.00 hrs, our first night demos. The met man told us that the winds at two thousand feet would be in the region of twenty knots, and that anabatic and katabatic turbulence within the bowl was likely to be pronounced. We nodded sagely in agreement, then went away to find out what he meant (updraughts and downdraughts). We went to look at the place the next morning and, as can be seen in the photo, this first viewing provoked some thoughtful expressions among the brethren. Before we did any jumping, however, we also decided to recce and photograph all the Drop Zones from the air at two thousand feet; as usual it all looked easier from upstairs. The only proviso we decided was to put an eight-hundred metre limit on the spot for the night jumps.

Our jumpships were to be 28 Squadron Westland Whirlwind helicopters, based at Kai Tak. These aircraft could only lift four jumpers, so we had to use three helicopters for each sortie, with myself in the lead aircraft doing the spotting. The crews were more familiar with operating at low level, whereas we required 10,000 feet on most occasions; so on the Monday for purposes of crew familiarisation we flew three high lifts at Sek Kong in the New Territories. This was followed the next day with a camera run with Bob Souter and Ray Willis from altitude into Victoria Park on the waterfront. This turned out to be a real rock'n roller in winds gusting eighteen knots, between the skyscrapers, everyone piling in backwards on the dusty soccer pitch with feet and knees tight together, legs reaching and turned off, with chin on chest and elbows tucked well in.

On the Wednesday we did our first rehearsal in daylight into the Government Stadium. As already mentioned, this was quite a tight area and we ran in at 3,300 feet with three Whirlwinds in line astern at one minute intervals, with a strict briefing to observe good stack discipline. As usual, we were reliant on the balloon/theodolite to provide wind information, the balloons being tracked at night by the attachment of a small candle suspended below each balloon. The day rehearsal went well, so on the Thursday we followed up with our first rehearsal at night, also without complications. Thus reassured we carried on with a high rehearsal into the Happy Valley racecourse on Friday, and a high demo for our hosts on to the airfield at Kai Tak on the Saturday. We jumped on Sunday afternoon at Sek Kong on the mainland, then prepared for the official opening demo at the Stadium that evening. I was designated to spot from the lead aircraft. As I noted at the time, in an extract I wrote for Peter Hearn's "*Falcons*":

*"We waddled out to the choppers at Kai Tak about nine o'clock in the evening for our first demo, festooned with 'chutes, life jackets, smoke brackets, torches to illuminate the canopies when they were open, lights to illuminate the altimeters – all the paraphernalia pertaining to a night demo close to deep water. As the aircraft flew over the harbour towards Hong Kong the view from the open door was dramatically spectacular; the whole waterfront of Wan Chai was a blaze of lights with bejewelled towers jutting up from the illuminated ribbons that were the main highways, while the mountainside of the 1600 foot Peak loomed in the background, totally black.*

*From the lead chopper I could see at least six floodlit stadiums. Which was mine? I hoped the pilot knew… . Then I recognised it as he made straight for it. I started my stopwatch as I left the aircraft over the mountainside about 800 metres past the stadium, tucked up into fast fall, and pulled on exactly eleven seconds. As the canopy came out, I saw the shape of Snowy going past me, still in freefall. Wrong. He should have been above me. He opened below me and started running hard for the stadium, with the sodium flare in the centre and its smoke blowing towards us. Wrong again, especially as I was by then right over it at 1000 feet facing into the upper wind and being blown backwards towards the harbour. Worrying moments, but all at once, as we came below the level of the ridgeline, the 20-knot uppers decreased to zero and we were left with a gentle approach to the bowl and we could take those Para Commanders just wherever we wanted. As we came into the radius of the stadium lighting we pulled the smokes and slid comfortably one after the other into the centre circle of the soccer pitch in a series of light running standups. Judging by the din, thirty thousand highly vocal Orientals thought it was magic. We were a bit impressed ourselves… ."*

Our next foray was an afternoon high show at Aberdeen, a fishing village on the south side of the island. The opening point was inland and, as we tracked back below the ridgeline down through the wooded valley toward the small stadium, the treetops appeared pretty adjacent. The surface wind dropped out and unfortunately caught five of the guys the wrong side of the fence, it happens, and just served to sharpen everybody up. The same evening we jumped again into the stadium with everybody in the centre circle. We jumped the stadium once more on the Wednesday night and two days later we were back at Sek Kong, this time with a C130, for some useful filming with Bob Souter and Ray Willis. This was to be Ray's last jump on the trip; he was involved in a low canopy collision with Snowy, and came off worst, being airlifted out and ending up with a leg in plaster. That evening was to be our fifth and final night descent into the Government Stadium, which was captured on film by the MOD movie unit; the accuracy was first class with every jumper touching down in the centre circle.

Saturday the 4th was another high show, this time at the Happy Valley racecourse from the C130. This was a vast oval, some five hundred metres long with a dozen football pitches in the middle, and should not have been a problem. We had ten fit team members and put in a spectacular bomb burst right over the top, with respectable accuracy for most of us. One unfortunate non-attendee was Henry MacDonald, who overcooked his outbound track, and failed to come back in time and opted for the nearest clear undershoot, which just happened to be Wednesday's DZ, the now deserted Government stadium five hundred metres the other side of the ridge. Today, however, was Saturday, and after the lineup and presentation to the Chairman of the Jockey Club we repaired to the Clubhouse to find Henry there, having hitched a ride back, with a cold beer already in front of him. We were scheduled for a final night demo on the Sunday, but had to cancel in view of the forty-knot winds at two thousand feet. The DZ party reported a near riot as this news was relayed to the thirty thousand full house waiting inside; "Falcons chicken" was the cry.... . In our final few days we also found time to sample the local culture, with visits to various floating restaurants and street markets. A real highlight was a cruise around the island, courtesy of the Hong Kong and Shanghai Central Bank, who loaned us the company yacht (plus crew) for the day. We anchored in Repulse Bay on the island's south side for lunch, taken to the accompaniment of music provided by the jazz section of the RAF Central Band.

On Monday the 6th of December we gave our final demonstration in the Crown Colony at Yuen Long. This was an industrialised area in the northwest of the mainland territory, surrounded by canals and paddy fields and was, perhaps more significantly, situated right on the border with Red China. We had previously overflown with the Whirlwind at low level for an aerial recce and I had remarked to our pilot that no doubt the border guards had us under close observation with their binoculars. Not binoculars, he assured me; surface to air missiles. Accuracy was obviously paramount on this occasion; any incursion over the border could well have provoked a diplomatic incident and seriously spoiled Christmas for anyone who missed the stadium on the wrong side. In the event, we were allocated the Hercules for this one, and mustered up our full remaining strength of nine jumpers. Ray Willis, Alan Rhind, and Dave Ross were out with injuries and Snowy was sick. Peter Hearn joined us for a high demo with bomburst and we all put down in light winds smack in the penalty area in front of another wildly vociferous full house. And that, finally, was that. After a farewell evening out, the Falcons left Hong Kong the following day, burdened with Christmas shopping; having tried with some success to buy up half the island with half a month's pay. We were given a tremendous send-off by the Royal Air Force Central Band, who paraded to play the team aboard the C130 for the five-hour flight back to Singapore.

On landing at Tengah, our intended night stop was unexpectedly extended; in familiar parlance it had "all been changed". On the 3rd of December war had broken out between India and Pakistan and our Hercules aircraft was handed over to a new crew to evacuate British citizens from the war zone. As Hansard recorded on the 13th of December:

The Secretary of State for Foreign and Commonwealth Affairs (Sir Alec Douglas-Home)

*"Over 1,300 persons were airlifted out of Pakistan by the Royal Air Force in three days; this was no easy task and in the case of Dacca in particular it was carried out in circumstances of considerable difficulty and danger. I am sure the House will wish to join me in expressing congratulations and thanks to all those in the Services and in our posts in the subcontinent who were involved in this fine achievement. Our Deputy High Commissioner and a residual staff remain in Dacca".*

This was the background to a swift re-organization of our itinerary: all the kit had to be offloaded from the Hercules and stacked in a hangar, which meant that a rear party was required. There were three Flight Sergeants on the trip – Jim Hurford, Ron Ellerbeck and myself; we tossed for it and I lost. Bob Souter, with the falcon, also stayed behind as the rest of the team dispersed back to the UK over the next couple of days by civilian charter. Bob, myself, and falcon Fred were regrettably compelled to remain billeted in the 5-star Singapore Hyatt Regency for a further six days, on full local overseas allowance, until the Herc returned from Pakistan with tales of hairy takeoffs on bomb-cratered runways. On Wednesday the 15th of December we supervised the re-loading of all the Falcons' gear and returned to Lyneham on a twenty-four hour flight via Gan, Masirah and Akrotiri, picking up fifty Royal Marines and a couple more slip crews en route. The freight bay was choc-a-bloc but we were more than happy to be back for Christmas.

Thus ended Falcons '71; a year which started with two months in Australia and finished with three weeks in Hong Kong, through continental Europe from Gothenberg to Gütersloh and on to the island of Cyprus. On a personal level, it entailed a tally of one hundred and seventy two jumps and provided me with a series of unforgettable experiences. On a professional level I considered it a unique privilege to have worked for two seasons with two great Falcon leaders and an outstanding team of friends and jumpers. I did not know it at the time, but this was to be my final year on the team. When we finally returned to Abingdon, the Boss called me into his office.... .

# Chapter 8

# *RAFSPA*

*1972-1973*

I walked out of the boss's office a happy man. Peter Hearn had asked me to work full time at Weston to expand and upgrade the weekend Royal Air Force Sport Parachute Club into a full time Centre. This was a dream job indeed. We were now to run parachute courses for service personnel under the auspices of the new Adventure Training Scheme, with the following remit:

> *"The aim of Adventure Training courses is to provide an opportunity for personnel to participate in adventurous activities which are challenging and involve controlled exposure to risk. The training is designed to develop many of the personal attributes and skills vital to operational capability, including leadership, teamwork, physical fitness, self-reliance, physical and moral courage, initiative and determination. This aim will be met through the medium of training in basic static line and freefall parachuting. "*

All the basic facilities were of course already in place; now the Club was to be expanded into a full time Association. The directing staff were Flight Lieutenant Peter Burgess, OC Weston, as Association Secretary, and Flying Officer Peter Smout as officer in charge. Snowy Robertson and myself were to provide the experience and freefall expertise. I handed over the Falcons to Andy Sweeney, put on my tracksuit, and headed for Weston.

Early 1972 was a period of expansion and innovation on the British parachuting scene; full time Centres had now been opened by John Meacock at Sibson and by Charlie Shea-Simonds at Grindale. Bob Acraman had also opened RSA full time and was shortly to move to Thruxton. The BPA headquarters remained at Artillery Mansions in central London, with Bill Paul firmly in place as Secretary General; Headcorn's Lawrie St John became the Association's second civilian

Chairman, succeeding Gerry Turnbull; while Jim Crocker had taken over from Peter Sherman as Chairman of the STC. At Weston we were ready to play our own part and we had already put in a successful bid to host the National Championships later that year. During the first few weeks we made staff liaison visits to the APA at Netheravon, who were going through the same process as we were, setting up their own Joint Services Centre. The OC was Don Hughes, chief pilot was Major Gerald Stacey of the Royal Greenjackets, with Gus Martin, ex Red Devils, as Club Chief Instructor. We jumped at Netheravon and Upavon intermittently until mid-March, then settled down at Weston with our own Rapide G-AGSH, as always still piloted by Gerry Schellong and Con Grieves. At RAFSPA we were well served by our weekend instructors, PJIs Tony Dale, Bob Souter, Harry Parkinson, Ken Jacobs and Ian Harper; backed up by Bob Kirkham, Tony Oliver, and Dave Bennett (who were all serving aircrew), plus Tony Born, Kevin Dineen, Mike Deakin and Norman Addison from other trade groups. The other good news was that Ken Mapplebeck had returned from Cyprus to ensure we were excellently placed to expand full time with great backup at weekends. Nonetheless at the same time, I instituted a recruitment drive in the PTS crewroom with subsidised jumping on offer for instructors wishing to become BPA qualified.

One urgent priority was to expand our parachute inventory; we required new student rigs as well as more advanced canopies for staff and experienced jumpers. The basic student kit had remained largely unchanged for ten years – the canopies were C9 double L, in a B4 container; sleeve deployed, with static line break ties on the cones replacing the ripcord. For advanced kit we decided to go with short line Mk 3 Para Commanders; we also went for Mini System containers manufactured by North American Aerodynamics. In March, RAFSPA went square, the second team in the country to do so; we invited Peter Schofield and the Red Devils to Weston to demonstrate Steve Snyder's (Para-Flite) Paraplane canopies. The Freds turned up at Weston on Saturday 25th March, with team commander Peter Schofield and Ted Lewington as team Sergeant

Major. We were given a most comprehensive professional briefing, a canopy handling demonstration, and shown how to pack. We made a couple of familiarization jumps and ordered three on the spot. These Paraplanes were the first viable ram-air canopies on the market in the UK; although the Russians had had a prototype at the Graz WPC four years previously, they had not jumped it as they were unable to control the opening shock. The deployment on these canopies was controlled by a top reef – a system of rings and ropes on the upper surface, attached to the pilot chute, the canopy opened against the resistance exerted by the pilot chute. (Pilot chute controlled reefing, PCR, patented by Para-Flite). On packing, we included a slipknot on the lines before the mouthlock to slow the opening still further. The canopy itself was about 180 square feet, with a speed comparable to a PD 170 today. The lines were long, it had no stabilizer panels; it was certainly not an accuracy canopy, but it was a real crowd pleaser and we had no hesitation in buying three of them as demo canopies. After a dozen jumps I had a bag lock at two thousand feet over the Ben Jonson pub at Weston on a sub-terminal delay. I made a clean cutaway (one and a half shot Capewells) on to my Irvin Talisman reserve, which delivered me safely back to earth in the pub's beer garden. Next day we were straight down to Aldershot to discuss the matter with Peter Schofield's riggers, and it was decided the malfunction was caused by canopy slump inside the bag. We had all the bags modified to a smaller size and thereafter suffered no deployment problems at all, either at terminal or sub-terminal.

There were a variety of other canopies on the scene at the time, one of which was the Irvin Delta 2. The opening was controlled by a velcro wrap, which was colour-coded and wrapped around individual line sets; opening times were variable indeed; it was not a ram-air canopy and we saw no particular advantage in it. We also jumped the Para Sled, produced by Aerofoil Systems. The reefing system was not perfected and the manufacturers themselves recommended it should not be used on delays longer than five seconds. Also around, although we did not jump it, was Pioneer's

Volplane, which relied on a hydraulic reef to control the opening. Anecdotal evidence pointed to the hydraulic fluid freezing under certain conditions. No chance. We did, however, build a cutaway rig to use both in demos and also for training purposes; at that time a cutaway jump was a pre-requisite for the Advanced instructor qualification. All these deployment issues were, however, to be shortly resolved as in 1973 the slider as a retardation device was invented/perfected by Pioneer's Greg Yarbenet.

The Parachute School suffered another hammer blow in April. The Falcons were over in Italy for pre-season training using a 46 Squadron Andover at the Siena/Ampugnano airstrip. After a final demonstration jump on the 8th, the team emplaned for the return flight to Pisa and thence to the UK. The aircraft suffered an engine failure on takeoff, cartwheeled, then caught fire. Two crewmembers were killed, as were PJIs Squadron Leader Bill Last and Sergeant Ron Bullen. Ron had survived the water at Akrotiri six months earlier, but for him, this time, it was not to be.

Bob Souter remembers it thus:

### *"The Day I Got Lucky…*

*My account of this aircraft crash is dedicated to the memory of those who lost their lives on this day April 8th 1972. Sqn Ldr Bill Last P. J. I. Sgt Ron Bullen P. J. I. A. L. M. Brian Barnstable. Sgt. . . . Ground Engineer.*

*The Falcons were off to Pisa for pre-season Parachute Training 1972. It was our first time training in Italy, care of the Italian Air Force. There was always a buzz of excitement about a new venue. I was 23 years old, it was my second season of Falconry.*

*Duly billeted and admin attended to, we started jumping from our Andover. It was a good jump platform, ideal for a small Detachment. The ride to altitude took about 20–30 mins, everyone liked to have their own piece of "aircraft space," I took up a seating position forward on the starboard side, towards the nav's desk, over the wing. In between rehearsing the jumps in my mind on the way up, a lot of banter with others was the order of the day. I noticed opposite me was an emergency exit sign, which read. . . . In case of emergency lift flap, turn handle, push out window. I would look at this sign a lot. My gaze was turned to this on about every occasion whilst getting to altitude.*

The Detachment was going well, jumping underway and the Italian weather was behaving. A demo was arranged for the locals at the D. Z, which was a small airport, Ampugnano. It was ideal, as the runway on site, allowed quick turn arounds between lifts. We were due to fly back to base after the demo for lunch. A good demo completed, we embarked for the journey back to Pisa. The loadmaster Brian Barnstable, told us to strap in as the Skipper was going for a "Tac Take-Off" on departure. Strangely, I strapped in on this occasion, something I never bothered to do, it probably saved my life. The aircraft lined up at the end of the runway with engines revving. Brakes off, we started to accelerate down the runway on full power. I gazed out of the overwing porthole window as we sped along towards take off. With the aircraft only just airborne, I realised something was not quite right. All of a sudden I saw the wing tip crumple and starting to smash into the runway distance markers alongside of the runway… . I suddenly realised what was about to happen. . . we were going to crash… .

It was a weird sensation, everything started to happen in slow motion, I committed myself to die, thinking how it would be and that my head would be sheared off by the parachute static line attachment cable above me. I clung onto the ditching curtain for dear life. I heard the ground engineer seated opposite me yelling out "Oh No!! Oh No!! No, No." He was to die during the crash.

All hell broke loose, we were being beaten, bashed and pulverised as the aircraft crashed and went into its death throes cartwheeling down the runway nose over wingtip. Quite extraordinarily, everything stopped as soon as it started. I may have been unconscious, I don't know. As I came round, I opened my eyes, questioning myself if I was still alive, or was I dead, very strange. I tried to get up… . I was strapped in of course, thank the heavens. There was so much dust and debris about; everything was just a tangled knot of mess and broken metal. Acrid smoke filled the air. I heard others about and saw them through the murk further back from me. They seemed panicked, shouting and screaming. I remember shouting "Don't panic, don't panic there is a gap," I had noticed shafts of light forward of where I sat beaming down through the huge amounts of dust. At this moment, maybe I could have done something… . Could have, should have. Remembering the sign… . In case of emergency lift flap, turn handle push… . Doing this was not in my thoughts. It certainly was not in my head; even though I had read it to myself many times before… . No one was paying any attention to me anyhow, that's if they even heard me. Thank

God that further to the rear of the fuselage Davy Ross had the presence of mind to push out an emergency exit porthole window. Quite a few of the lads got out there.

Suddenly a thought completely overwhelmed me, she is going to blow, the whole lot is going to explode. It was time to leave, and quickly. I probably panicked. I fought my way forward through the tangled mess of metal wires and cables, towards the shafts of sunlight and fell out onto the grassy ground below. I bumped into the Aircrew, who were trying to do their best outside saying "is everyone out?", we all seemed dazed, in shock by what had just happened. Someone needed to get a grip of the situation. I felt better now, out in the sunshine; I could even hear the birds singing, how strange. The aircraft was starting to smoke and crackle quite badly now,

Team Leader Gwynne Morgan had lads grouped around him 50yds away, they shouted to me "Come over here for a head count Bob!" I looked towards the rear of the wreckage and noticed some lads spilling out. I ran to the area, and looked into a crack in the tail segment. Sid Garrard had just extricated himself, I looked into his eyes and shouted "Is there anyone else still inside Sid?" His eyes were dazed wide shut, as he scrambled out and away. Others got out from this crack in the tail.

A feeling of total shame and guilt overcame me. I was out in the sunshine, were there any others still inside? We had to restrain Chris Buchan who wanted to scramble back in to look. We reluctantly joined the main group, feeling totally useless as we watched the Aircraft burn. Someone said they saw Bill Last and Ron Bullen trying to open the rear door, but they also heard a very loud hissing noise as if the survival dinghy had burst open and was inflating right by them at the rear of the aircraft. Later, nobody said they saw the Loadmaster Brian Barnstable, we all thought he also died during the crash. The Airport Fire Truck had arrived by now at the scene after trundling out of its shed, the other side of the strip. It was obviously antiquated. It started on an angle, from the runway towards the wreck, which was burning away quite fiercely by now… . It immediately bogged down in the soft ground.

We all tried to push it out, no chance, it was up to its axles in mud. Its foam was turned on, but dropped woefully short of the wreckage well alight by now. The firemen in their firesuits and head protection were banging on the outside of the wreck with their pickaxes and turning around putting their arms up into the air in a sign of hopelessness and despair. It was all over, we all watched as the wreck popped and burnt away. We were lucky, we were alive. The head count revealed there were 4 unaccounted for out of 22 airmen. None of us sustained serious injury, only superficial cuts and bruises. No Sqn Ldr Bill Last, Sgt Ron Bullen, A. L. M. Brian Barnstable or Ground Engineer Sgt... .

A feeling of relief was experienced by all. We were alive, we were o. k. No matter how this had happened, it would become clear later, we all felt the same; we were the lucky ones.

The Italians did those four Airmen proud, holding a Service of Remembrance in the local Cathedral. All four coffins were draped in Flags of the union. When we got back to the U. K. if a demo was scrubbed with the team on board the aircraft, the aircrew stopped any low flying in respect. Someone said they saw the Skipper at a Drop Zone, years later. For still a young man, he seemed totally broken, carrying a huge burden."

Nonetheless, as always, life had to go on and our big priority was the National Championships, which were held at Weston at the end of May. The events were Individual Accuracy, Team Accuracy and Style, and attracted eight teams and sixty-seven individual entrants. Meet Director was civilian jumper John Cole (not PTS), and the Chief Judge was Marc Schneebeli of the Swiss Aero Club. This was a significant appointment as we had very limited experience of judging in this country; Marc was the first International judge to appear here and we took full advantage to learn as much as we could from him. Scoring was by manual measurement out to ten metres, with a 10cm disc. 1972 was a World Championship year, and the results would determine Team selection. These results were of particular personal interest, as I had been appointed Team Coach by the BPA. The RAFSPA team was Ken Mapplebeck and Tony Dale, plus civilian Club members Bob King and Bob Hiatt.

The Championships were concluded in five days with six Accuracy rounds, five Style, and four Team Accuracy. Standards were high, with John Meacock winning both the individual Style and individual Accuracy events. RAFSPA performed very well, with Ken second in Style and fourth overall; Bob Hiatt was fifth and Bob King sixth. The prizes and trophies were presented by Air Vice Marshal Fred Sowery, erstwhile Station Commander of RAF Abingdon, and a long time BPA member and supporter. Following the Nationals, the BPA Council decided that the top ten overall-placed competitors be invited to a series of training camps for final selection. These took place at RAF Abingdon, and after a further thirty jumps each, the six selected were John Meacock (Peterborough), Brian Standring (Red Devils), John Kemley (RAPA), Ken Mapplebeck and Bob King (RAFSPA), and Dave Savage (Old Warden). Wing Commander Alan (Doc) Johnson was Head of Delegation. The British Team were highly indebted to the Target Trust Group for sponsoring the trip to the 11th World Championships which were to be held in Talequah, Oklahoma from the 6th to the 17th of August. We had also decided, following recommendation by Peter Schofield, that we would run a two-week training camp at Gene Thacker's Raeford Drop Zone in North Carolina. I had known Gene Paul since 1962; he was ex US Army Team Golden Knights, who had retired from the military after being wounded in Vietnam, and had set up a Drop Zone at Raeford, just down the road from Fort Bragg. The British team were seen off from Heathrow on the 15th of July by Bill Paul and his wife Dorothy. We night-stopped in New York before flying down to North Carolina the following day.

We spent two very valuable weeks at Raeford, with expert coaching critiques from Gene Paul on telemeters and in the target area. Despite temperatures in the high nineties and with eighty percent humidity, the team made some seventy jumps apiece, including thirty Style. At the end of the period the selected five were Meacock, Mapplebeck, King, Standring and Kemley. Dave Savage was the nominated alternate. In addition to the professional expertise of Gene Paul himself, the hospitality at Raeford had been outstanding and the home cooking provided by Gene's wife Billie superb. We set off for Oklahoma fully acclimatized, relaxed and confident.

We arrived in Talequah the next day, to be accommodated on a college campus, some three miles from the airport itself. Over the next few days we were able to make half a dozen practice jumps from the National Guard UH-1 Hueys, detailed for the Meet. The competition commenced on Sunday the sixth of August with Team

Accuracy, which was, realistically, our best chance of a medal. The first round was jumped in upper winds in excess of forty knots, with many teams missing the airfield completely; nonetheless, we carefully worked out the run-in and opening point, ensuring us of a good first result, with dead centres from Mapplebeck, King and Standring and John Meacock short by a metre. On Monday we jumped two further rounds of Team, and were in first place at close of play with a third round total of 70 centimetres, and real prospects of a podium finish. On Thursday we completed the final two team jumps; we held on to second place after round four, only to slip to third after a highly disputed Swiss rejump. Despite our own score of less than one metre on round five, the Czechs were closer and we finished up with fourth place in Team Accuracy, and seventh Overall Nation. We had thus dropped one place in each classification since 1968, albeit without any serious deterioration in performance. Square canopies were jumped for the first time in a World Meet arena; the shape, literally, of things to come was apparent in the performance of US Team alternate Bill Hayes, who jumped the Paraplane Silver Cloud six times on wind dummy loads, and totaled 4. 06 metres in the process. The era of the round canopy in competition was coming to a close, although it would be six more years until it was entirely superseded by the ram-airs. I provided a full account of these Championships for the BPA Magazine of December 1972, which is reproduced in Appendix 1. We returned to Weston in good shape to see out the rest of the season. We jumped a couple of demos with the Paraplanes at Pangbourne and at Cosford, then finished the season with a photo session at Abingdon, and produced some useful action shots of our square canopies in flight.

New Year 1973 opened for me with the news that I had been awarded an Air Force Medal. This was a most unexpected honour, shared at that time with only twenty other instructors. In February I attended the Palace with my family to receive the medal from Her Majesty the Queen. Car parking in central London was no problem; we simply showed our pass to the policeman and drove our VW Beetle straight through the Palace main gates. After the event, we celebrated with an afternoon tea at a Lyons corner house on Marble Arch.

Back at Weston, my crewroom recruiting campaign was starting to bear fruit, with several more volunteers to work weekends; among them Terry Cooke and Graham Pierce. On the staff, Ken Mapplebeck had now taken over full time from Snowy, who had been promoted and was working on the floor. In March I ran a Paraplane conversion course for Ray Willis, Bob Souter and Joe France at Compton Abbas, home of the Thames Valley Airsports Club, assisted by Chief Instructor Bill Boot, an early Volplane jumper; Peter Schofield also spent time with us and the three PJIs clocked up some twenty jumps apiece. By now I was jumping the Paraplane consistently as a demo canopy and had replaced my Mk 3 PC with a French EFA Papillon. I packed it in a POD (Parachute Opening Device), fitted twin MA1 extractors and thenceforth jumped it all the time. The Rapide had had a respray and was now resplendent in red, and we organized several photo sessions at Abingdon again featuring the RAFSPA Robins Display Team. This venture was Peter Hearn's idea and was most enthusiastically organised by our RAFSPA Secretary, Peter Burgess. Peter wanted a high profile, and kitted us out with new red Pioneer jumpsuits and rather natty blue scarves. We had a lot of publicity and a full calendar of weekend demos. The team was a mix of Falcons alumni, talented young instructors and the occasional invitee. The Robins were thus christened, slightly tongue in cheek, as the "birds which picked up the Falcons' leftovers. " We were, nonetheless, offered some pretty high-profile venues ourselves.

Also in March, the Robins enjoyed a unique opportunity to make one final parachute descent in commemoration from the Blackburn Beverley, our original display aircraft from ten years back. This last Beverley was to take off from Farnborough airfield on its final sortie en route to Luton with freight, and we were invited to jump with the Red Devils team onto their Queens Parade DZ over the road. The RAF jumpers were Peter Hearn, Peter Smout, Ray Willis, Graham Pierce and myself on the port side, plus six of the Freds from the other door at 3,000 feet. The RAF DZ party should have done the drift calculations with balloon and theodolite, but after takeoff we received word that the hydrogen cylinder was empty and they were therefore unable to pass any dropping instructions. I was accordingly given the honour of spotting this final lift as I had brought along a couple of WDIs just in case. The stack went OK from 3,000 feet in a twelve-knot wind, we all made the pit. The Beverley, piloted by Squadron Leader McCartney, then flew on to Luton never, to the best of my knowledge, to be jumped from again.

In May, Weston hosted the Army Championships, followed by a visit from the AOC 38 Group, Air Marshall Sir Denis Crowley-Milling. The staff showed off the Paraplanes to best advantage and the AOC pronounced himself duly impressed. Later that month RAFSPA ran the Nationals again. Civilian jumpers Bob Hiatt, John Meacock and Bob King dominated the Individual event, with Brian Standring of the Red Devils in fourth place. In the Team Overall the Red Devils team of Sooty Standring, Dane Kenny, Scotty Milne and Jackie Smith came first. The RAFSPA quartet of Pete Smout, Graham Pierce, Dave Bennett and Alan Layton were placed second. This was Jackie Smith's first season in competition; within five years she was to become a World Champion. The Meet Director once more was John Cole, with Marc Schneebeli again doing the honours as Chief Judge. This was the second successive year that Weston had hosted the Nationals, a tribute to the drive of Peter Hearn, the organization of OC Weston Pete Burgess, and the enthusiasm of all the staff. In June I spent five days in Holland at Teuge as Chief Judge at the Dutch National Championships, by invitation of Doc Johnson, who was now the Station Medical Officer at RAF Brüggen.

Following my return to the UK, RAFSPA were approached by the Ford Motor Company to give a series of demonstrations into the Royal Artillery barracks at Bramcote, north of Coventry. Fords had set up a large motor show on site and we contracted to give ten demos over a two-week period from the beginning of July. This necessitated a little juggling with instructors on a RAFSPA course, but we successfully fulfilled our commitment using first our Rapide and then the Red Devils Islander, taking off from the Bruntingthorpe airstrip near Lutterworth. The DZ was a pretty tight arena, a cricket pitch nominally one hundred metres in diameter encircled by trees, but with numerous stands encroaching. We decided to use the Paraplanes exclusively for these demos and on most days these were jumped by Ken, Pete Smout and myself. Ken and I jumped with Ford banners suspended from a line with a smoke canister as weight, the idea being to fly the canopies around the area to demonstrate the speed and movement of these canopies to the maximum advantage. This was the brief, but Pete had his own theory, which was to apply full brake to the canopy over the centre of the arena and descend vertically in a high-speed stall enveloped in orange smoke before recovering into a high-speed swoop and flare onto the target. We were unable to dissuade him and, in fairness, he was invariably given terrific applause. All was well until, on the fourth day, Ken was on duty back at Abingdon and was unable to jump. I gave Pete the brief to jump the flag with the smoke, and reminded him of the required pattern – fly it about, etc. etc. … No chance. Pete went out at five thousand feet, pulled at about two and a half with myself stacked above him, with a grandstand view. Pete pulled his smoke grenade, dropped the flag, then went into his high speed stall routine. As he dropped, the smoke bomb flew horizontally to one side and shot straight back through his risers, like a shuttle through a loom, completely jamming his brakes. Fighting to clear the red-hot canister, blinded by the smoke and at fifteen hundred feet over a tight arena on a nil wind day with no brakes Peter Frederick Smout was in a tricky situation. From five hundred feet I saw him land at full speed on the target cross, then bounce in the manner of a caber being tossed at the Highland Games before ending up in the thicket at the deep fine leg boundary. He emerged, macho rugby player that he was, limping only slightly, to sustained applause, albeit with a somewhat strained smile wreathing his features. Pete learned about parachuting from that… . Two weeks later it was to be my turn.

The venue was the new National Water Sports Centre at Holme Pierrepont near Nottingham, the date was 27th July and the occasion was the Opening Ceremony performed by Prime Minister Edward Heath. The course was some two thousand metres long; DZ Control was exercised by Squadron Leader Mike Stamford and Norman Hoffman, and was set up on a grassy mound behind a large concrete grandstand at the finish line. Surface windspeed was about fifteen knots and the WDI gave us a run in up the course toward the start line at a slight angle. We had decided to make two passes, first pass Peter Hearn, John Mace, Graham Pierce and Harry Parkinson on Para Commanders, followed by Pete Smout, Ken and myself on the Paraplanes. The aim was to land in the water in front of the grandstand; Mike Stamford was to co-ordinate with the race officials to ensure the course was clear. We were given clear drop and the sodium flare was ignited, so I put out the jumpers on the first pass and went round again for ourselves. On the downwind leg we noticed four crews heading down the course at about the same speed and direction as the Para Commanders. Wrong… . The result was a dead heat between the crews and the jumpers, the finish line awash with multi-coloured Mark 3s, four PJIs treading water and an equally surprised quartet of coxless fours all in front of the Prime Minister of Great Britain and assembled VIPs. What the hell – we got clear drop for the second pass, out we went at the top end of the course and set up the stack. No problems getting back and I turned into wind at about two hundred feet, flew in and then hit turbulence from the grandstand at about forty feet. The canopy dived and dropped me hard on the cobbled bank, missing the water by a couple of metres. Luckily, because of the smokes, we were all wearing para boots and this saved me from a worse injury; as it was I got away with a broken fibula. Another learning experience – beware of roll-over turbulence… . The injury put me out for a couple of months, which turned out to be academic anyway as I was shortly informed of my posting to RAF Germany.

It is said that things come in threes and the excitement was not quite over, as on August Bank Holiday Monday I went out to Weston by road, complete with plaster cast, early morning to cover the programme only to find the DZ completely fogbound. The Rapide was due to leave Abingdon about the same time, Gerry Schellong was the duty pilot and I knew he had passengers on board – his wife Iris, son Steven and a couple of Club jumpers, Mike Hand and Mick Skinner who were hitching a ride. I called Abingdon to hold the Rapide, only to be told Gerry had already left for Kidlington to refuel. Weston was still completely out and at about eleven, I received a call requesting my presence back at Abingdon. I arrived at the Belfast hangar to find Wing Commander Harry Baxter, who was acting CO for the weekend, along with Gerry and his four passengers all of whom were exhibiting various degrees of agitation. Gerry himself was pacing up and down with a slightly embarrassed expression on his face. In the background stood the Rapide with a mass of foliage and medium sized branches sticking out from the lower wing surfaces and with heavily dented undercarriage fairings. It ensued that, after taking off for Kidlington, the fog had rolled in and Gerry was forced to return to Abingdon. The visibility deteriorated further en route; Gerry was by then flying IFR* and descended to search for the A34. In zero visibility, some five miles from the airfield and directly in line with the main runway, he brushed the treetops of Marley Wood on Wytham Hill, at an elevation some two hundred feet higher than the said A34. He immediately applied power and surged free, continued on his bearing, and found a gap in the fog over the airfield. He put down on the grass parallel to runway 18 at RAF Abingdon, narrowly avoiding an itinerant mushroom picker trespassing on the airfield. He had chosen the grass in preference to the runway, as he had no way of knowing the state of his undercarriage, or indeed whether he still had one. Gerry certainly learned something else about flying from that. G-AGSH was soon back on line with a new paint job and continued at RAFSPA for another eighteen months. When she was replaced early in 1975, Gerry, too, retired from parachute flying and concentrated on his equally beloved garden. A true legend, covering two decades of Sport parachuting, no account of the period would be complete without acknowledging the sheer enthusiasm, unstinting

* I Follow Roads.

support and professional expertise which Gerry Schellong rendered to RAFSPA. He was simply one of the very best.

At the end of September the club treated Helen and I to great send-off dinner at the Weston Manor hotel; we then traded in our Volkswagen for a duty-free Opel Manta and in mid-October headed across the Channel bound for the East German corridor and the Sports Section at RAF Gatow. Parachuting was temporarily on hold. Temporarily.

**80.** *Helen at Berlin Checkpoint Charlie, Easter 1974.*

**81.** *The Brandenburg Gate behind the Berlin Wall, looking towards the Unter den Linden. Photo by the author on the Wall patrol in February 1974.*

82. *On the summit of the Zugspitze in February 1974. So far, so good…*

83. *Back at base in Oberammergau, in the aftermath of the Zugspitze pileup.*

154

**84.** *Dawn exit, Berlin Checkpoint Bravo, June 1974. Our Opel Manta on the way back.*

**85.** *British Team Training at RAPA, Bad Lippspringe in July 1974.*
Back row: *Scotty Milne, Deke Wright, John Meacock, Bob Hiatt, Self, Dane Kenny.* Kneeling: *Bob King, Jane Cain, Tracy Rixon, Annie McKie, Jackie Smith, Dave Waugh.*

**86.** *With Helen on the Appalachian Trail, north of Culpeper, Virginia in March 1975.*

**87.** *Paddy Byrne exits the RAFSPA Cessna 206 at Weston 1975. Note stopwatch as his only instrument.* *Photo Mike Hand*

**88.** *Air Chief Marshal Sir Denis Smallwood, AOC in C Strike Command, after flying the Cessna at Weston October 1975. With Keith Field (hidden) Squadron Leader Fred Marshall, Sir Denis, Wing Commander Brian White OC PTS.*

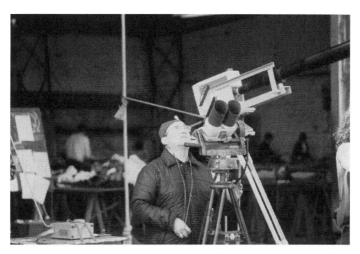

**89.** *The legendary French instructor Michel Prik, on telemeters at Bergerac. Note Style video camera behind.*

**90.** *British Team training at Bergerac, 1976.*
*Bob Hiatt, Bob King, Jackie Smith, Dickie Bird, Chris McGuire, Sally Smith,*
*Scotty Milne, Ken Mapplebeck, Self, Sandy Milne, Jane Waugh.*

**91.** *Bob Hiatt exits the Bergerac Antonov, August 1976.*

158

92. *Robin Mills Style tuck exit from the Antonov. August 1976.*

93. *Charlie Shea-Simonds, our Head of Delegation for the 13th World Parachute Championships, at the Hotel Sylvan in Guidonia.*

**94.** *British Team emplane with New Zealand jumpers in the Huey at Guidonia. Scotty, Ken, Robin, Bob King. Bob Hiatt was out, injured on the previous team jump. Note Robin Mills equipment: Hogback assembly with one and a half shot Capewell canopy releases, reserve blast handle, leg strap hand deploy and belly band.*

**95.** *Bob King poised for the disc at the 13th WPC, Guidonia 1976.*

96. *German Team Leader Helmut Schlecht with telemeter-mounted video camera. Guidonia 1976.*

161

# Chapter 9

# *Berlin to Budapest*

*1974-1975*

Monday 15th October 1973 was my birthday. At 16. 00 hours that afternoon I arrived at Checkpoint Bravo, the Dreilinden crossing point into West Berlin. I had changed into uniform and driven that morning from Gütersloh, crossed the East German border at Helmstedt Checkpoint Alpha, successively negotiated the British, Russian and East German checkpoints before cautiously traversing the A2 autobahn for 110 miles, adhering strictly to the 50mph limit and periodically scanning the verges for signs of non-existent landmines. At Helmstedt your mileage was checked by the Military Police, you were briefed not to deviate from the corridor, not to stop, not to engage in any contact with the East German police; if you were stopped you had to ask for a Russian officer. You were given a minimum journey time of two and a half hours, if you arrived earlier you were automatically charged with speeding; if longer than four hours they would send out a search party as you were probably lost, and half way to Warsaw. At Dreilinden the sequence was reversed – first the East German border guards, then the Russian checkpoint, finally you booked in with the British MPs. Mine was a petite redhead who greeted me with the words "You must be Dougy Peacock". Gatow sports section had contacted them and, in the person of Corporal Jimmy Robb, shortly arrived to escort me to the base.

Royal Air Force Gatow had been the Cranwell of the Third Reich, a former Luftwaffe Staff College situated in the southwestern outskirts of Berlin. The airfield was bounded by the Wall to the north side, six hundred metres from the main runway, and by the Havel River to the south. A near neighbour was Rudolf Hess, former deputy Führer of the Third Reich, currently serving a life sentence in Spandau Jail, just up the road. When I arrived, Gatow was home to No. 26 Signals Unit, monitoring Warsaw Pact military communications traffic from their base at the Teufelsberg in the Grunewald Forest. Gatow was also the base of 7 Flight AAC, flying Sioux light helicopters. I had complete charge of the Sports Section, comprising the gymnasium, an athletics track, two football pitches, a cricket square, tennis courts, golf course, and an indoor swimming pool. There was also a hangar down by the airfield which housed an archery range and an indoor ski slope. My staff were three civilians and my PTI Corporal, Jimmy Robb. The Manta was parked next to the gym. There was certainly enough going on to keep me busy, and I was really looking forward to a new challenge. I reported to the Wing Commander Admin through the Catering Officer, who had the Sports Section as a secondary duty; in other words I was virtually my own boss. Helen joined me shortly and we settled into a parachuting-free routine for the first time in sixteen years.

Berlin was unique in that we were paid in BAFSVs (British Armed Forces Special Vouchers), exactly as we had been on my previous tour in Germany twenty years earlier. These were to spend on base at the NAAFI, or to exchange for deutschmarks; and we took full advantage of our unaccustomed free weekends to tour the Western sector, enjoying the shopping and cafes in the Kurfürstendamm, sightseeing at the Wall, and generally enjoying the change of pace. We watched Bundesliga football at the Olympic Stadium and dined out at the Funkturm restaurant. We sailed on the Havel and went to a James Last concert. I also flew with Charles Murray-Twinn of 7 Flight on a couple of Wall border patrols, and managed a few aerial shots of the city at that time. Visits to the Russian sector were permissible, although under strictly controlled conditions; we had to wear uniform and photography was forbidden. I had been there once before Helen arrived, with Jimmy Robb and his wife; we passed through Checkpoint Charlie and went for a coffee; once inside the café we were immediately and openly approached by Russian soldiers and East German civilians alike for cigarettes. Our main objective was the Soviet military cemetery and war memorial in the Treptower Park, the final resting place of five thousand of the eighty thousand Russian soldiers who died in the battle for Berlin less than thirty years previously. The central feature of the cemetery was a well-maintained lawn lined by sixteen sarcophagi, decorated with carvings of battle scenes. There were quotations from Joseph Stalin on both sides of these white stone coffins, one side inscribed in Russian and the other in German. Apparently this is the sole location in Berlin where Stalin's writings are still on public view. We returned to the Western sector, doubly conscious of the deep divisions prevailing in this historic city.

Christmas passed under deep snow, and in February I volunteered for a ten-day ski expedition in the Bavarian Alps. RAF Germany had a ski centre based in Oberammergau and I thereupon drove Helen home to Geilenkirchen, left the Manta there, and boarded the train south. I had never skied before, but, having put in a few hours on my Gatow dry ski slope, I felt sure I would have no problems with the real thing. We assembled at Oberammergau but the ski run behind the village was solid ice and we could not operate. Thereupon the Command Physical Fitness Officer, who was running the course, decided we should transfer our activities to Garmisch-Partenkirchen and the Zugspitze, the highest mountain in Germany, some ten miles to the south. We reached the summit by rack railway and cable car and, at just under ten thousand feet, strapped on our skis; my first impression, lying flat on my back, was that this was bloody FAST, and in no way resembled my previous dry runs back in the hangar at Gatow. We soon got the hang of it, the weather was perfect, and for three days we practised on the nursery slopes, gradually building up confidence and technique. The final day we were turned loose on a free run; ten adrenaline-charged novices hurtling round the vast bowl of the summit to the accompaniment of piped music from the restaurant terraces above. I was to the back of the line, approaching the finish at a small ridge topped by a notice marking the start of the red run. Justifiably alarmed by this information, the leaders came to an abrupt halt, and everyone piled in on top like a collapsed rugby scrum. I hit this human mass at speed and finished up skewered with a ski pole in the knee, millimetres from the kneecap; the pole itself was buried up to the basket, and bowed by the impact. The pole was removed, shell dressing applied, and I was then evacuated off the hill by a two-man American ski patrol, skiing on one leg with arms around their shoulders down to the rack railway and thence to the US Forces hospital in Garmisch. Skiing was a great experience, I loved every minute; but that pole could have gone anywhere... Just as with the cattle trough at Fox Covert on the night jump two years earlier, I got lucky.

In addition to running the Sports Section, I had spent time at Gatow managing the Station soccer team and also attending German language lessons at the Education Section in Spandau. In March I was able to follow this up with a couple of weeks full time at Rheindahlen on an advanced course, which qualified me as a Civil Service Linguist. In May I took a week off and travelled down to Lippspringe, made ten jumps to keep my hand in, then settled back into the sports routine. Life in Berlin was relaxing, the job was interesting, and I was settling down quite happily for a three-year tour when one morning, shortly after returning from RAPA, I was called in to see the Catering Officer who had some news. "Good morning, Flight; how would you like to be called Mister?" My first reaction was that I had been selected for early redundancy, but no. My promotion to Warrant had come through and, eight months into my tour I was posted back to PTS. I actually considered for a moment turning it down, but was rapidly persuaded otherwise. So it came to pass that at the beginning of June we packed all our worldly goods into three shipping crates, handed over the Married Quarter, drove to Checkpoint Bravo and thence back down the A2 autobahn heading for Ostend and Abingdon. Good while it lasted... .

My new job was Station Warrant Officer at Weston on the Green and I was responsible for administration and discipline on the Station, which was home to the PTS Balloon Unit and Adventure

Training Flight. I was also jointly responsible for DZ Control for all military parachuting programmes along with OC Weston, Flight Lieutenant Stan Cooper. The Club was flourishing and, once reinstated as RAFSPA CCI, Berlin receded into memory as a transient and pleasant interlude.

Within a week of my return, we were plunged into the National Championships which were being hosted by Weston for the third year in a row. I was welcomed by Bill Paul who had arrived from BPA HQ, and had thoughtfully arranged transit accommodation for Helen and myself in the Jersey Arms. This was the first week in June, and the Meet attracted sixty competitors for the Accuracy and Style events. BPA Council had decided that the top six men competitors should represent the UK at the upcoming 12th WPC at Szolnok in Hungary. The top three jumpers overall were now firmly established civilians – Bob Hiatt, Bob King and John Meacock. Fourth, fifth and sixth were all from the Red Devils, Dane Kenny, Deke Wright and Scotty Milne respectively. We had also decided for the first time to enter a women's team. Four ladies were selected; Jackie Smith, Tracy Rixon, Jane Cain and Annie McKie. Jackie had distinguished herself in the Individual Accuracy event, being placed third from the sixty competitors. As for the men, Bob Hiatt had outjumped all the opposition on his Paraplane Cloud. The BPA had again requested my services as Team Coach and I was granted special leave. Wing Commander Alan (Doc) Johnson was again Head of Delegation with Dave Waugh as Team Leader. We ran a couple of preliminary training sessions at the Peterborough Parachute Centre and at the Wilstead Duck End Farm, before flying out to the Rhine Army Centre at Bad Lippspringe for two weeks concentrated training.

As an interlude, and two weeks prior to this, I had already been out at RAPA with the Robins display team. We had been asked to jump at the RAF Gatow Air Display and I was looking forward to a return to Berlin as a jumper. We flew down the air corridor from Bad Lippspringe in the Army Islander, with Peter Hearn on the team. We took three Paraplanes for Ken, myself, and Graham Pierce, (always game for anything) who was to perform the cutaway on to the Plane. On arrival, we caught up with the Falcons team, who were also scheduled to appear. Proceedings were delayed by a thunderstorm before we finally got airborne late afternoon. We all exited at six thousand feet, wrong side of the wall, deep inside the Russian sector. Graham performed his cutaway routine onto the Paraplane, I had a spinning malfunction on mine which cleared itself at 2,000 feet just as I was about to chop it, and somehow we all landed on the cross in front of the crowd This was one of the few occasions both PTS teams, Falcons and Robins, had appeared jointly – shades of Hucknall 1962. I said hello to old friends on the base, then disappeared back down the corridor to RAPA in the Islander. I would not see Berlin again for nearly forty years.

Two weeks on, with the British team at Lippspringe, we were greeted by the Commandant, Major Tom Oxley and CCI Sergeant Major Geordie Lang – both old jumping buddies. Everything was laid on, except for the weather, we made as many accuracy team stacks as possible, but style training was severely restricted. After two rather frustrating weeks we said our farewells and flew out to Budapest from Frankfurt. We arrived to a clammy heatwave and after a most detailed scrutiny at immigration we were bussed to our accommodation at the Tiszagilet youth holiday camp in Szolnok some sixty miles to the southeast of Budapest. The facilities here were excellent; comfortable bunkhouses, mineral baths, athletics track and volleyball courts all on site. We settled in and the following day travelled the six miles to the airfield. This area of Hungary had been severely affected by flooding so the competition site had been switched to a neighbouring military airfield with all the attendant security restrictions in place.

Practice jumps were strictly limited to one jump only. We made a team stack in high winds from the AN2, then hung around for three days awaiting the Opening Ceremony, which turned out to be a most protracted affair conducted under blue skies and a temperature of 96 degrees. Meanwhile Doc Johnson had arrived, and the Meet got underway the next day with Style from the Mi-8 helicopters. The minimum three Style rounds were completed by

Wednesday and at midday we went into the first round of Individual Accuracy. For the first time at a World Championships we had an electronic scoring system which consisted of a Russian-made pad reading out to 15cm. The dead-centre disc remained at 10cm. Scotty Milne and Bob Hiatt both scored 0.00 on the first round, Hiatt was doing particularly well on his Paraplane Cloud. The rest of the Meet was dogged by bad weather – rain and high winds – and also marred by communication failures between organisers and competitors. Chief Judge Sven Brostedt from Denmark was the hapless go-between, and did a great job under difficult meteorological and political conditions. In the end, the Meet was called on a minimum programme; six Accuracy, three Style and three Team Accuracy. The Individual Accuracy was won by Stanislaw Sidor of Poland after a jump off, totalling 0. 01 cm over six rounds jumping a Soviet UT15 canopy. It was to be the last victory ever for a round canopy on the World stage. At these championships the Soviets emphasised their domination with a virtual clean sweep of the Overall Individual titles, both men and women. From a National viewpoint, the British team lost ground in overall international standings, dropping to 12th position from 7th two years previously in Talequah. On the credit side, Bob Hiatt showed the way to go with his square canopy; whilst 1974 was the first time we had entered a full female team at a WPC. The Brits returned home on the Monday with a few lessons learned, but certainly with Bob Hiatt, Bob King, Scotty Milne and Jackie Smith firmly established as our leading jumpers.

Back at Weston, we carried on with our routine of courses and demos. On the second of September we ran a basic course for the Birmingham University Officer Training Corps. We were weathered out for the first week, and jumping started the following Monday. Because the Rapide was off the road, we brought in a Cessna 182 with a step exit, basically the same exit as the Rapide, only from a smaller platform. The static line system was still a sleeved C9 canopy in a B4 container, with 50lb break ties through the cones tied round the static line. On the second lift we were to experience our first fatality since Neil Perry's ill-fated over-delay seventeen years previously. The jumper was Marian Hicks, making her first descent, static line, poised exit from the right hand step. As she left the aircraft, she rotated backwards and fell away back down. The pilot chute came out and wrapped round her left arm, a classic horseshoe malfunction. The main came out of the sleeve, but the extractor snagged round the lines, preventing any canopy deployment. The jumper remained upright holding the risers, but made no attempt to operate her reserve and she landed over the road to the west of the airfield. This tragic death was the starting point for a basic rethink of our systems. We switched to a static line bag deployment system, in common with several other Centres, using a bag with an elasticated mouthlock and an apex tie. The fatality was a sad backdrop to Peter Hearn's last days as OC PTS, as in the same month he finished his tour, and handed over to Wing Commander Brian White before departing reluctantly to an appointment at the Ministry of Defence.

On the civilian scene, the Association's Council had approved the relocation of the BPA headquarters from London to Leicester. We had been informed the previous year that the rent on the Artillery Mansions offices was due to be increased by 400 per cent, and staff costs in the capital had in any case become prohibitive. Bill Paul had investigated alternatives, and, together with the British Gliding Association, decided to move to Leicester. This move was effected early in 1975, the new HQ was located in Kimberley House, a recently constructed office block not far from the city centre; and the BPA Council held its first meeting at this new venue on Wednesday the 19th of February 1975. The most significant agenda item at this inaugural meeting was the confirmation of the establishment of the post of a full time National Coach and Safety Officer. This resulted in the appointment of Charles Shea-Simonds with effect from the first of July 1975. Charlie, of course, was already a prominent Council member and Editor of the Magazine. Formerly commissioned in the Parachute Regiment, he was a qualified flying instructor, and had successfully established a full-time Centre at Bridlington Grindale, following his retirement from the Army. Charlie occupied a desk in Kimberley House, but his role was in the field. Charlie bought a ten-foot touring caravan, which he hitched on to his Renault, and started a round of all BPA Clubs, accompanied by his Jack Russell terrier, Boomerang. This was an appointment long overdue. Charlie was the ultimate enthusiast; with his military background and civilian sport parachuting expertise, he was, in my book anyway, the ideal appointee. He and I had worked together at many competitions and instructor courses, and were to continue to do so closely for most of the decade.

In March 1975 Helen and I took a couple of weeks out to visit old friends in the States, first to Washington to see Bob Muller and Bill Ramey from Cyprus days; we stayed with Bob in Culpeper, Virginia, then flew down to Raeford to catch up with Gene Paul and Miss Billie. In all we spent a most enjoyable three weeks touring the Eastern seaboard, before flying back to the UK. Within two days I was out at Weston checking out our new jumpship – a five place Cessna 206, registered G-ASVN. This aircraft was the replacement for our Rapide, which had been sold; concurrently, and to his vast disappointment, Gerry Schellong had been deemed redundant. He was replaced at ATF by our first established pilot, Flight Lieutenant Keith Field. Courses were running as normal and, following the Marian Hicks fatality the previous year, we had introduced a static line bag system, using a bag with elasticated mouthlock. To date, in the course of over six hundred jumps, this had proved fully satisfactory; we were aware of the technical constraints, static line length and dropping speeds etc. On the fourth of June on a student sortie, although these parameters were strictly observed, we were forced radically to revise our ideas. Bob Souter despatched the last jumper at 2500 feet, the canopy emerged prematurely and struck the leading edge of the tailplane. The canopy sustained minor damage, and the student did not notice anything amiss, did not even deploy his reserve, and landed safely. On the instruction of Keith Field, Bob exited smartly and Keith landed the aircraft successfully with the leading edge of the tail severely dented. Keith subsequently received a Green endorsement for this feat of airmanship. As a result, the Civil Aviation Authority banned all static line jumping from this aircraft type until further notice. In co-operation with Irvins, RAFSPA launched a trials programme, using a modified bag featuring a centre base tie as per the military PX canopy. We filmed deployments both at Weston and Abingdon, and trials continued until December. The upshot was that we decided to adopt a static line bag deployment system which utilised a one hundred pound centre base break tie in place of a mouth lock. This system was approved by STC and adopted at RAFSPA early in the New Year.

At Weston we continued to be occupied with competition training, and it was encouraging to see the emergence of new Classic competitors from our Club jumpers. Prominent were Peter Dowling, a solicitor, based in Reading and Paddy Byrne, a Junior Tech based at RAF Benson; Paddy went on to make the National team at the Zagreb WPC three years later. Mike Hand, although not a competitor, was an ever-present on the scene and a very useful air-to-air photographer to boot. In August we hosted the Nationals at Weston for the fourth year in succession. Our best result was that of Ken, who took second place in Style, whilst RAFSPA took second place in Team Accuracy behind the Duck End team starring Bob Hiatt and Bob King. Top jumpers at this Meet were established as John Meacock, Ken Mapplebeck, Scotty Milne, Bob Hiatt and Bob King. All five were all to continue to figure prominently at future World Championships. Although not directly within my remit, PJIs Ray Willis, Bob Souter, Joe France, Ty Barraclough and Henry MacDonald won the National 4-Way event at Dunkeswell and represented Great Britain at the first World Relative Work (Formation Skydiving) Championships in Germany.

The Cessna came back on line in September and the following month we were visited by the Air Officer Commanding in Chief Strike Command, Air Chief Marshal Sir Denis Smallwood. The Weston cloud base was about fifteen hundred feet solid; nonetheless the AOC expressed a wish to fly the 206 on a live sortie. Squadron Leader Fred Marshall (OC Advanced Training Squadron) volunteered to accompany me in the back. We threw a WDI below the cloud, then climbed and ran in toward the bottom end of the DZ at three thousand feet above the white shining carpet. I could see nothing at all. The AOC glanced back over his shoulder seeking enlightenment and, not wishing to disappoint him, I gave him a confident five right correction. A momentary gap revealed we were right above the turkey farm, very deep, so I gave the cut, hopped out and pulled high on five seconds. I came out of the cloud, fortuitously set up for the cross in front of the control tower, and touched down right on target. Fred Marshal followed close behind, and we were both standing in front of the tower as the AOC landed and taxied over. We naturally congratulated him on his excellent run in and everyone was happy, OC PTS Brian White in particular. The year ended on a quiet note, with basic courses and bag trials ongoing. Now that I was back in the UK for the foreseeable future I decided to stand once more for election to the BPA Council after an absence of six years, and in this I was successful. If 1975 had been a year of change, the following two were to prove still more decisive.

**97.** *Briefing German Airborne troops at the Pitts Road Depot, Aldershot 1976.*

**98.** *Peter Sherman's United Arab Emirates Team at the 10th CISM competition in Wiener Neustadt, August 1977. Ali Nasser, Mohammad Yousuf, Abdulrahman Ali, Said Khalifa.*

173

**99.** *En route for Zagreb in the BPA Maxi. Paddy Byrne, Paul Slaughter, Dane Kenny, Trish Bird, Bob King. August 1978.*

**100.** *Jackie Smith at Manifest prior to her 10th Round of Accuracy. 14th World Parachute Championships at the Zagreb Lučko Airfield. September 1978.*

174

**101.** *World Champion Jackie Smith on the podium. September 1978.*

**102.** *Ladies Individual Accuracy Result, 14th World Parachute Championships 1978.*

175

**103.** *CIP Sporting Code sub committee Arnhem 1979. With Canadian Buzz Bennett, Uwe Beckmann from Germany and Australian delegate Claude Gillard.*

**104.** *CIP Delegates outside the Hartenstein Hotel in Oosterbeek, February 1979. Charlie is kneeling in the centre, and I am in the front row, fourth left.*

**105.** *Roger Flinn behind the BPA Van at the Bulgarian border en route for Kazanlak. August 1980.*

**106.** *With Sven Brostedt (Denmark) and John Mirus (USA) at the 15th World Parachute Championships in Kazanlak. The Bulgarians had a first class video backup camera; this was the last time the Style event was to be judged on telemeters.*

**107.** *Off Duty in Kazanlak. John Mirus (USA), Helmut Schlecht (Germany), Chief Judge Buzz Bennett (Canada), Ken Mapplebeck and BJ Worth (USA). August 1980.*

**108.** *Scotty Milne on his Parafoil at the 15th WPC 1980.*

178

**109.** *Scotty Milne with Bronze Medal and trophy at the Closing Ceremony in the Kazanlak city centre.*

**110.** *12th CISM Competition in Chile, September 1980. Pete Sherman sits with two American Golden Knights team members. Next are UAE Team captain Said Khalifa, Team leader Major Bakhit Salim, and our Head of Delegation with local Interpreter.*

179

# GULF NEWS

DUBAI  THURSDAY OCTOBER 22, 1981

## 13th World Military Parachuting Championship

### Chief judge from neutral country

By A Sports Reporter

Handling a complicated and extremely crucial job at the 13th World Armed Services Parachuting championships is Doug Peacock belonging to a team of judges belonging to different countries.

Speaking to Gulf News in between watches of brief intervals, who is not scrutinising the performances of the parachutists though, said the "brass" of a high-powered Pakistan is. Greg Peacock said the standard of play had been very high and the pilots were handling their part of the job very well.

The UAE has done a magnificent job in organising this event, said the chief judge taking a long and searching look at the sun-lit scene and then marking down the points on a pad on his side. He has attended many such events in this capacity. The present one could be compared with any one in the past, said the skeleton defence experience. The skies were...

Doug Peacock and Britain was not a member of CISM which was founded way back in 1948. Why, he would not say. "I am completely neutral," quipped the Yorkshireman who happens to be the national coach of the British parachuting team which secured the third place in a world meet recently.

## U.S. suffer setback at Pakistan's hands

Chief Judge Doug Peacock—in touch with players in the sky. —Photo by Javed Nawab

Individual Style Champion Christian Labbe of France on his way to complete the final jump  —Gulf News photo

## Style Event ends in a blaze of glory for Lubbe

By Rangi Akbar

### Last attempt to salvage tour of India

## U.S. capt

By A Sports Reporter

Parachuting is fast used...

Al Nasr ca
Leag

Eagle Printing
Airlines from Pakistan,
India, Sri Lanka
Philippines Thailand
Booking Tickets for all the world
ALWASL GENERAL SERVICES EST.
P.O. Box 5141 Tel: 555628 DUBAI

111. Chief Judge at the 13th CISM, held in Dubai at the Chicago Beach Drop Zone.
Extract and photo from the Gulf News 22nd October 1981.

180

# Chapter 10

# *Rome to Vienna*

*1976–1977*

In the April of 1976 No. 1 Parachute Training School was relocated from RAF Abingdon to RAF Brize Norton. Abingdon had been the home of the Parachute School since 1950, following a four-year sojourn at Upper Heyford. For many of us this was quite a wrench, a move from a base where we had been a major unit along with Nos. 47 and 53 Squadrons, equipped first with Hastings and latterly with Beverley aircraft. We were comfortable there, we had our own No. 2 Sergeants' Mess with a more relaxed dress code, where we could have a drink wearing our flying suits after evening parachute sorties. *Pace* the flying squadrons, No. 1 PTS to us was first amongst equals at Abingdon. Brize was totally different; PTS was now just another unit on a large station. Abingdon had been my home for twenty years, we had lived in three different Married Quarters as postings and promotions dictated. I was working anyway at Weston as Station Warrant Officer; but rather than make another move, we decided to remain in the area and buy our own house. Thus, for the first time in twenty years, we left the security of Service accommodation and joined the outside world. This decision was shortly to have a profound career effect. All the Army basic courses were relocated to the Aldershot detachment for a month during the move to Brize, and I took advantage of this brief break to spend three weeks in Germany at Bad Lippspringe to assist Tom Oxley and make some useful training jumps.

In the sport parachuting world, the main event of the year was the National Championships, held at the Hereford Parachute Club.

RAFSPA entered a team consisting of Ken Mapplebeck, Paddy Byrne, Dave Bennett and myself, with Mick Geelan as alternate. The World Championships were on again later that year in Italy and the team would be selected from these results. I had again been asked by the BPA to coach the National Team, but nonetheless decided to compete to keep current and maintain a level of credibility. The jumping opened at Shobdon on 13th June in decidedly mixed weather conditions, with Charlie Shea-Simonds as Meet Director and Dave Waugh as Chief Judge. Because of the indifferent forecasts, early starts were the order of the day, with the first lift airborne at 05. 00 most mornings. Significant visitors were a military team from Dubai, coached by Pete Sherman, entering their first competition and jumping French Papillons. This was the first time we had seen Pete in the UK for some eighteen months and he had quite a tale to tell. Although I did not know it then, this team were to play an important role in my future, more of which later. As always, Style was the deciding factor in regard to team selection, and at the end of the competition the top placings were Meacock, Milne, Mills, Mapplebeck, myself, with Bob Hiatt in sixth. In the event, John Meacock declined selection for business reasons, and I was already designated as coach. Thus the men's team for Rome was Milne, Mills, Mapplebeck and Hiatt, with Bob King and Dickie Bird from the Red Devils to make up the six. Following the precedent set in 1974, it was also decided to send a full women's team, consisting of Jackie Smith, Sandy Murray, Sally Smith, Jane Waugh and Chris McGuire. Charlie was Head of Delegation and Dave Waugh was to travel as Team Judge. The final day coincided with the start of the 1976 heatwave, which gave us the opportunity for a further eight weekends team training at Sibson and Weston.

This year also saw the introduction into the UK of two technical innovations – the slider and Bill Booth's hand deployed pilot chute. The slider had been unveiled a couple of years earlier but had not yet achieved universal acceptance and most jumpers on the 5-cell Strato Stars and 7-cell Strato Clouds were still using Pilot Chute Controlled Reefing(PCR) otherwise known as rings and ropes. Robin Mills, a very talented jumper and ever ahead of the game, was jumping a Strato Star in a hogback system with a hand deploy, and a slider to control the opening. The hand deploy was a new one on me, when I first checked his rig at Weston I queried the fact he had no ripcord, whereupon he showed me a pocket on his right legstrap with a small plastic toggle visible at the mouth, and invited me to watch his exit. He hopped out of the Weston 206 at 2500 feet, reached down for the toggle, extended his arm and let go the pilot chute. The sub terminal deployment was absolutely faultless, and certainly impressed me. Although the pocket was subsequently to be re-positioned on the bottom of the container (BOC) it was obviously the way to go, and the main ripcord was destined to follow the competitive round canopy into the dustbin of history.

The 13th World Parachute Championships were scheduled to take place from 11th–25th September at the Guidonia airfield just outside Rome, and we had decided to use the Bergerac Parachute Centre in the Dordogne for the training camp. At that time, Bergerac was one of the leading French centres, with a very strong competition ethos, and home Drop Zone to Jean-Claude Armaing, the reigning World Style champion who had won successive gold medals at Talequah 1972 and Szolnok 1974. Ken and I had been granted special leave for the event and Bill Paul had obtained sponsorship from the Fiat Motor Company, who provided two estates and two saloons for Team transport. On 23rd August Robin Mills, Scotty, Sandy and myself left Ramsgate on the hovercraft as advance party in one of the estate cars, arriving at Bergerac the following day. We were greeted by Chief Instructor Jean-Jacques and Michel Prik, a veritable legend of the early days of French parachuting. http://michelprik.jimdo.com/parachutisme/bergerac-1967-1978/. Charlie, Dave Waugh and the rest of the team arrived a couple of days later, and we settled down to a routine of Team Accuracy and Style training from the Antonov and the Broussard, interspersed with some good old fashioned road runs and general fitness work when we were weathered out. The Style training was particularly valuable as most jumps were recorded and debriefed on video, not yet available in the UK. Unfortunately we suffered a couple of training injuries; Bob King was out for three days with a shoulder injury, whilst more seriously, Scotty missed ten whole days with a torn back muscle, which ultimately affected his performance in Rome. The Japanese team was also training there; also in residence were the French 4-man sequential RW team, Les Cénobites, who were preparing for the forthcoming World Cup in South Africa. The training camp ended on 7th September and we entertained Chief Instructor Jean-Jacques and Michel Prik and their wives at the local hostelry; we had a great evening and, to their surprise, I had brought along a copy of André Suire's book (Chapter2) http://www.priceminister.com/mfp/12830/chute-libre-suire-andre#pid=161244955. Michel Prik was prominently featured in this book, and was delighted to sign his photograph for me.

The following day our first car set out for Rome, with Scotty, Robin and I sharing the driving. We had an overnight stop in Genoa, and settled in for an early night. The Fiat Estate was parked outside in the street and about five o'clock the next morning Scotty and I were awakened by the landlord with the news that the car had been broken into. We hared out into the street and collected Robin's para bag which had been abandoned by the thief as too heavy to carry, then returned to assess the damage, luckily confined to a smashed windscreen and side window. The other para bags were still in the car. Repairs delayed us for most of the morning and we eventually continued in the direction of the Eternal City. We arrived late on the evening of the 9th to be accommodated in the Hotel Sylvan, about three miles from the DZ at Guidonia, a dozen miles from Rome city centre. This hotel featured a superb restaurant and a very hospitable staff, with great facilities including a swimming pool. The remainder of the party arrived the next day, and we went out to the DZ on Friday for a recce and team photographs.

The serious business started on Saturday 11th with one practice jump each. Denmark's Sven Brostedt was Chief Judge again, Dave Waugh had been nominated as Event Judge for Accuracy and I was pleased once more to catch up with another old friend, the German Team Leader, Helmut Schlecht, who I had first met as a competitor in Leutkirch in 1963. Although Style was still being judged at World Meets on telemeters, many teams were already mounting video cameras on their own telemeters for training purposes, and the German team were forerunners in this innovation. Helmut and I jumped together on WDI loads and we took advantage of a rest day to tour the inner city together. I also took the opportunity to visit the World Heritage site of the Villa d'Este Tivoli Gardens, only a few miles from the airfield, and spent a great morning exploring this magnificent estate, reflecting once more, as I so often had, how fortunate we were to be able to travel the world in pursuit of our sport.

Back to work again, the competition continued apace, and a full contemporaneous account of the Meet is given in Charlie's writeup for the BPA magazine, http://www.bpa-archive.org.uk/mag_archive/magazines/056-1976-5.pdf. Our outstanding performer in Rome was without doubt Bob Hiatt, who totalled five centimetres over eight rounds in the individual event, with six consecutive discs in the first six rounds, and who missed third place by one centimetre, despite being injured in the first team jump. Bob was jumping a 230 Strato Cloud, as were Kenny Mapplebeck and Scotty Milne. Bob King had a 180 Parafoil, while Robin Mills was happy on his 180 Strato Star. Our team results were disappointing; with Ken our best performer totalling eight centimetres from the time he took Bob Hiatt's place for the second round. Suffice it to say that as a group we built up more experience and achieved individual accuracy results which were the foretaste of medals to come at two succeeding WPCs. This World Championships was notable for the fact that by now over one third of competitors were using square canopies. The individual accuracy winner was Jean Dermine of France, who scored eight consecutive dead centres, a World first.

On return to the UK, I continued running Weston military Drop Zone Control, and was sent on a short detachment to Aldershot to act as interpreter and assist Pitts Road personnel on a German Airborne exchange visit. On the 5th of November I made what was to be my final military descent – number 1037 – from a Wessex helicopter, 10,000 feet at Weston, following a student jumper. This was, to within a week, the twentieth anniversary of my first ever parachute jump on my basic course at RAF Abingdon – a balloon descent from 800 feet on 16th November 1956.

At the turn of the year, BPA Council elections saw the retirement of Lawrie St John as Chairman after a five-year tenure. He was succeeded by John Meacock, owner and Chief Instructor of the Peterborough Parachute Centre, multiple National Champion and British Team member at two World Meets. John was one of the leading personalities of the decade, who combined the running of a busy commercial Drop Zone with a highly successful competitive career. His vice chairman was Dave Waugh, whilst Jim Crocker was STC chairman. Charlie Shea was starting his third year as National Coach and Bill Paul remained firmly ensconced as Secretary General. These five were the power brokers of the day, big hitters every one; all were destined to play a part in my future parachuting career.

At the beginning of 1977 I began to take stock of my options. Since leaving the Falcons Display Team five years previously I had had the good fortune to combine a Service career with an almost full-time involvement in Sport parachuting. I was now a BPA Council member, Advanced Instructor, Examiner, FAI international judge, and had been British team coach at the last three World Parachute Championships. It was becoming increasingly apparent that, in my position as a Royal Air Force Warrant Officer, this state of affairs could not continue indefinitely; and that a choice had to be made between my civilian sport parachuting commitment and a Service career. I had a further ten years to serve and, from where I stood, the options in the RAF were not too appealing. Accordingly I applied for premature voluntary release after twenty-six years service, effective from 1st August 1977. This move was viewed with some scepticism by the PTS hierarchy, but I knew my own mind and I successfully enrolled in a three-year German Language degree course at the Oxford Polytechnic, with a view to a career as translator and linguist. This was to start in September; meanwhile there was still plenty of parachuting left in the summer, starting with the Army Championships in May where I assisted Charlie in the judging.

My final day in uniform came on Thursday 30th June 1977, when I left Brize Norton in a low-key exit on my four weeks terminal leave. I certainly felt a surge of emotion as I drove past Station Headquarters and the Ensign for the final time; this was instantaneously replaced by an overwhelming sense of freedom. My future was in my own hands, there were no constraints, no boundaries, and I was looking forward immensely to whatever might lie ahead.

On the 2nd of July I headed for Hereford and the British National Championships as Chief Judge, with Charlie as Meet Director. We were favoured with excellent weather, and the Meet was completed in three days. Scotty Milne won the Style and overall; Sandy Murray took the ladies overall title. Bob Hiatt took second in Style and second overall. It was good also to see ex-RAFSPA jumper Paddy Byrne take third place Style. Red Devil team members Dane Kenny and Jackie Smith had left the Army to jump as professionals in the States; they had teamed up with Robin Mills and Tony Uragallo to form Team Symbiosis, all four jumpers equally at home in RW competition as in the classics.

Two weeks later I was back at Lippspringe as Chief Judge at the RAPA Meet, which encompassed Style, Accuracy and RW. The Meet was completed in seven days, and one of my most memorable descents ever came at the conclusion of the competition, on the 31st July, my final day in the service of her Majesty the Queen. I was invited to join the Rhine Army team on a demonstration at a German *Feuerwehr* (Fireservice) open day in Rödinghausen, thirty miles away over the ridge of the Teutoberger Wald. The other jumpers were RAPA Commandant Tom Oxley, Jack Fowler, Geoff Payne, Tim Andrewes and jumpmaster Derek Thorne. The pilot was RAF Flight Lieutenant Hugh Thomas. We flew over the tiny DZ and dropped the streamer which landed 1700 metres downwind. We all piled out at 3,000 feet, over a mile away and trailing smoke, everybody running back at top speed for the DZ before hooking into wind at low level and obliterating the target cross with the canopies. It was a baking hot afternoon and the crowd loved every minute; as a guest jumper RAPA gave me a red beret to wear on the lineup; for my part I could not have wished for a more satisfying conclusion to my military career. After a tremendous barbecue, we flew back to Lippspringe to continue the party, which cost me two crates. I was among friends.

Also at Lippspringe was Pete Sherman, who had brought over his team from Dubai for the competition, and stayed on until mid August in training for the forthcoming CISM parachute championships in Austria. We made a couple of jumps together and exchanged notes. I had known Pete since the early days; he was on one of the first SAS freefall courses at Abingdon in 1961 (Chapter 2). He went on to serve in Malaya during the emergency; he returned to the theatre later to became one of the very few Army personnel to be awarded an Air Force Medal for his pioneering work on freefall tree-jumping techniques. He was an Advanced instructor/Examiner and member of the BPA Council in the 1960s. He left the Army in 1969 to become chief test parachutist for the GQ Parachute Company who were then based in Woking. In 1974 he became a victim of company restructuring and, along with Billy Foulkes and ex PTS Wing Commander Gerry Turnbull, was made redundant. Co-incidentally, a delegation from Dubai was in the country at the time, seeking advice on military parachuting. Pete was contacted and, together with his two colleagues, formed Parachute Services Ltd to travel to the Gulf to build up a parachute school from scratch. Pete was given *carte blanche* with regard to training apparatus and equipment; the full story of his seven years in the Gulf is far beyond the parameters of this chapter, and is surely a book in its own right.

The Conseil International du Sport Militaire(CISM) http://www.cismmilsport.org was founded in 1948 after the end of the second World War. Its purpose was to organize various sporting events between military teams; parachuting was introduced as an event in 1967. Unfortunately, for whatever reasons, Britain had decided against becoming a member and thus missed out on an annual world parachuting competition. This year, the 10th CISM Parachute

Competition was to be held at the Austrian Parachute School in Wiener Neustadt and the United Arab Emirates had entered a team. Pete told me there was an open slot on the delegation for a judge, and wondered whether I would be interested. I needed no further invitation and accompanied the team forthwith. I joined the military judging team under the leadership of Helmut Schlecht and gained invaluable exposure to judging at international level, as, although I held an FAI rating, I had only limited experience outside the UK. CISM were in fact far ahead of the International Parachuting Commission (CIP) in the field of International competition. The Accuracy event was more streamlined; there was no separate event for individuals. Instead, nations jumped as a team of five with the best four scores to count as team score, with individual results extrapolated. Style was already judged by ground to air video, an innovation not to be adopted by the CIP for another five years. After the Meet I spent a couple of days in Vienna with the UAE team before returning to the UK to go back to school. I settled down at the Oxford Polytechnic as a mature student, and took a six month break from parachuting with only half a dozen jumps until the following April. In December I was once again elected to BPA Council, and took the position of Chairman of the Competitions Committee. 1978 was a World Championships year and I intended to be there.

112. *Guardroom at SOPR Rostaq in 1982.*

113. *Parade square SOPR 1982. The HQ building is in the foreground centre, with the parachute training area behind on the left.* "Al Abyad" *is in the background on the right.*

**114.** *Taking parachute landing refresher training with the RSM. The PJI under training is Arif Rashid Salim. SOPR April 1982.*

**115.** *Early morning with the Skyvan at the Hazm DZ.*

*Photo Dave Hayward*

191

*116. With Chris Lyall on the Hazm DZ in 1983.*

*117. Royal Aero Club November 1982. HRH Prince Andrew presents Mary with my Tissandier Diploma.*

**118.** *En route to the Jebel Dawi in December 1983.*     *Photo Dave Hayward*

**119.** *Villagers of the Jebel Dawi.*     *Photo Dave Hayward*

**120.** *The Sorcerer returned: Jake with Jack Hiley at the Hazm DZ 1984.*

**121.** *Freefall training. Static line tailgate exit from the Skyvan at Hazm.*

122. *Troops deplane from the C130 at the Hazm DZ in 1985.*
*Photo Jake McLoughlin*

123. *Road runners. With*
*Ron Greenhalgh on the*
*uphill section of my circuit.*

195

**124.** *Jake with his Gemini inflatable at Al Sawadi in 1984.*
*Photo courtesy Jake McLoughlin*

**125.** *With HM Sultan Qaboos; Chris Lyall is to my left. Muscat, Sultanate of Oman 1984.*

126. UAE Coach Eugen Melles pours the champagne for Mohammad Yousuf at the Altenstadt CISM 1984. I am next to Tiger; Helmut Schlecht is right foreground, whilst Mohammad extends his glass behind Helmut. This shows a rather unorthodox modification of a reserve container.

**Chapter 11** | *BPA*

*1978-1979*

My new identity as a mature student proved to be short-lived. I certainly had found the work to be interesting and my grades for the first two terms were wholly satisfactory. The fates, however, decided that an academic career was not to be, as, at the last Council meeting of 1977, Charlie Shea-Simonds announced his resignation as National Coach after three years in post. This was for overriding family reasons. I was sitting halfway down the table and, as his words sank in, I knew immediately where my future lay. College had proved a most useful interlude, a break in which I could assess my options, but when this opportunity arose there was only one decision I could make; Council invited applications for the post and I submitted my own within the week. I attended for interview and was confirmed in post at the Council meeting of the 8th of February, job to start on the 1st of April. There was to be a four-week handover period in which I was to work with Charlie before being turned loose on my own; we had worked closely together at many competitions and Instructor courses and the transition was virtually seamless, although not entirely incident-free.

Our first task together was at Sibson, the job was a five-day Relative Work seminar conducted by American skydiving guru Roger Hull. This was attended by about twenty earnest seekers after knowledge; Formation Skydiving, as we now know it, was in its relative infancy (no pun intended) in the UK, but was already well-advanced in the United States, particularly on the West Coast. The Second World Championships in Relative Work had been held the previous November at Gatton in Australia and had attracted entries from nineteen countries. PJIs Ray Willis, Bob Souter, Joe France and Ty Barraclough represented Great Britain in the 4-way event, finishing in a creditable seventh position, but obviously with still a lot to learn. Hence the popularity of the current seminar, conducted by an acknowledged master of the art. Charlie was at Sibson with the BPA caravan (Chapter 9) hitched to his Renault; the BPA had provided me with a company car in the shape of an Austin Maxi complete with towing bracket. The seminar was a huge success, and was concluded on the Friday morning. Our next task was the Army Open Classics Meet at Netheravon, where I was to be chief judge. Charlie was to take Roger Hull down to Heathrow, whilst I was to tow the caravan with the Maxi the hundred and fifty miles down to Netheravon. The previous day I had had a total of thirty minutes towing and reversing practice around the airfield; I had always enjoyed driving and felt reasonably confident I could handle the job.

Charlie helped me load the caravan with the three sets of telemeters, full DZ kit, competition impedimenta, personal kit and a couple of dozen tins of dog food for Boomerang. Weight and balance seemed OK to me, so I left Sibson after lunch and proceeded in a southwesterly direction at a genteel 40mph until I got the feel of the combination. After about an hour I was bored almost to death, wondering how on earth anyone could drive in such a fashion. Everybody and his brother was passing me, and, proceeding along the A45 behind an articulated truck at about 35mph, I checked the mirror and pulled out slightly to observe my options. That particular section was then a single carriageway with three lanes; there were no bends for over a mile and the road ahead was absolutely clear. I accelerated and pulled out smoothly, gave the truck about fifty yards clearance and very gently eased back over into the inside lane. Almost immediately, the van started to fishtail with increasing violence. On the principle that one never accelerates into a hazard, and not daring to brake, I took my feet off everything and hung in there. The oscillations increased until the van overtook the car on the outside; the whole combination turned through one hundred and eighty degrees and came to a juddering halt in a fortuitous layby facing the oncoming traffic. The wheels of the van hit the kerb, the towing gear swivelled on the ball joint and in two nanoseconds the BPA caravan was matchwood in the ditch. I sat in the upright Maxi as the articulated truck drew up alongside and stopped. "You lucky young bastard" was the verdict of the trucker. I was grateful for the "young".

The mobile phone had yet to be invented so I unhitched the Maxi and drove to the next garage where I contacted Sibson CCI Ronnie O'Brien, who organised a breakdown truck. I then phoned Bill Paul at the office. My first question to him was whether the van was insured, and he immediately got my drift; in a nutshell, I had been in the job for six days and had already totalled the BPA's caravan. I returned to the scene to find Ronnie there with the breakdown truck. Together we offloaded the telemeters, dog food, DZ kit etc. into the Maxi and supervised the loading of the wrecked caravan onto the breakdown truck. I then drove home to Abingdon for a nightstop. Next day I pitched up bright and early at Netheravon to give Charlie the bad news. He received this information in a manner befitting an officer and gentleman, no harsh words were spoken and we proceeded with the competition as planned. I was grateful that no ungracious comments were made, at least not to my face, and Council tasked me with finding a replacement van. Meanwhile I made do with the Maxi, which at least had adequate carrying capacity.

The APA Classics Meet was concluded on the Sunday, with five rounds completed. The following weekend I visited John Hitchen's DZ at Wickenby; this turned out to be a working visit as I found myself flying in the Cessna 172 for an hour, despatching four student lifts for him as he found himself inexplicably a little short-staffed. Next weekend I was at Elvington, inspecting and assisting Tony Keoghan in similar fashion. The last weekend in April was spent with Charlie Shea-Simonds on his final weekend in post. We decided to make a tour of the Northern clubs in a Cessna 172 from East Midlands Airport, starting with a one-hour flight to Bridlington. Charlie, helpful enthusiast as he was, gave me basic flying instruction and exercises 1–4 in aircraft handling, thus displaying a generosity and confidence in my co-ordination and control despite my having destroyed his beloved caravan only three weeks previously. We jumped together at Grindale and flew up to Sunderland the next day to visit Jim Barnes at the Tyne and Wear Parachute Club before flying west to Dave Prince's Northwest Parachute Centre at Cark, where I jumped together with Charlie, Dave, and Biff Burn. On the Sunday we flew to Tilstock, home of the Manchester Freefall Club in atrocious weather before returning to East Midlands Airport, coming out of cloud at two hundred feet perfectly lined up with the runway. I was most grateful to Charlie for easing me into the job so smoothly, and doubly impressed with his professional flying capabilities.

The next day I settled in at the Leicester office with my own desk, National Coach in my own right for the first time. I was directly answerable to Council on all matters parachuting, via the Safety and Training Committee. I had no formal terms of reference; I just took over the whole spectrum from Charlie. I assumed operational and judging responsibility for all domestic Classic competitions and handed over the Classic team coach slot to Bob King, whilst maintaining my role as FAI judge. I was responsible for running four Instructor courses per year. I introduced the concept of scholarship/progression courses for promising newcomers. I aimed to make a liaison visit every Club and Centre in the land; there was no formal inspection system, I just needed to show the face of the BPA around the country and offer assistance and advice if so required. It was also my task to update and advise the Safety and Training Committee and take the minutes at all meetings. The BPA Chairman was John Meacock; Dave Waugh was Vice Chairman, with Jim Crocker as Chairman of the Safety and Training Committee. Charlie was still editing the Magazine and was co-opted to Council as BPA delegate to the International Parachuting Commission (CIP) of the FAI. I was alternate delegate and attended all CIP meetings, which in those days were rotated in alternate years between the Paris headquarters and member countries.

At BPA HQ we had a staff of five including myself; Bill Paul who was now in his tenth year as Secretary General; Dorothy, his wife and Assistant secretary; plus Helen Curry and Susie Bates as junior staff. I knew Bill Paul of old, I had worked with him when he was a Syndicate Officer at PTS; he retired in the rank of Squadron Leader. Bill was an old-school jumper, albeit never involved in sport parachuting; he was an administrator of the highest calibre with an even temperament and we enjoyed an excellent personal and working relationship. Since the unfortunate incident with the caravan, I was tasked with finding a replacement; it was immediately apparent to me that a towed caravan was a gross liability and I decided that a Mobile Control Unit would be much more manageable. I envisaged a Transit-type vehicle fully kitted out for DZ control. In the event, I decided on a 2-litre Ford Transit van with a sliding side door and a tailgate. I needed a custom-built interior with racks for the telemeters, a ground to air radio and an anemometer on a telescopic mast, plus storage space for DZ panels and other impedimenta. There remained enough space for a camp bed in case of emergency. Council were immediately in favour of this project and applied for Sports Council funding. This all took time, of course, and in the meantime I continued to load up the Maxi to capacity and travelled wherever required.

In those days, there were four major domestic Championships every year; the first being the APA Championships for the first ten days in May. We ran eight rounds of Accuracy, three of Style and three rounds Relative Work (now Formation Skydiving). There were ninety-two competitors in total; Pete Sherman turned up in a brand new Ferrari with two teams from the United Arab Emirates; there was also a team from the 25th German Airborne Brigade and one from the US Special Forces. Aircraft support was the two APA Islanders and Cessna 206, augmented by an Army Scout and a Navy Wessex. Ken Mapplebeck was now out in Germany on the staff at RAPA and took the individual accuracy event with 0. 08cm total over eight rounds. We were still using a ten-centimetre disc with manual scoring. Scotty Milne became Army Champion, placing second in Accuracy and first in Style. Dougie Young was runner up in both events.

In between competitions I still had a job to do and the next week I was at Grindale Field, Bridlington, where I ran my first PI course (Potential Instructor – now Basic Instructor), assisted by ex-PJI Tony Keoghan. For the next ten days I was on the road, visiting BPA Clubs at Chetwynd in Shropshire, Brunton in Northumberland, Strathallan in Scotland and Netheravon in Wiltshire, before finishing up the following month at Sibson for the National RW championships, with Biff Burn as Chief Judge. Five 4-man teams entered, with judging by ground/air video camera and the Meet was concluded in three days with the Army team of Tim Andrewes, Pete Hough, Mike Smith and Wally Wallace taking the honours over the ten rounds.

Back to Bridlington again in July for the Classic Nationals; this year held particular significance as the 14th World Championships were to be held in Zagreb in August, and the team would be selected from the Bridlington results. Bill Paul had done a great job and had engineered sponsorship from Smirnoff Vodka in the shape of a cash grant that was used to reduce the competitors' general entry fee. We had 44 competitors, fifteen of whom had spent time at Raeford with Gene Paul Thacker for intensive training. Dave Prince was the Meet Director, bringing with him the Cark Cessna 182. His pilot was known only as Ben, who flew the machine most expertly in green Wellington boots and who had attached a tin box on the instrument panel just inside the door, for tips. True. My judging team was John Meacock, Bob Burn, Roger (Doc) Flinn, Richard Atherton and John Hitchen. The target area was the 30-metre pea gravel pit and we had a ten-centimetre disc with manual scoring. Despite a few weather holds, the Meet was completed inside a week. The top six overall men were, in order: Doug Young, Scotty Milne, Dickie Bird, Paddy Byrne, Dave Tylcoat and Bob Hiatt. These were selected for Yugoslavia, together with the only two girls who made the qualifying standard – Jackie Smith and Sandy Milne, both of whom had jumped in Rome two years previously. Bob King was to travel as Team Coach, with myself as FAI judge. This was still six weeks hence and the Rhine Army Parachute Association (RAPA) Meet beckoned.

This was held over five days at Bad Lippspringe from 31st July to 4th August, and was, as always, a hugely popular event. I drove over in the Maxi a couple of days early to catch up again with the Commandant, Major Tom Oxley, and Chief Instructor Mac McQueen. This was of course, the anniversary of my final day in the Air Force twelve months previously and I was looking forward to meeting old friends again. In the event, we made over one thousand Accuracy jumps, one hundred and fifty-five Style plus fifty-seven 4-way RW. The Meet closed on Friday the 4th August, complete barring the final two rounds of RW. I was Chief Judge again, and wrote up an account of the competition for the October edition of the BPA Magazine, which is reproduced in Appendix 2.

Once back from Germany I busied myself with routine admin and planning the forthcoming trip to Zagreb, whilst Bob King took the team to Raeford for two weeks training. We decided to take the Maxi on the nine hundred mile trip to Yugoslavia, and hired a Dodge minibus as team transport so that we would be independent on arrival. The advance party consisted of Bob King (Team Coach) Paddy Byrne (Team Alternate), myself (FAI judge), Paul Slaughter of the Metropolitan Police (driver, photographer) plus Dane Kenny and Dickie Bird's wife Trish as the supporters club. Paddy and I took the Maxi, with the other four in the Dodge. We left the UK on the Sunday, drove through Germany and Austria, crossing into what was then President Tito's Yugoslavia, and arriving in Zagreb after lunch on Tuesday. Once out of Austria, the autobahn system was far from complete, the dual carriageway deteriorating into single track a few kilometers outside main cities; signposting was equally sparse and in Cyrillic script; on more than one occasion we stopped to take a compass bearing at some particularly obscure crossroads.

Two days later, the team arrived along with BPA Chairman John Meacock as Head of Delegation. The Meet proper started on Sunday the 27th August, with Sven Brostedt of Denmark as Chief

Judge for his third consecutive World Meet. Aircraft in use were once again the AN2 Antonovs and the ubiquitous Mi-8 Russian helicopters. I managed one jump from each, but was kept pretty much continuously employed in my judging role – we totalled 1700 Accuracy jumps and 360 Style, the latter still being judged on telemeters. The electronic scoring pad was now established for the accuracy, with a ten-centimeter dead centre disc. The main story from a British perspective is the historic achievement of Jackie Smith in becoming not only the first Brit to win a gold medal at a World Meet, but the first person ever in World Championship history to score ten consecutive dead centre landings in the process. She scored her first two discs on day one, whilst her main rival, Cheryl Stearns of the USA, dropped two centimeters on her first jump, a deficit she was never to make up although she shadowed Jackie jump for jump thenceforth right up to round ten.

Jackie's ninth accuracy dead centre was on the Wednesday; the next day she was jumping style. This ensured that she had to sweat out her last round for two whole days. Friday saw the final round of female accuracy and I was judging in the pit. It must be remembered that in those days individual accuracy was just that – one jumper out per pass. The first girl out suffered a spinal injury reaching for the pad, which caused a thirty-five minute delay; the situation was further compounded by the next two jumpers being waved off, each landing out on opposite sides of the pit. As the Antonov circled, door closed, with Jack next to jump, she did not know whether there had been a wind hold, or wind change, or whatever. Because of the language barrier the on-board judge could not explain the situation to her. The uncertainty thus engendered dramatically heightened an already highly charged situation and British Head of Delegation John Meacock had already drafted out a potential protest. As the Antonov was finally given clear drop, every competitor on the Drop Zone encircled the target area to witness history in the making. I crouched down directly on the windline behind the pad as Jackie turned in on finals at two hundred feet, flying her 5 cell Strato Star steady as a rock right on line but a little hot. Her hands barely moved, apart from slight application of brake as she adjusted the angle. The last ten feet she braked smoothly and dropped her right heel, for my money, dead centre again. I glanced up at the electronic readout for confirmation and there it was – Jackie Smith, **0. 00** and thus Ladies Accuracy World Champion 1978. The whole British Team invaded the pit and carried her out shoulder high. I joined in and had to dash back to take up my own position. This was one truly great parachuting achievement, and nobody could take it away from her. Second placed Cheryl Stearns of the USA tried to steal some of her thunder by persuading the organizers to allow her to continue jumping in order to create a record for the number of consecutive dead centres; the fact remained that she was second on the podium behind the lass from Middlesbrough.

Following this individual triumph, there was still all to play for in men's Team Accuracy. We went into round four, requiring four dead centres to clinch third place. The team jumped brilliantly; with discs from Scotty, Dickie, and Bob Hiatt; Dave Tylcoat scored one centimeter, which dropped us to fourth behind the Soviets. Third in Graz, fourth in Talequah, now fourth by a whisker again; the Brits had a history of solid team jumping success, although we were never able to meaningfully challenge the state-subsidised Eastern bloc countries. Scotty's four dead centres were a tribute to this most consistent competitor and were a harbinger of things to come two years down the line. All four rounds were completed as follows: with Great Britain scoring as follows:

| Milne | 0.00 0.00 0.00 0.00 | 0.00 |
|---|---|---|
| Bird | 0.00 0.02 0.00 0.00 | 0.02 |
| Tylcoat | 0.00 0.00 0.00 0.01 | 0.01 |
| Hiatt | 0.04 0.00 0.09 0.00 | 0.13 |
| | **Total:** | **0.16 cm** |

Paul Slaughter's write-up of the competition appears in the October edition of the BPA Magazine, http://www.bpa-archive. org.uk/mag_archive/magazines/068-1978-5.pdf, and all results can be found at Bob King's website: https://sites.google.com/site/

bobkingsparchutingarchive/1978-wpc-results. I jumped with Scotty, Dickie, and Paddy Byrne as the Brit representatives on the final demo, two thousand feet from the Mi-8, to round off a momentous ten days. Back then to the office, blissfully unaware of the storm brewing up back home.

I arrived back at work on Monday the 11th September; a routine Council meeting was due on the coming Thursday, and Bill Paul warned me of a possible rocky ride ahead. The subject was staff salaries. All the BPA staff had been assimilated into the Sports Council grading and salary scales since October 1975; this situation had been accepted by Council and had never been a subject of dissent or indeed discussion. For the past three years Bill had applied these scales to all staff without question. The 1978 scales came into force on 1st April, and Bill applied them as a matter of routine. This time, BPA treasurer Peter Mitchell queried the figures and raised the point that Council had not been consulted on what was a modest salary increase for all staff, myself included. When the agenda item came up, Bill and I were requested to leave the meeting and Council sat *in camera*. On our recall, we were informed that Council had resolved that Bill had acted without authorisation and that furthermore, they had no confidence in his conduct of Association affairs. Council issued Bill with a reprimand and requested his resignation. The meeting was then adjourned until the following Monday to complete the agenda.

At this subsequent meeting, Bill Paul was invited to make his observations on the matter. The atmosphere was pretty tense, and Bill's main stance was that he had always been granted total autonomy over routine financial matters. We were then again requested to sit outside. On recall, Council re-iterated their demand that Bill resign, failing which he was to be given three months notice. Bill Paul was a very proud man, and one of the utmost integrity. He declined the offer to resign, with the inevitable consequences. His employment was terminated at the end of the year and Dorothy left shortly thereafter. Bill subsequently appealed to an Industrial Tribunal on the grounds of wrongful dismissal. At the hearing in March 1979, this tribunal unanimously found in Bill's favour and awarded him

207

damages for the wrongful dismissal and loss of income. Bill obtained another post with the nascent British Parascending Association in Leicester, where he remained until he suffered a heart attack the following year, from which he tragically never recovered.

Bill's successor was Charles Port, also ex Royal Air Force, where he had specialised in Intelligence as a linguist fluent in Chinese and Russian. Following a brief spell working with an insurance company, he had successfully applied for the BPA post and started the job on the first of January 1979. Although totally devoid of any parachuting background, Charles was a most capable administrator and a very willing learner; we shared an office and I was able to fill in any technical details for him whenever required. I was, however, mostly on the road. In February the annual International Parachuting Commission (CIP) meeting was hosted by the Netherlands Para-chuting Federation at Arnhem and I drove across in the Maxi with Charlie Shea-Simonds, by now himself a fully elected Council member, for the three-day session. My main role was as member of the Sporting Code sub-committee, chaired by Canada's Richard (Buzz) Bennett, with Uwe Beckmann from Germany and Claude Gillard (Australia) making up the quorum. Apart from the working meetings and plenary session, our Dutch hosts entertained us royally, culminating in an official banquet at a medieval castle. We were also given a tour of the Arnhem battlefields in Oosterbeek, including a visit to the military cemetery and the recently opened Airborne museum at the Hartenstein Hotel. It was impressive to note that our guides were mostly young persons, steeped in the history of the battle which took place thirty-five years previously, before most of them were born. This meeting was personally significant in that it gave me an insight into the workings of CIP and complemented my two previous outings as an International Judge at the 1977 CISM and the 1978 WPC.

Back then to the UK and the next trip was to sunnier climes. Peter Sherman had organised a National competition in the United Arab Emirates and had invited a team of British judges to officiate. In the event, the Meet was cancelled, but we went anyway, Pete having organised a training camp instead. Along with Jackie Smith, Dave Waugh, Roger Flinn, Jim Walmsley and other BPA judges I travelled out for two weeks in Dubai to assist in coaching the UAE team. Doc Flinn brought along his electronic pad for further evaluation. As well as unlimited jumping, Pete and Billy Foulkes extended us tremendous hospitality, including a couple of sailing lessons in Billy's yacht. This was a most welcome interlude, and was my first introduction to parachuting in the Gulf – an experience which was to extend a further thirty-five years to the present day.

Later that year I took delivery of the custom built Ford Transit Mobile Control Unit. This vehicle was equipped for Drop Zone Control with full ground/air and ground/ground communications, and was to prove great value for the following three years. Its first outing was in April to the Scottish Nationals in Glenrothes, then down to Sunderland where I ran the second Instructor Course of the year. In June I was Chief Judge at the Army Championships at Netheravon where we completed 750 competition jumps in the three days permitted by some appalling weather. This was followed one week later by the National Championships at the same venue. This year we combined the Classic disciplines (Senior, Intermediate and Novice) with Relative Work (FS) 4-way and 8-way. The Third WPC in Formation Skydiving was to be held later that year and teams would be selected on these results. The Meet was highly successful, thanks to good weather and the highly professional APA organisation. Statistics for the Meet were 420 Accuracy jumps, 80 Style jumps (judged on telemeters) and 160 RW (FS) 4-way and 8-way; these latter being judged by ground to air video camera. As a follow-up, we can see that international jumpers Jackie Smith, Robin Mills, Dane Kenny and Bob Hiatt had effortlessly transferred their Classics skills to Formation Skydiving. All four were selected for the British teams to compete in the Third World Parachuting Championships in Relative Work, which were to be held in Châteauroux, in central France at the end of August.

After the July RAPA Meet, I took the van over to France, this time in my capacity of Team Leader of the British Delegation to the 3rd WPC in Relative Work. Charlie Shea-Simonds was Head of our Delegation, with John Laing as Team judge; Biff Burn was given the prestigious task of Head of Training Judges. The Meet was organised by the French Armée de l'aire, the jumpships were Nord Atlas transports, and judging was by ground/air video with the exit being called from the ground. Chief Judge was Uwe Beckmann who I had met at the CIP meeting in February; Meet Director was Michel Rogovitz who I knew from CISM, whilst in charge of the crucial video/telemeter operation was my old friend Desiré Mignam who had been instructing at Châlon during my first visit there sixteen years previously (Chapter 3). The Meet was completed after ten days and proved most profitable for the British team, who achieved a silver medal in the 4-way sequential event with the Symbiosis team of Will Grut, Dane Kenny, Rob Colpus, Geoff Saunders with Jackie Smith as alternate. Thus Jackie won medals in two consecutive World Parachute Championships in separate disciplines, following her Gold the previous year in Yugoslavia. The 8-way team of Tony Uragallo, Robin Mills, Jackie Smith, Fred and Jim Keery, Steve Newton, Mike Smith, Tim Andrewes with Bob Hiatt and Tim Kirkstead-Moore as alternates, were placed fifth; sandwiched between the Chinese and German teams.

Exhilarating as this European competition circuit was, my main task was back in the UK organising and staffing four Instructor courses each year, running scholarship/progression courses, and maintaining constant liaison with clubs and centres. A balance with competition work had to be maintained, and I was invariably given total support from my fellow examiners and from all club and centre CCIs. On the training side there was an ongoing debate regarding our progression system, with some very knowledgeable instructors anticipating AFF training, which was still some three years in the future. One of the most prominent was Dave Howerski, an extremely enthusiastic coach and accomplished RW jumper; author of "Body Flying", a treatise on relative work published in June 1979. Dave assisted me at his Shobdon Drop Zone on the July progression course, and wrote a thought-provoking article in the October 1979 edition of the magazine, outlining his training philosophy. It must be remembered that at the time students were jumping low-performance round canopies with all the weather restrictions and frustrations thereby imposed. Over time, these problems were alleviated by the introduction of Accelerated Free Fall training (AFF) around 1984, and by the Ram Air Progression System (RAPS) in the UK some two years later. In 1984 Bryan Dyas became one of the first BPA instructors to obtain the USPA AFF qualification at the Deland DZ in Florida, and became a strong advocate for its adoption by the BPA.

Meanwhile, the New Year was fast approaching, with three major National and two World Championships on the horizon.

**Chapter 12** | *Judge*

*1980-1982*

The New Year opened for the BPA with a change at the top. John Meacock had retired after three years as Chairman and eleven on Council; he was succeeded by Dave Waugh with John Laing as Vice, whilst Jim Crocker remained as Chairman of STC. On the international front Charlie and I again were to attend the annual CIP Conference, this year held at FAI Headquarters in the Rue Galilée in central Paris. We travelled separately; I drove from Leicester to East Midlands airport in good time and presented myself at check-in only to discover to my slight embarrassment that, for the first time in some twenty-five years travelling, I had left my passport behind at home. Border Control were most reluctant to let me through but eventually relented, albeit with the dire prediction that French Immigration would inevitably refuse entry and return me to the UK in short order.

Suitably chastened, I landed at Charles de Gaulle International some forty-five minutes later and joined the queue ministered by the most sympathetic looking gendarme I could see. When called forward I explained in my best O level French that I had regrettably left my passport back in the UK. He then asked whether I had any other ID, and I produced my driving licence. He examined this at some length and came to a decision, closing the barrier to the queue behind me and requesting that I follow him. This I did, marching down a long corridor a couple of paces to the rear. He knocked on the door and we both entered. Sitting behind the desk was a shirt-sleeved civilian, evidently his boss. The dialogue proceeded roughly as follows, in English, interspersed with some pretty feeble O level French from me:

**Gendarme:** "This Englishman wishes to come to Paris, but has forgotten his passport"

**Bossman:** (to me) "And what is the purpose of your visit?"

**Me:** (grovelling) "Monsieur, I have come to your beautiful city at the invitation of the International Parachuting Commission for the Annual Conference"

**Bossman:** "You are a parachutist?"

**Me:** "Oui monsieur"

**Bossman:** "So if you were to jump out of your aeroplane, would you forget your parachute as well?"

**Me:** (diplomatically smiling at this uproarious Gallic pleasantry) "Non, monsieur"

**Bossman:** "Do you have any identification?"

**Me:** "Oui monsieur"(producing Driving Licence)

**Bossman:** "And do you have any other identification?"

**Me:** "Oui monsieur, American Express" (offering said card for inspection)

**Bossman:** (on cue) "That will do nicely thank you"

And I was through. The above dialogue is absolutely authentic; all I had now to worry about was getting back in again to the UK.

Our Sporting Code sub-committee was involved with discussions involving fundamental changes to the International Judge Rating system and the composition of the Jury at World Meets. We also wished to add a Canopy Relative Work (now CF) Category to world records. These proposed amendments were then submitted to the plenary session for ratification, only to be informed by the Director General that these could not be accepted as the FAI General Conference had ruled that changes to the Sporting Code could only be effected every four years. There was nothing to be done about this at the time, but Committee chairman Buzz Bennett made it pretty clear that this issue should be resolved next time to allow the sport to progress without any bureaucratic holdups.

Returning from France I was on the road to Netheravon running a PI course followed by an Exam course; because of the sheer numbers involved, I had introduced the two-week format which is now standard procedure. For my own personal parachuting I had been jumping a 230 Strato Cloud, which was, along with the 252 Parafoil, one of the two standard accuracy canopies used in the western world. I was happy with this rig, but in March the GQ Parachute Company offered me a GQ Unit on permanent loan. This was a 7-cell 200 sq. ft. canopy, which could be either packed in a bag or freepacked with the lines stowed on a diaper. http://www.flickr.com/photos/vintageparachutegear/sets/72157627694440463/html GQ had introduced Kevlar suspension lines to reduce drag; albeit with mixed results. Whilst drag was undoubtedly reduced, Kevlar had a low abrasion tolerance and the lines had to be closely inspected after each jump. In addition to the abrasion problem, we found that the low stretch factor was placing an undue strain on the canopy fabric on deployment. This having been said, it was a most enjoyable demo canopy to jump with an advertised airspeed of 22 mph and slider deployed opening.

In March I was invited to jump on the Langar Hitachi demo team then run by Tom Sawyer and Dave Hickling. Tom was a pilot and old-style entrepreneur who harboured ambitions to compete with the Red Devils demo team nationwide. He engineered simultaneous sponsorship from Barclaycard, Subaru, Jeep, and Fuji Film as well as Hitachi. This project eventually ran out of steam, the logistics proving insuperable, but it was good while it lasted. My particular involvement was confined to four jumps onto a miniscule lawn at Belvoir Castle at a Sony Corporation symposium. One rehearsal, carried out by Dave and myself in doubtful visibility at the minimum D licence height of 1500ft, resulted in an eight hundred metre overshoot; GPS having not then been invented. Happily I was able to lead the team stack on target for the four live shows. These jumps were interspersed with a demo into the Wolverhampton Wanderers Molyneaux stadium with Dave Turner; this was no area for a fast canopy and I reverted to the Strato Cloud to take the match ball into the centre circle for a home game. The previous weekend Wolves had won the League Cup; the wall of sound as three of us came in over the stand at the northern end was absolutely mind-blowing, even surpassing the Hong Kong Government Stadium experience (Chapter 7). I had always enjoyed the challenge and novelty of demonstration jumping, these interludes provided the perfect counterpoint to the mechanics of competition training; this was pure fun, my release from the day job, and I seldom turned down an invitation to make up a team going into an arena or sports field.

A particular instance occurred one Saturday during the Army Championships in May, when jumping was suspended for the day as the westerly airflow exceeded thirty knots at ground level. Don Daines from Biggin Hill was flying his Islander at the Meet; he supported a particular charity, the Carshalton Queen Mary's Hospital for children and that afternoon he had promised a demo jump for the Hospital fete. Shady Silverlock of the Royal Artillery team was running the DZ, we phoned down and he gave us a surface wind of ten knots, and on this highly unlikely intelligence we decided to give it a go. On the aircraft were Nick Harrison and Rod Burgess of the Royal Artillery team, plus John Hitchen, with myself as jumpmaster. We covered the sixty miles from Netheravon to Carshalton in about twenty minutes flat thanks to the aforementioned westerly airflow. On arrival at the DZ we had a 1700 foot cloudbase and a thousand metre spot – typical demo conditions for the UK in June... . Hitchen was pointing aghast at his altimeter as we ran in through a hailstorm; I turned it up to 2000 feet for him as I hopped out of the door. We all made it in, to the delight of the children and also to Don Daines, a great pilot and friend. I later received the following letter forwarded from the hospital:

*Dear Sister Collis,*

*I am writing to thank you for taking Richard and I from Ward 3B to see the parachute jump on Hospital Fete Day. We left the field and returned to the ward when it started raining. As we were leaving we heard people saying the jump would not take place because of bad weather and so we were delighted when you came to take us out again and allowed us to have some crisps. It was very exciting to see the plane circle and the parachutes open and twist and turn as they came down over the field. We thought the men were very brave to come down among all the tents and stalls, they were really fantastic to land on the right spot. I was very excited and it was worth having my operation to see it. Will you please thank the parachute men for me. I am getting better from my operation now and I hope that you and all the nurses and children are well.*

*Thank you Sister Collis*
*Neil*

**BPA Magazine August 1980**

What more could one ask for?

The British National Championships were this year held at Sibson, once again encompassing Accuracy, Style, plus 4-way and 8-way FS. The Meet was bedevilled by bad weather, but we had sufficient jumping to select a team for the upcoming 15th WPC in Bulgaria. For the first time we had Roger Flinn's electronic scoring pad for accuracy; Style was still judged on telemeters. The video camera, operated by Graham Pierce, was by now firmly established for judging the FS. This year no ladies had met the selection criteria, and accordingly Bob King was nominated as Coach of an all male team. A squad consisting of Scotty Milne, Dougie Young, Dave Tylcoat, Deke Wright, Paul Slaughter, Paddy Byrne and Jim Coffey flew out to Raeford for a training camp a couple of weeks later.

The 15th WPC in Style and Accuracy was held in Kazanlak, Bulgaria from the 16th to the 27th of August. Ken Mapplebeck and myself were the British Judges, with Roger (Doc) Flinn and Martin Rennie travelling to attend the trainee Judging seminar. Ken and I drove over in the BPA van, in convoy with Roger Flinn and Martin Rennie in Doc's Mercedes. We drove through Germany and Austria into the then Yugoslavia and continued southeast into Bulgaria. We were held at the border for a couple of hours as, although our visas were valid, and I was by now a civilian, our passports gave our occupation as "Government Service" with the inevitable military connotations. The Balkans autobahn system had not improved either since our last incursion to Zagreb two years previously. The dual carriageway was constructed of wide-jointed concrete blocks which rattled the van with a continuous thumping, adhesion was made all the more treacherous by the torrential downpour which lasted most of the journey. We finally reached Kazanlak, a distance of sixteen hundred miles covered in three days. Kazanlak turned out to be a medium sized town with a population of some 50,000 situated at the eastern end of the Valley of the Roses, one hundred miles inland from the Black Sea coast. The organisers had constructed a four-star hotel especially for the competition, and the remainder of the team flew in a couple of days later with Charlie Shea as Head of Delegation. From the Raeford training camp Bob had selected his team of Scotty Milne, Dougie Young, Deke Wright and Dave Tylcoat from the military, with Paul Slaughter (Metropolitan Police) as the sole civilian representative.

We had a most experienced judging panel, including Sven Brostedt who had been Chief Judge at the last three WPCs. This time the Chief Judge was Buzz Bennett of Canada and he appointed me as Style Event Judge. I was ably backed up by Brostedt, Ken Mapplebeck and John Mirus from the USA. The Bulgarians had provided a first class video system for Style judging, which we evaluated for the CIP, and used as a backup. The prime judging was on telemeters; as it turned out this was the last time they were ever used at a WPC. We made 708 style jumps with only one rejump for cloud and no protests; Ken and I had a great relationship with Buzz, himself an expatriate Yorkshireman. We certainly both enjoyed jumping with him, taking the Antonov up to 10,000 feet on a couple of occasions, revelling in our somewhat rusty FS skills.

As far as the Brits were concerned, our main hopes centred once more on the Accuracy event. Two years previously we had seen ex Red Devil Jackie Smith go head to head with Cheryl Stearns of the USA for the title. This time it was our own two top jumpers, Red Devils Scotty Milne and Dougie Young vying for third place. Dirk Boidin of Belgium and Craig Winning of Canada had each scored ten dead centres and jumped off for first and second; Winning jumped first and dropped five centimetres, whilst Boidin scored an eleventh consecutive disc to take the Gold. Bronze was now up for grabs with Scotty and Dougie both on one centimetre for 10 rounds. Dougie went first on the jumpoff, and hit 0.01. Scotty made no mistake, smashing out another disc to take the Bronze medal. Extramural activities included a tour into the surrounding hillsides, spent in the company of our German, Canadian and American colleagues. Luminaries included Helmut Schlecht, by now one of the top figures in European parachuting, whilst American jury member BJ Worth had already achieved international renown as an aerial stuntman, first coming to prominence with the skydiving sequences for the Bond film *Moonraker* the previous year. The Competition ended on the 27th August with the closing ceremony and competitors jumping into the town square. 1980 had given Great Britain a third consecutive medal at the last three World Championships, and we set off for home on the long trek across Europe totally content with a job well done.

One month later, I applied for two weeks leave from the BPA. Pete Sherman was taking his UAE team to Chile to compete in the 12th CISM Parachuting Championships, and had invited me along once more as Team Judge. I accepted with alacrity and flew across to Frankfurt to meet up with the team before embarking on the eight thousand mile transatlantic flight into the Southern hemisphere. We had a long stopover in Rio, then across the continent and over the nineteen thousand feet Andes peaks before dropping steeply into the Santiago Arturo Merino Benítez International Airport in the valley behind.

We were accommodated at the Bernardo O'Higgins Military Academy on the outskirts of the capital, and were rapidly introduced to our two escorting officers, one of whom was a statuesque brunette who carried a Browning automatic pistol in her handbag. The competition Drop Zone was some thirty miles away at the Chilean Special Forces base in Peldehue, deep in the coastal foothills to the west of the city; every morning a cavalcade of buses left the barracks with a heavily armed escort, including a helicopter in close attendance. The bus drivers were themselves armed with Uzi submachine guns. The Chile of 1980 was ruled by a military government following the coup of 1973 and was under constant threat from the left-wing guerrilla movement MIR, hence the massive security. We had only eight teams at this particular competition, which comprised Accuracy, Style and RW, all flown by Army UH1 Huey helicopters. At the opening briefing, conducted by Chief Judge Pinon, I was appointed Event Judge for both Style and RW. Both were judged on video, with the exit called from the ground. This was fine by me, although I was confronted by one particular technical problem in that the 7,000 feet winds were consistently blowing at 50 knots from the west, and the DZ was in a valley surrounded by 5,000 feet high hills, opening height being of course 2,000 feet. We had to run downwind for style, and the trick was to get the jumper out far enough on line to give a fair chance of landing on the tight dropzone, but close enough to avoid hitting the 5,000 feet hill in freefall. This we managed to accomplish, and the one hundred and sixty style jumps were concluded without scaring anyone too much.

Only a few teams entered the RW event, and we judged only 14 jumps. These were flown into wind at 10,000 feet; ground spotted, and passed off without incident. At the end of the Meet we flew a Judges load consisting of Pete, myself, and three other CISM judges, one being a Moroccan named Tahidi. Brazilian judge Nelson Palma did the honours on the telemeters for the ground spot. We put Tahidi out on the exit call, I pinned him and Pete closed third. On opening we found ourselves two miles downwind in the immediate vicinity of a medium sized mountain. Tahidi and the other two other judges made for a ledge they thought they could see on the hillside; Pete and I turned downwind and made for the only clear area down the valley. The DZ was out of sight a good three miles away on the other side of the hill. We hopped over some power cables and touched down without incident in a wide gravel-covered stretch by the riverside. We gathered up our rigs, and turned around at the clip clop sound of approaching hooves. Half a dozen immaculately attired gauchos pulled up beside us, mounted on magnificent horses, and accompanied by what seemed to be the entire population of the neighbouring village. They announced they were there to help, and escorted us back to a clear area where the Huey eventually touched down to fly us back, having previously rescued the other three judges from their perch on the mountainside. Nelson Palma, who had put us out, signed my logbook and asked me to log it as a military tactical insertion.

Our UAE team distinguished themselves by taking the silver medal in Team Accuracy, ahead of the American Golden Knights, whose team included a smartly uniformed Cheryl Stearns. We were each presented with a commemorative plaque and Chilean military wings. Our hosts then laid on an excursion to the coast at Valparaiso, about 70 miles from the capital. The Pacific did not appear so peaceful, waves lashed the shore and it rained non-stop; nonetheless we were treated to a superb equestrian show by the Chilean Army display troop and a farewell barbecue liberally laced by an inexhaustible supply of Pisco Sour cocktails. We flew home on the first of October, content in the aftermath of a most informal and friendly CISM interlude.

The New Year opened with the AGM, held at the Centre Hotel in Leicester on 9th January and which saw a reshuffle of Council members. Dave Waugh retired as Chairman to be succeeded by Charlie Shea-Simonds, Jim Crocker moved from STC Chairman after an invaluable ten-year stint to become the Association Vice Chairman, his place at STC being taken by John Laing of the APA. Shortly thereafter Charlie somewhat reluctantly stepped down after eight years of editing the magazine, handing over to Dave Waterman. The stage was thus set for the first important event of the year – the Annual CIP Conference which we were to host for the first time ever. This was held at the Bisham Abbey Sports Centre near Marlow, and was masterminded by Charlie in his capacity of UK CIP Delegate and CIP Vice-President, assisted by myself. The initial rendezvous for most delegates was the Army Parachute Association Centre at Netheravon, hosted by Commandant Gerry O'Hara and Chief Instructor John Laing. The Army provided food, accommodation and jumpships for a great parachuting weekend before all guests were bussed down to Bisham for the Meeting on the Sunday evening. At Bisham, my technical input was confined to the Sporting Code sub-committee and several fundamental rule changes were incorporated. At the previous WPC in Kazanlak, Belgium's Dirk Boidin had scored eleven consecutive dead centres on a ten-centimetre disc; this target was now by common consent reduced to five centimetres. Because of the improved performance of ram-air canopies, wind limits for Style and RW were increased to 9 metres/second. Finally, and following the contretemps at the 1980 Paris CIP meeting, certain sections of the text were transferred to Annexes, which could then be amended annually without reference to a four-yearly FAI General Conference.

With these international affairs behind us, I returned to the day job; my next jump of note was for Tom Sawyer's Subaru team into the West Bromwich Albion FC stadium at the Hawthorns, just off the M5. We jumped in from 1700 feet, all putting down in the centre circle to be greeted by the manager, Ron Atkinson no less. He recognized me from his National Service days at Abingdon in 1961 (Chapter 2). We were all given seats in the directors box for the match against Ipswich, and entertained in the directors lounge after the game, further enhancing my street cred with the Langar based team. My next three demos were with a BPA team into the National Exhibition Centre at Birmingham for the National Action Sports Show; I put the Strato Cloud dead centre on the lawn outside the main entrance by the lake, followed a week later by a water jump into the Edgbaston Reservoir. Finally at the end of the month I made a return to the Queen Mary's Carshalton hospital with the Royal Artillery team. Thenceforth to the Army Championships at Netheravon, once again encompassing Accuracy, Style and RW. Scotty Milne took both the Accuracy and Style quite comfortably, whilst Issa Mohammad of Pete Sherman's visiting UAE team took second place for the visitors; a warm-up for his future success in the Nationals at the same venue two weeks later.

The 1981 British National Parachute Championships were held at Netheravon from the 4th–12th July, with priority being given to RW, as this was a World Meet year. The RW event 8-way and 4-way was won by Symbiosis, consisting of Geoff Saunders, Rob Colpus,

Jim Keery, Fred Keery, Dane Kenny, Kathy McCormack, Jackie Smith, Will Grut, Tony Uragallo and Robin Mills. Both Symbiosis teams finished comfortably ahead of the field, having benefitted from an intensive three-week training camp in Raeford; all were selected to represent Great Britain at the 4th WPC in RW, which was scheduled for Zephyrhills in October. Once again Classics jumpers Jackie Smith, Dane Kenny and Robin Mills had proved their versatility and sheer skydiving ability to excel in both disciplines. In the Accuracy event Issa Mohammad of the UAE took the gold, whilst Scotty Milne, who had himself spent eleven weeks in Dubai at the beginning of the season coaching style and accuracy, dropped into second place behind his star pupil. Said Khalifa, also of the UAE, was in third place. This Dubai-based team had made great strides under Peter Sherman since their first appearance at the Hereford Nationals five years previously (Chapter 10), and had already hosted the Army Competition Cadre and the Red Devils on training camps in Dubai earlier in the year.

The Dubai profile was further raised as the United Arab Emirates were the host country for the 13th CISM to be held later in the year, with Pete as Meet Director. He asked me to officiate as Chief Judge, and I accordingly booked leave and travelled out to Dubai in October with RAF PJI Graham Pierce as video operator. The Competition site was in Jumeirah, at that time a deserted sandy coastal stretch ten miles outside the city, alongside the Chicago Beach Hotel, (now the Jumeirah Beach Hotel) where all the seventeen teams were accommodated. Helicopter landing pads were provided by the simple expedient of closing off one thousand metres of the main north-south highway to all traffic. The UAE organization was superb, all credit due to the Central Military Command; Pete did a great job as Meet Director, masterminding the whole show with effortless diplomacy and characteristic thoroughness.

The Meet itself comprised eight rounds of Team Accuracy, with individual scores extrapolated from team scores; four rounds of Style, and four rounds of sequential RW (FS). The jump ships were Bell Huey 214s; Style and RW were judged on the best colour video I had ever seen, expertly handled (except for once) by Graham Pierce. Accuracy was judged on a ten-centimeter electronic disc, over eight rounds. This led to a nine-way tie for first place, which was reduced to five finalists, after five alternate foot jump-offs. The final five were each awarded a first place Gold medal. This certainly convinced me that the 5 cm disc was here to stay and that CISM must follow the CIP ruling in future. Christian Lubbe took the Style with a total of 25.79 seconds for the four sets, including an incredible 5.4 sec clean right series, which the French were proud to submit as a world record. His technique was to exit immediately on call, and dive vertically for a full nineteen seconds before tucking and throwing his first turn at the maximum horizontal distance from the camera. I was calling the exits to the aircraft, and watched and timed this jump on telemeters. I checked my stopwatch, turned to Graham on video and said "How about THAT then?" "Missed him", said Graham.... . He had, indeed, failed to pick up the jumper on exit and Lubbe had to jump the round again. This he did, and repeated his 5.4 clean on the rejump. The overall team winners were the French who, as well as taking two Style medals also won the RW Gold. They were closely followed by the USA with Helmut Schlecht's rebuilt German Army team in third place. I jumped on the final day with Pete and Helmut on a 34-man mass exit with smoke from the G222 tailgate at 12,000 feet. A slight problem was caused by all the smokes being pulled on the red light, and then the pilot forgetting to switch on the green; nevertheless an impressive 15-way was built out over the sea, coupled with some pretty impressive tracking from those of us at the back, far out over the Gulf. Everybody finally made the arena aided by some even more impressive winds on the deck. For me, this was an important experience and an opportunity to meet many old friends and judge some top class jumping.

The emergence of the Dubai based competition team had engendered massive interest in freefall parachuting throughout the region. In addition to Pete, British instructors included Dave Howerski in Saudi Arabia, Tony Keoghan on contract at the Sultan of Oman's Parachute Regiment, and Chris Lyall, also in the Oman, with the brief to set up a freefall team with SOPR personnel. Chris had come to see me in Leicester for advice a year previously, just before he went out to Muscat. Six months after the Dubai CISM we were running the Oman team together.

**127.** *Closing fourth on the three-way at the Seeb Go-Kart Demo in December 1984.* *Photo Chris Lyall*

**128.** *Omani National Team at the Raeford training camp in May 1985.*

**129.** *Raeford owner Gene Paul Thacker on the video camera. May 1985.*

**130.** *With Chris, Guy Jones and Denise after our 4-way hook up at Raeford on 29th May 1985.*

131. *Farewell to David Baxter in June 1985. Obaid Salim is on the right of the group.*

132. *With Bill Cook and Jake on the Hazm DZ, 6th May 1986.*

**133.** *Jump number 3000 on 6th May 1986.*          *Photo Chris Lyall*

**134.** *Fazil Mubarak set up for a dead centre landing at the 18th CISM Meet in Morocco 1986.*

228

**135.** *German Army Low Level Parachute T–3F Triform. Demonstration jump at the Altenstadt Intersprung competition in 1986. Not much control here.*

**136.** *Demo for the Minister of Defence. Muqaddam Nasser Sultan and Obaid.* From left to right: *Said Nabhan, Hassan, Shanin, Rashid and Said Saif. Rostaq 1986.*

**137.** *Team Accuracy Winners at the Rhine Army Open Championships at Bad Lippspringe, July 1987. Hassan, Shanin, Obaid, Muqaddam Nasser Sultan, Fazil, Said Nabhan, Rashid.*

**138.** *With Jake under canvas on recce at the Barzaman DZ. September 1987.*

**139.** *With my eldest daughter Mary at Al Ain in September 1987.*

**140.** *Ali Sohail, Said Saif, Abdullah in the SOAF Defender in September 1987.*

231

**141.** *Team demo on the Rostaq Airstrip September 1987. Bomb burst track pattern par excellence.* *Photo Jake McLoughlin*

**142.** *Final jump at Hazm on 252 Parafoil. December 1987.*

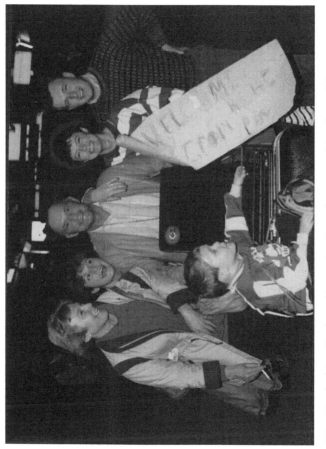

143. *Terminal 4 at Heathrow Airport, 31st December 1987. With Helen, Heidi, Mary, Steve and grandson Joe.*

233

# Chapter 13 | *Rostaq*

*1982-1983*

One afternoon just before Christmas 1981, I received a phone call which was to have far-reaching effects on my future. The Abu Dhabi Armed Forces were looking for a freefall instructor, and would I be interested? Although I was committed to my present job, and secure with the BPA, as a professional instructor all options had to be examined; the short answer was "yes". Helen was in agreement and arrangements were made for me to travel out in January to visit the Abu Dhabi Special Forces Parachute School. No one else was in the know, and I booked two weeks leave for the New Year. The BPA Dinner and AGM were scheduled for the 8th and 9th of January at the Central Hotel in Leicester and I was fully occupied with organising the Instructor Convention to follow the Saturday AGM. My flight to Abu Dhabi was booked for Sunday morning 10th January.

Immediately the Convention was over, I set off down the M1 for Heathrow in a blizzard. Driving conditions were atrocious, as the UK and most of Europe were in the midst of a mini Ice Age; I slept in the van overnight in the terminal car park with my jumpsuit over my clothes to keep warm. The flight suffered a twenty-four hour delay because of icing and I finally arrived in Abu Dhabi on the Tuesday morning, where I was welcomed by the team commander and the team staff sergeant, and ensconced in the Abu Dhabi Meridien hotel. I worked and jumped with the team for a week; they had a few members freefall cleared for short delays and plenty of kit, but no rigger, and nobody qualified to pack the reserves. I gathered that their previous instructor had been from the Jordanian military who had apparently reached the limit of his instructional capabilities. The setup was very promising indeed, and at the end of the week I was offered the job, to start immediately. I was happy to accept, but had to explain that, attractive as this proposition was, I had to go back to the UK to hand in my three months notice. It was agreed that a formal contract would be forwarded, along with flight tickets, in due course.

Back in the UK, the next job was the CIP Conference in Paris and there I took the opportunity to tell Charlie the news. He understood the situation, and accepted my decision with his usual grace. I made it official and handed in my written notice, penned my valedictory Coach's column for the Magazine, and settled down into my usual weekly routine to await the call from Abu Dhabi. Meanwhile the wheels were turning out in the Gulf; Pete Sherman had left the Dubai team and Tony Keoghan (Chapter 12), who had been Chief Instructor at the Sultan's Parachute Regiment, was on his way back from the Oman. The Bournemouth based Airworks agency then advertised this Omani vacancy in the national press and I applied by way of a backup to Abu Dhabi, from whom nothing had been heard. I contacted Airworks and went down to London for an interview. This was successful and they gave me a couple of weeks for a decision. Came the end of March and still nothing heard from Abu Dhabi. At this juncture, I decided to take the bird in the hand and go with the Oman option. My flight to Muscat was confirmed for 16th April. Tickets arrived from Abu Dhabi on the 15th. *C'est la vie...* and the job was eventually taken by 1980 World Accuracy Champion, Belgium's Dirk Boidin.

In March the BPA had advertised the National Coach vacancy, and three senior instructors had expressed interest. As already mentioned in the previous chapter, Pete Sherman was back in the UK looking for a job; he applied also and was immediately taken on. I drove down to Heathrow on 16th April in the BPA van, met Pete there, shook hands and gave him the keys; the handover was as simple as that. I was on my way again and, in a strange parallel to my arrival at the Parachute School in November 1956 on the day that 3 Para jumped into Suez, the South Atlantic Task Force was outbound for the Falklands as I left for Muscat.

I arrived at Seeb International Airport early in the morning of 17th April 1982 to be met by Jack Hiley, driving a pickup truck. I knew Jack as a rigger back in the UK; Jack was there on contract, having teamed up with Chris Lyall two years previously when Chris came out to run the freefall team. Chris has a unique story to relate, more of which in the next chapter. The Sultan of Oman's Parachute Regiment was based at Rostaq, in the foothills of the *Jebel* (mountains) of the southern Al Hajar range some seventy miles west of the capital, Muscat. We drove west along the Batinah coast road to Barka then turned inland toward the village of Nakhl, a small township surrounded by masses of date palms, behind which lay a clay and stone fort built over thirteen hundred years ago, typical of the interior region. The single carriageway then wound its way through steep outcrops of volcanic rock for a further thirty miles, before we turned off to the right up a dry *wadi* (river bed) leading to the camp. We were quite definitely out deep in the boondocks.

The Oman Armed Forces were organised on the British model and were at the time heavily dependent on expatriate British Officers and NCOs working there on contract. When I arrived the total British contingent was seven: Commanding Officer *Raa'id* (Major) David Baxter, Quartermaster Tom Hazel, Chris and Jack, plus Safety Equipment Fitters Dave Hayward and Nigel Boreham, both ex-RAF. We were shortly joined by Charles Lynch-Staunton and later by Ted Carrington to bring the numbers up to nine. Our bachelor living quarters were self-contained two-room units (*bayts*) in a single-story stone block; we used our individual resources to make them as comfortable as possible. The accommodation block backed onto the *wadi,* which in the rainy season sometimes flooded in spectacular fashion. We shared a common Mess with the Omani Officers, and frequently breakfasted on the adjoining lawn. There was also a miniscule ten-metre swimming pool with a shade area, with a *falaj,* a stonewalled irrigation channel, running behind the *bayts.* Alcohol was permitted in the Mess; the rest of the camp was completely dry. Entertainment was a nightly video, or a couple of beers at the poolside. That was it. Telephone contact, even with

Armed Forces HQ in Muscat, was intermittent at best and if we wished to make a private call to the UK we had to drive the seventy miles to the capital to phone from one of the hotels.

The situation at SOPR, of course, was that I was purely concerned with the static line operation; Chris and Jack ran the freefall team. I had been out of military parachuting for five years, but certainly had the requisite qualifications to fill this post. The CO, who was wearing British parachute wings, briefed me in his office the morning following my arrival and I took stock of the situation, which certainly demanded my full attention. All static line parachuting had been suspended, at the *diktat* of the Sultan's Air Force (SOAF). Apparently one C130 Hercules sortie had been mounted and the aircraft drills had been less than satisfactory. There was also an issue with the Al Hazm Drop Zone, involving an unacceptable level of canopy damage from thorn trees. In the short term I had to resolve the DZ issue and restart the parachuting operation using the Short Skyvans based at Seeb. I was also to run a basic static line course starting immediately. The question of the C130 conversion was shelved, pending the arrival of a loan service team from No. 1 PTS.

Chris, Jack, and I got together that evening over a beer; we knew each other well from the BPA and were all three Yorkshiremen born and bred. They immediately invited me to join in a programme out at the Hazm Drop Zone; I had brought along my GQ Unit and, in the event, made my first jumps there two days later. We jumped a Pilatus Porter from the Police Air Wing who were currently supporting the freefall team because of the SOAF embargo. Nonetheless, I was not involved in any way with Chris's operation; I was purely a guest jumper and in any case had plenty of work on my own side of the hangar, which I reviewed in company with the CO that first morning. We had a matted training area, with a Skyvan mockup, landing ramps, and flight trainers. There was a fully operational parachute packing section under the control of *Wakeel* (Warrant Officer) Mohammad Ahmed. He controlled ten parachute packers with an iron rule, and was backed up by the two Airwork contracted

Safety Equipment Fitters, Dave and Nigel, both ex RAF. The parachutes were American T10s. It was clear that this side of the operation was in safe hands and completely autonomous. My own staff consisted of two Omani *Arifs* (corporals), who were working as PJIs under training, Rashid Salim and Amor Rashid.

After one week, the basic course assembled and were detailed for a P Company type exercise. This consisted of a helicopter lift to the five thousand feet summit of the *jebel* overlooking the camp, known as *Al Abyad* (the white mountain). Once assembled, we were to make our way down at speed. This was obviously a test for myself as well as the troops; I was an unknown quantity and was invited to make the descent with the CO. There was a roughly marked trail with various short cuts and I reached the bottom in reasonably good shape ahead of most of the recruits. So far, so good; the next task was to look at the DZ.

The Hazm drop zone lay some ten miles north of Rostaq, on the southern fringe of the Al Batinah coastal plain. The DZ was at twenty-three and a half degrees North, bisected precisely by the Tropic of Cancer, on the loop road heading to the coast at Muladdah. There was a hard dirt airstrip parallel to the road, and the DZ they had been using was an area two kilometres to the south, consisting of sloping dunes, covered with thorn trees, and which backed right on to a high rocky outcrop. These trees, unsurprisingly, were causing a lot of damage to the parachute canopies; the plan, apparently, had been to uproot the trees and clear the area. This to me was a non-starter and the location in any case was not ideal. Accordingly, together with Amor Rashid, I recce'd another area 1000 metres closer to the road and adjoining the airstrip, set between two low ridges, one of which provided a natural reviewing stand for any visiting VIPs. I had this new DZ ratified by SOAF HQ; one problem resolved. A further concern was the role equipment in the Skyvans. There was no provision for retrieval of a hung-up parachutist, and I was not prepared to operate without this. In the absence of HUPRA (Hung Up Parachutist Release Assembly), or a winch, I recommended that a simple block and tackle be installed. This was done and we were ready to operate again. Jumping, however, remained suspended at the insistence of SOAF HQ pending the arrival of a PJI Officer from the UK, and I used the opportunity to take three weeks UK leave. We had moved house from Leicester back to Abingdon, which was more accessible from Heathrow; Abingdon was home territory, closer to Netheravon and Brize, which were both possible detachment venues. The Rostaq post was unaccompanied; we worked a three-month stint followed by three weeks home leave. Helen and I had discussed this at length before I signed the contract, and agreed we would go along with it until we jointly decided otherwise.

At the end of July, the loan service team from No. 1 PTS arrived in Muscat. This comprised Squadron Leader John Cole, WO Peter Keane, and Flight Sergeant Brian Davies; all seconded to SOPR. We heard they had arrived in country and I had been looking forward to working again with my fellow PJIs. Chris and I contacted their hotel and offered to pick them up from Muscat; this gesture was declined. The three of them eventually arrived at Rostaq under their own steam some seven days later and duly installed themselves in the hangar. Somewhat disappointingly, however, John Cole showed zero interest in any of the work we had put in, and proceeded from scratch with his own team and his own agenda. This notwithstanding, static line jumping resumed on the 4th of August from the Skyvan on to my new DZ. Fittingly enough, the pilot was Flt. Lt. Bob Kirkham, jumper and former RAFSPA instructor (Chapter 8). Operations continued throughout the month in which we flew twenty-six sorties jumping tailgate. These all passed without incident, and we carried on for a few more weeks with Peter Keane and myself both employed as Warrant Officers in the same post. Peter and I got on well, there was no friction whatsoever, but it was an extremely anomalous situation which had to be resolved, and early in September John Cole suggested that I move across the hangar and join Chris's freefall section. This arrangement certainly suited me and, as the team were shortly to travel to France to compete in the 14th CISM at the French Airborne School, it was decided that I should accompany them in my capacity of CISM judge.

We landed in Pau on the 23rd of September; Chris, Jack and myself in the team uniform of rather natty green blazers and grey slacks. We had a young Omani captain, Nasser Musabah, in charge of the team. He was extremely personable, and very keen to progress in freefall, a great guy. Nasser, Chris and I were at the rear of the aircraft when we landed and consequently last to disembark. Jack Hiley (WO2) was in the first group to step on to the tarmac. We were met by an immaculate French paratroop lieutenant who immediately saluted Jack and escorted him to a VIP staff car and drove him off to the Officers' Mess. Jack departed with a gracious wave in our direction whilst Nasser, Chris and myself at the rear of the group looked on in amazement. Jack was rotund in build, with a swarthy complexion and an impressive moustache; with his plausible Middle Eastern appearance the French officer assumed he was our Head of Delegation and addressed him as *Emir* (Prince). On his return, we swiftly and politely disabused him of this perception; Chris and Nasser went to the Officers' Mess whilst Jack retreated to the SNCOs' quarters with the rest of us… .

This CISM was the first competition of real significance for Chris's team; indeed it was only the second time they had been out of the country. The team leader was *Raqib Awwal* (Staff Sergeant) Obaid Salim; backed up by *Raqib* (Sergeant) Said Nabhan, with the two *Arifs* (Corporals) Hassan Salim and Said Saif. Two *Jundis* (Privates) Gharib Amor and Hamood made up the six-man team. The competition was won by the USA, with the French in second place and the German Army third. We were only there for the experience. This naivety was displayed when Hamood, a veritable loose cannon in any company, went AWOL from the team tent and jumped in on a Siki load, notwithstanding he was a competitor. How he got through Manifest is not known, neither did my fellow judges at the target pick it up. I played it down and escorted him out of the target area before handing him over to Chris to deal with. After the competition we spent a few days in Paris; Chris and I visited the Au Fanion parachute equipment store (Chapter 3) near the Gare de l'Est and purchased two sets of telemeters for DZ Control. Over a couple of beers we soon decided we could work very well together; Chris would run the show and concentrate on RW training, whilst I would work with the Accuracy and Style jumpers. Chris was a first rate aerial cameraman and an excellent all round skydiver, attributes which would come to the forefront in dramatic fashion a couple of seasons later.

Back at home, I received news that Charlie Shea Simonds, in his capacity of BPA Chairman, had been generous enough to recommend me for the FAI Paul Tissandier Diploma, and that my eldest daughter Mary had accepted it on my behalf from HRH Prince Andrew at the annual Royal Aero Club awards ceremony. That year I spent my first Christmas in the Oman and became fully employed on team training and team demonstration jumping. In 1983 we brought in new team members Fazil Mubarak, Shanin Jumma and Rashid Khamis to augment the squad. The Air Force were now very much onside and we were allocated a military Defender (piston Islander) aircraft five days a week out at Hazm. Working hours were 07. 00–13. 00 and we breakfasted out on the DZ. The team were still jumping the GQ Units and we were in urgent need of some decent accuracy canopies. We ordered Strato Clouds, and were promised delivery in March. Meanwhile, the UAE team in Dubai had appointed a new team coach to replace Peter Sherman; this was Eugen Melles, a German ex-military instructor from the Airborne School in Altenstadt. The Dubai team invited us across in early February and we spent a most valuable three weeks jumping at their Minhad Airbase DZ fifteen miles out in the desert. This detachment was of inestimable benefit to our team; they were able to speak to their more experienced neighbours in their own language and compare training and competition techniques to great advantage.

Back at SOPR, and one week after Minhad, I jumped with the team on a military demonstration at the artillery ranges at Mudaybi, which lay on the southern side of the *jebel* one hundred miles to the southeast of Rostaq. Chris and I led in the team with a tracking demo from eight thousand feet, with a two kilometre spot. Jumping the GQ Units, we all put down in a twenty-knot surface wind smack in front of the assembled military brass and local dignitaries. From a vantage point overlooking the plain we then witnessed an awesome artillery barrage, the ordnance screaming overhead from some twenty miles to the rear and obliterating the target area below with a myriad of overlapping craters. These demos served to raise the team profile even further and assured us of substantial support from the Army High Command for the forthcoming season.

At the end of March we took delivery of the Strato Clouds and stepped up our accuracy training. We had entered the next CISM meet, which was to be held in Switzerland in June. As a warm up we had applied to put the team into the APA Championships at Netheravon in May, and, despite some initial opposition from OC PTS, the detachment was authorised. We got in some good practice at Netheravon but, for once in my case, the main event was personal; the birth of my first grandson at the Radcliffe Infirmary in Oxford. I had a phone call at nine in the evening that events were progressing; I told Nasser I needed the team transport to travel the sixty odd miles in a hurry. So far so good, but the tank was almost dry and at nine o'clock in the evening on Salisbury Plain all the gas stations were closed. The APA came to the rescue; we went down to the pumps at the aircraft hangar and filled the motor with high octane Avgas. I covered the sixty miles inside the hour and was able to make the hospital in good time. Once again, as so often in my parachuting career, the Army had come to my rescue.

In June we travelled to Switzerland for the 15th CISM at Frauenfeld. This was my fifth consecutive CISM on the judging team; the Chief Judge was Gilbert van Damm of Belgium and I was again nominated as Style Event judge. Once again, it was a steep learning curve for the team but our results showed a distinct improvement from the previous year. A personal highlight was undoubtedly the chance to jump from a Junkers 52 – "*Tante Ju*"– the German WW2 paratroop aircraft. My exit was delayed by the Chilean judge who overestimated the height of the door and smacked his head on the top of the doorframe; luckily for him he was wearing a hard helmet.

After the Frauenfeld competition I flew directly from Zürich to London on three weeks home leave. On returning to Rostaq I found that there were some changes in the established order. The CO had been promoted to Lieutenant Colonel and was now *Muqaddam* Baxter. John Cole was still in post but shortly afterwards returned to the UK permanently, leaving Peter Keane as Chief Instructor. As the cooler weather approached we remained on base and concentrated on senior team training and bringing in new members. We also jumped another high profile demo at the International Go-Kart rally at the track opposite Seeb International Airport which engendered further welcome publicity.

Frequent marches into the local foothills, exploring the spectacular scenery just on our doorstep, were a regular feature of our time at Rostaq. These excursions, known as "wadi-bashing", were sometimes extended overnight on the Friday/Saturday weekends. The stony dust trails off the main road narrowed sharply until they became impassable to vehicles. One weekend in late December a few of us hiked deep into the *jebel* to the village of Limqasil, on the far side of *Jebel* Dawi. It took us a good four hours hiking and scrambling from Rostaq to reach it. On one particularly precipitous stretch we were chastened to come across a small flip-flop, abandoned by a child seemingly some four years old who had obviously passed that way quite recently. We reached the village shortly before nightfall and enjoyed spontaneous hospitality from the villagers, who first provided coffee, then roasted goat meat followed by sweetmeats. We spread our sleeping bags on the gravel and slept pretty soundly until dawn. Dave Hayward was an enthusiastic participant and a keen photographer to boot, and provided evocative pictures of our overnight stop.

Back at base, the departure of John Cole had left a vacancy, which had to be filled. This omission was shortly to be rectified, as I had been in touch with my old mentor Jake McLoughlin (Chapter 3), who was by now a Squadron Leader in the RAF Regiment, and looking for a move. I advised Colonel Baxter accordingly and Jake was successfully interviewed for the post by Airwork. Jake retired from the Royal Air Force, and I spent my second successive Christmas at Rostaq, awaiting the imminent return of the Sorcerer himself.

# Chapter 14 | *Return of the Sorcerer*

*1984-1987*

Jake McLoughlin arrived on the unit early in February 1984. Having left PTS in 1963, following the breakup of the original RAF Display Team (Chapter 3), he had been posted to the Jungle Rescue Team at Changi in Singapore. From there he went on to Henlow to be commissioned into the RAF Regiment, subsequently serving with No. 2 Field Squadron (Para) for the intervening seventeen years. Jake took over as OC PTS Rostaq, and Peter Keane remained in post as School Warrant Officer. Jake hit the ground running as if he had never been away. He initiated an immediate integration of the static line and freefall programmes and the Skyvans were now used both for conversion and progression training, giving us most welcome extra capacity. There was a new sense of progress on the unit, engendered by the arrival of a highly experienced professional jumper, with exceptional interpersonal skills. The sorcerer and the apprentice were now reunited after twenty years separation.

The year saw a further expansion in personnel and, along with Jake, the expatriate contingent was reinforced by the arrival of equipment officer Ted Carrington, plus MILAN (anti-tank) expert John Tomlin, and armourer and fitness fanatic Ron Greenhalgh. The Officers' Mess could no longer cope with this influx and accordingly a new expat WOs' and Sergeants' Mess was built, which rapidly became the social hub of the unit. In those days at Rostaq our working hours were 07.00–13.00 and we were required only to make a token check of the mail at 16.00. This left us with every afternoon to kill and I was myself by now into a regular winter fitness training routine, alternating between seven kilometre road circuits and workouts on the weights in the hangar, with Ron as a frequent companion. The spirit of Stan McCabe (Chapter 1) was very much still alive. Meanwhile, Jake had acquired a Gemini inflatable boat with a massive outboard motor, which he shared with us at weekends at Al Sawadi, a popular picnic beach on the Batinah coast.

In February the UAE team from Dubai paid us a return visit during which we trained together at Hazm using both Skyvan and our Defender. I took leave in June and in July we travelled to Germany for the RAPA Championships at Lippspringe, and for the 16th CISM, which this year was hosted by the German Airborne School in Schongau/Altenstadt in southern Bavaria. We were joined at RAPA by the full Dubai team and trainer Eugen Melles. From Lippspringe both teams travelled south to Munich by coach where we enjoyed a couple of days checking out the sights before moving down to Altenstadt for the Meet. The organisation was, as expected, absolutely first class; aircraft support ranged from the C160 Transall and CH 53 transport helicopter to the ubiquitous Huey. Accompanying the team as liaison officer and team manager was *Wakeel* Mohammad Ahmed who was in charge of the packing section at Rostaq. By now well past his fortieth year, he was not known as a prolific jumper back home but he certainly impressed us all at Altenstadt by jumping static line on a demonstration jump from the Transall from 800 feet in a twenty-knot wind, shod in trainers. I managed half a dozen Siki jumps, plus one memorable sortie with Altenstadt veteran *Oberstabsfeldwebel* (Sergeant Major) Tiger Schultz. This was at 1500 feet from the Huey; the occasion was the promotion to Captain of Mohammad Yousuf of the Dubai team. I jumped my Foil and Tiger had an old 1972 vintage long-line Paraplane with a front-mount reserve. We duly arrived in the pit, whereupon Tiger opened his reserve to reveal not a canopy, but a bespoke drinks container complete with bottle and glasses from which he proceeded to dispense champagne to everyone around.

On our return to the Oman it became apparent that our work had not gone unnoticed, and Chris and I had the honour of being presented to His Majesty Sultan Qaboos following a military review. In September we recced a new DZ ten miles up the road from Hazm at Muladdah on the Batinah plain, which was on more open terrain away from the *jebel*. We made our first jumps there from the Skyvan on the 18th of September; I made two T10 static line descents, the second of which was certainly my last ever military night descent with equipment. I then took three weeks UK leave, unaware of the dramatic events which were to unfold on the sixth of October at the Al Hazm drop zone. This was the day that Chris Lyall made the most crucial jump of his life. I returned to SOPR and was given the news by Rashid Khamis; he told me that during a routine RW exercise that Gharib had been knocked unconscious when he collided with Shanin Jumma, and that Chris had dived down to catch him and open his reserve seconds before impact. This was indeed a fantastic act of skill, instantaneous reaction, and sheer courage by Chris, which was duly recognized by the Sultan himself through the award of the Oman Distinguished Service Medal for Gallantry. His bravery was also recognised back home, through the subsequent award of the Royal Aero Club Gold Medal, which is only given for outstanding aviation achievement. This latter was presented to Chris the following year by Her Majesty the Queen; seldom, if ever, has this honour been more deserved. Gharib was unconscious and defenceless; CYPRES was seven years in the future and FXCs were only fitted to our student kit.

In 1980, Chris had been recruited to train SOPR personnel in freefall techniques with the specific task of organising a night demonstration in honour of the tenth National Day celebrations into the downtown Watayah stadium. This was an outstanding success, and Chris was given a permanent contract to build up a competition team. This is his account of the rescue:

> *"We had a routine and disciplined approach to our training schedule; there was always the eye for detail and meticulous planning. As a result of good,*

predictable weather we were able to plan ahead to every individual team member's requirements and therefore to plan the training sequence for the next day. At the end of every working week we would perform a demonstration jump onto the parade ground back at Rostaq Camp. We had this down to a fine art and we would usually build an eight-way round formation with smoke on every jumper. I have to confess at this point that on one occasion I made the classic altimeter setting error. Al-Hazm drop zone is four hundred feet lower than Rostaq camp. I set the altimeters the wrong way and therefore doubled the error. Spectacular indeed to see the eight-way formation break off at 2,500 feet as opposed to the normal 3,500 feet. I was hoping that no one would notice – they did but saw the funny side of it. David Baxter thought it was the best demonstration jump we had ever made, I did not disillusion him!!

We were a happy and well run organisation and the morning of the 6th October 1984 began exactly the same as any other. We would meet up at 6am at the parachute school and load the vehicles, we possessed a pick up truck, a Landrover and one mini bus which made us entirely independent and self contained. There was one element in the training which I felt was a weak spot and should be addressed and that was the ability to close vertical and horizontal distance combined with the ability to lose the accumulated speed and effect a smooth docking onto a formation, swooping, as it is now known. I had two good flyers as I called them who could perform this exercise. They were Arif (Corporal) Gharib Amor Bin Suliman and Jundi (Private) Shanin Juma. Gharib had accompanied me to New Jersey USA the previous year, in order to select equipment for the next season. During the course of which both he and I became Star Crest Recipients (SCR) as it was known. To achieve this we were required to dock on a formation, either eighth or above in what was to become a ten way star. Gharib had achieved this without difficulty. The only problem we had experienced was the aircraft, this was an ancient Lockheed 12 L which with a full load of jumpers aboard had all the climbing characteristics of a house brick. Shanin Juma was showing a good deal of natural ability and so I was feeling confident of success. The previous day and also in the morning much time was spent in dirt diving the planned skydive. Quite simply, I would exit first, Shanin would wait one second and then Gharib, one second after him, thus giving us the required separation for the exercise.

The Sultan's Airforce Defender duly arrived flown by Neil Eden, a jovial rotund fellow who was a loan service flying instructor from the RAF. The second pilot was an Omani officer who was under instruction in the art of jump flying. We launched straight into the training programme. I believe from memory that we were on the second lift of the day. The aircraft for this lift was to be flown by the Omani Officer and both Jack Hiley, the team rigger and Neil stayed on the ground with Jack running the drop zone control. There were to be two passes made at exit altitude, 9,500 feet. The reason for using this altitude was that it is the exit height for the CISM, or Military World Championship Meet. Little point in going higher, this would only serve to give the team members a false sense of working time – 35 seconds is the standard competition working time allowing for break off and safe deployment. The first pass went as planned and the remaining three of us went round again for the second pass.

I spotted the aircraft and exited from a sitting position, followed by Shanin and then Gharib, all as planned. Shanin made a perfect exit and approach, slowing his accumulated forward speed by bringing his arms forward and slightly tucking his knees – perfect, good lad, he took up position flying no contact with me holding his station brilliantly. I gave him a thumbs up and then looked to my front to see how Gharib was doing. Horror of horrors, he was in an absolute vertical dive with everything pulled back, I thought, whatever you do, please do not pull out of your dive at this point in time. He did and came rocketing at us at enormous closing speed. I would estimate his closing speed to be about forty miles per hour in relation to us. It was obvious that he was not going to be able to stop. The eye witnesses on the ground said it looked as if I had jumped sideways out of his way. Shanin had turned ninety degrees to him and Gharib wrapped himself around Shanin's back. The impact was awesome to behold and clearly either one or both would be in a bad way, perhaps even worse. The inertia carried Gharib a long way from us and a lot lower than we were. At that same instant I saw a flash of Shanin's pilot chute so I knew he was ok and hopefully under a fully deployed canopy and not too badly hurt. This as it turned out, was exactly the case and he landed ages after us quite unhurt.

Gharib's situation was dire. He was miles away from me and much lower; he was on his back spinning, and even from that distance I could see that his goggles were off and he was obviously unconscious. I have tried to be as accurate as possible, but this is where matters become a little difficult. I have absolutely no idea of just how I closed the distance between us, I could I suppose invent all sorts methods by which this must have been done, but I really just don't know. What I do know is that he was now on my fingertips; the mind works in strange ways in these situations and I was horrified to see what for all the world looked like a fine smoke trail coming from his nose and mouth – it was blood and for all I knew I could well be chasing a dead body. Ultimately we found that his reserve was covered with blood, almost in the manner of a spray gun.

I also discovered that the unconscious human body does not fall to earth in a nice neat straight line; no, it rather follows the pattern of a falling leaf and every time I got close to him, over he would go and skid off into the next county, metaphorically speaking. I was getting desperate and I knew we were out of time. We are all flesh and blood and none of us wish to meet the ground, especially when one is doing one hundred and seventy six feet per second; it was a conscious decision and I clearly do recall repeating to myself – do not look at the altimeter, if I had, then I would have left him to the fate which was most assuredly awaiting him. One last despairing lunge, there was nothing delicate about it, and I managed to get hold of him. My intention was to roll him face to earth in order to give the reserve the best chance of a clean opening. Not so, there was no time for niceties and so I dumped out his reserve ripcord whilst he was still side to earth. I saw the deployment bag lift and allowed him to pull out of my hand. I then instantly put up my own main pilot chute, bad move; the reserve may have opened just that bit faster. In my defence, I think I was suffering a bit of sensory overload at this point in the proceedings. Once again, I have no clear recollection of just how long I was under the canopy. I landed very hard and ended up on all fours, looking at the piece of ground between my hands – the same piece of ground I had been looking at as my canopy deployed. I landed hard because the Parafoil was still in a braked configuration and secondly, I was not into wind.

Almost immediately down came Gharib under his reserve, still unconscious and landed very close to me, I shuffled rapidly across to him, still on all fours and grabbed him, my main intention was to stop him from moving but also to make sure he was still alive. He began moving and making groaning sounds. I can't say I could really blame him!!! We had both landed immediately adjacent to the airstrip, almost at the emplaning point. I was aware of the sound of feet pattering across the desert, it was Jack, he normally does not move too quickly for anything, this morning he did!!

Next on the scene was the medic complete with ambulance; he was always with us on standby. Gharib was clearly badly injured and there was little the medic could do for him. I asked Jack to radio the aircraft and to inform the pilot to be ready for an immediate evacuation to Seeb Airport. Gharib was loaded onto a stretcher and I grabbed another rig, we loaded him into the Defender and took off instantly for a low level journey back to Seeb which was some seventy miles distant. Gharib was obviously in great pain and his left upper leg was very swollen, clearly there was internal bleeding. I held on to his arms to prevent movement but he was really fighting me until, mercifully he would pass out again. On arrival we were met by Helen Tobin, the Sultan's Air Force doctor who immediately examined Gharib. He is going to be OK she said, just broken bones, although he had broken rather a lot of them!!

Then something happened which I shall carry with me to my dying day. We were under the wing of the Defender in the shade when Gharib who was calm and now conscious, looked me straight in the eye and gave me a thumbs up – somehow he knew what had happened. Later when he was interviewed by the Board of Inquiry he said he assumed that the instructor must have opened his reserve for him – such faith!! If I could bottle and sell it, I would make a fortune.

The next port of call was the main Hospital where Gharib was admitted immediately to the operating theatre. I waited for what seemed like an age when I was told that the Surgeon wished to speak to me. He was a very brisk Royal Navy Lieutenant Commander. I was asked what had happened to Gharib, I briefly explained about the collision and the unconsciousness. He asked – if he was unconscious in freefall, then how come he is still with us?? I caught him, I replied. Good job you were around he said. I can only agree. Gharib's list of injuries was impressive. Starting from the top: broken nose, fractured jaw – nine places, broken teeth, three fractured vertebrae, broken ribs, fractured left femur – two places. I am happy to say that he made a full recovery, although he did not jump again and his left leg ended up slightly shorter than his right. I hope he lives happily into ripe old age.

I was utterly staggered by the aftermath. At first I was told to say nothing of what had occurred. When I went on leave the following November, I spent some time jumping at Netheravon. My fellow jumpers said they were hearing all manner of strange rumours emanating from the Omani desert, I denied all knowledge of anything and said it was just that – rumours. Time passed and it was early 1985, I think February from memory that it was announced I was to be awarded the Distinguished Service Medal – Gallantry WkHM (G) by His Majesty the Sultan of Oman. I think I am *correct in saying that this was the last one awarded. On the 1st of May 1985 I was greatly honoured to be awarded the Royal Aero Club Gold Medal, by Her Majesty the Queen. This medal is not awarded annually. It is awarded for outstanding aviation achievement, I had joined a very exclusive club indeed and to have my name alongside those of my boyhood heroes was humbling in the extreme".*

It is difficult to overstate the skill and courage Chris displayed on that October morning; suffice it to say that it was typical of the Chris I knew. Above all, Chris was a practical man who dealt with each situation as it presented itself in a commonsense and efficient fashion. He was a most accomplished skydiver, cameraman, and instructor; and a modest youth to boot. It was truly a privilege and pleasure to have worked with him.

In early December we once again were invited to do a demo at the International Go-Kart Rally at Seeb, and this time Chris captured the action on camera. I spent my third Christmas in the Oman, then spent three weeks at home in March. Shortly afterwards Brian Davies was tour expired and was replaced by Terry Cooke. For me Brian, ex-professional player with Sheffield Wednesday, had done a great job, both on the parachuting side and coaching the Regimental football team. Cookie, of course, was a different personality; a total extrovert who transformed the Mess social scene within a couple of weeks of his arrival. He had visited the local hospital in Rostaq and arranged a guest night for a dozen of the European and Filipino nurses. This initiative was an immediate success and these guest nights became a regular feature in the Mess calendar. Terry had been a member of the Falcons Display Team for three years, and kept current with us at Hazm whenever the opportunity arose.

In March 1985 I attended a two-week colloquial Arabic course in downtown Muscat at Bayt al Falaj. I had worked hard from the outset to pick up the language, and although my Omani students did not always understand what I said, they almost invariably grasped what I meant. This three year practise had paid off, and I passed the course with a good grade. The main focus for 1985, however, was the 17th CISM, which was to be held in Abu Dhabi at the end of the year. Chris and I presented our programme to the CO for approval, the main feature of which was an extended training camp at Gene Thacker's Raeford DZ in North Carolina. In order to make maximum advantage, we took fifteen team members and trainees on the detachment. We travelled out at the end of April and were billeted in a motel just outside town. This was the first time out of Oman for some of the younger jumpers and they certainly made the most of the experience. Team discipline was excellent, controlled by Obaid and Said Nabhan; we loosened the reins occasionally and they all enjoyed the odd beer from time to time. We were welcomed everywhere, both on and off the Drop Zone, except on one occasion when racial prejudice manifested itself on a visit to a local restaurant where the staff decided to clean the floor around us with a noxious disinfectant whilst we were eating. Happily this remained only the one isolated incident.

Raeford was a big success and the whole team benefitted from working at this DZ, with its long tradition of Style and Accuracy training. During our five weeks Thacker's videoed style critiques proved invaluable, and in addition each man averaged over one hundred accuracy jumps using the Cessna 182 and the Twin Beech. Hassan in particular thrived on the training – I called him Geordie, after Geordie Charlton, as they definitely shared a hard streak and a highly competitive temperament. Gene Paul saw to it that we were invited to Fort Bragg for a day out with the Golden Knights, and we took advantage of the Raeford scene to enjoy our own jumping; we caught up with Guy Jones of the US Special Forces, last seen in the 1981 Dubai CISM (Chapter 12). I recall in particular a four-way dive with Guy, Chris, Chris's wife Denise, and myself closing fourth. We took one day out to visit the North American Aerodynamics Company in Roxboro, a two-hour drive north from Raeford. Gene Paul came along in holiday mood as we toured the factory and were treated to lunch by John Higgins and his directorate. We also ordered ten more custom made 252 Parafoil/Centaurus assemblies, to be delivered in time for the European season. We had a generous imprest, total control, and authority to purchase equipment as we saw fit. It was a good team, and Chris, Jack and I got along like a house on fire, with seldom a hard word between us.

We flew back to base at the end of May, following which I went on UK leave, spending some time helping ex Red Devil Ted Lewington at his Englefield DZ near Reading. On arrival back at Rostaq Peter Keane had now reached the end of his tour. Peter had done a great job under sometimes difficult circumstances; his replacement was Bill Cook, ex-Falcons with me in 1970, on loan service from PTS. David Baxter also came to the end of his tenure; the new CO was Omani, *Muqaddam* Nasser Sultan, with Major Mike Argue seconded in to SOPR as second in command. Mike, who won an MC with B Company 3 Para at Mount Longdon in 1982, was a very positive character, a fluent Arabist, and a Yorkshireman to boot. http://wwwtelegraph.co.uk/news/obituaries/1528389/Lieutenant-Colonel-Mike-Argue.html. David Baxter was dined out in the Mess and then afforded an appropriate send-off by the locals over the road in Rostaq.

By this time we had a new C130 mockup in the hangar; conversion from the Skyvan was proceeding apace, and we were soon using the Herc for both static line jumping and freefall at Hazm on a regular basis. We also made high-profile demos at Armed Forces HQ at Muaskar al Murtafa'a and the training depot, SAFTR Rusail. In November we traveled to Abu Dhabi for the 17th CISM competition. This was the second time in four years that the UAE had hosted this Meet, following the Dubai competition in 1981, when Pete Sherman was Meet Director and I was Chief Judge (Chapter 12). We were based at the Ramada Hotel, a stone's throw from the competition site; Chris took responsibility for the team, whilst I was selected as a judge. Helmut Schlecht was Chief Judge; once again the top three teams were France, USA, and the German team from Altenstadt. These three teams had dominated the previous four competitions, and finished in the same order as in 1981 and 1982. The sequence was only broken at Frauenfeld in 1983, when USA took top spot from the French. We still had a long way to go... .

Back home again, we finished the year with another high demo at the Seeb Go-Kart track. This time our jumpship was the de Havilland Canada Buffalo from the Police Air Wing, and we had a new pilot. He was obviously determined to make an impression as, after we observed the WDI, he set up maximum rate of climb of about 2500 feet/minute. He called running in after three minutes, the team got ready in a hurry, and I made the classic mistake of spotting from the tailgate in the climb. The WDI had gone about 800 metres, I got the angles all wrong and put us out about half a mile short. The team carried on regardless and put together a neat three way whilst I made a solo max upwind track. The smoke must have looked good from the ground, although the pattern was not strictly as planned. In the event we all made the target and in true PJI fashion I gave them all a rollicking for not looking where they were... .

1986 again promised to be a busy competition year, with meets scheduled in Belgium, Morocco and Germany. We were still using the C130 at Hazm from time to time, and in May we had the aircraft to ourselves (twelve men) for RW training. In a combined PTS effort Jake and Bill Cook ran the DZ, whilst Terry Cooke supervised the RW. Chris offered to film my jump number 3000, so we both exited on the second pass, with Chris recording some vanity footage for my album. The real work started in earnest a couple of weeks later with overseas training. By this stage, we were running two separate teams; Chris took the RW team to the UK whilst I was in charge of the Style and Accuracy team for Europe and CISM. In order to give the team more varied experience, I had made the case for a training camp in Chalon-sur-Saône, a known centre of excellence. I knew Chalon of old, Didi Mingam (Chapter 3) was now the Chief Instructor, and it proved an excellent choice. We flew into Paris, then took the train down to Chalon, hired a VW minibus, and checked in at the Hotel Mercure a couple of miles from the Drop Zone. Chalon had changed somewhat since my last time there twenty years previously (Chapter 5), with a new hard runway, and a Pilatus Porter in place of the Broussard but the ambience remained undiminished. We stayed five weeks in Europe, and after a couple of weeks at Chalon drove north to Belgium for a military competition at the Belgian Parachute School in Schaffen. At that time, the Belgians were the only parachute school besides PTS to use a static balloon for initial training and all the team, myself included, had a go. This was my first balloon descent for ten years, and almost certainly to be my last. We returned to Chalon for a couple more weeks work before heading back to the Oman.

We had a hectic five days back in country before our next venture. All domestics had to be completed and I had to make a couple of 150 mile round trips to Murtafa'a to complete the necessary travel admin and collect the imprest before flying out to Morocco on 25th June. The venue was the Rabat-Salé International/military airport, a couple of miles inland from the Atlantic. We started jumping on the 27th and I caught up with many old friends, amongst them being Jean Claude Helguers from France, Johnny Lakon from Belgium and Eduard Teschke from the German Airborne School. This year the French took top spot ahead of a revitalized Swiss team and the German Army. Our top competitor was second year jumper Fazil Mubarak. This competition attracted hundreds of local spectators who ringed the target area; they were extremely partisan and very noisy. In one jump-off they whistled, shouted and booed in an attempt to distract the jumper on finals in the manner of a football crowd behind the goal attempting to put off a penalty taker, a sight I have never witnessed before, or indeed since, at a parachute meet.

We flew back home again in mid-July and this time we had nine days in country before boarding the aircraft for Frankfurt en route to Altenstadt for their fifth own mini CISM, the Intersprung. Teschke was the Chief Judge with myself as the RW judge. Bob Charters was down with the RAPA team as well as Rico Deutsch from Austria – still going strong after we first met at Cork Farmer's Cross airfield twenty four years previously (Chapter 3) – and we all got together again in the same Siki load. The French team again took top spot ahead of the USA and the German Army. The Germans were demonstrating their newly developed T-3F low level parachute, a static line deployed assembly with three canopies. Exit altitude was

90 metres, or some three hundred feet, and Obaid volunteered to give it a go. The assembly was subsequently discontinued following a total malfunction in the United States the following year. The year ended with a visit to the Regiment by the Oman Minister of Defence, culminating with an impressive high demo onto the Rostaq parade square by the first team.

In February 1987 we entertained the team from Jordan to a two-week joint training camp at Hazm, an indication of the progress we had made, and the status we had achieved. Terry Cooke was tour-expired and his replacement was Gary Corkish from PTS, who joined us as cameraman and gave us some excellent in-air shots over Hazm. In March we again travelled to Dubai for their first ever Open International Meet, the equivalent of the Altenstadt Intersprung, using CISM rules. The event attracted eight teams; Mohammad Yousuf was Chief Judge whilst I ran the Style. We finished in third place overall, behind the UAE and Austria, and made useful contacts with the Austrian team who promised us an invitation to their International Open competition later in the year.

In June the teams again split, with Chris and Jack embarking on a UK tour with the RW group whilst I travelled to Germany and Austria with the Style and Accuracy team. The plan was to train at RAPA for a couple of weeks, fly down to Austria for the Invitation Meet, then back to Lippspringe for the Rhine Army competition. We arrived in Düsseldorf and hired a minibus for the onward journey, and stopped off the autobahn at Remscheid for a break. My lunch was interrupted by Rashid Khamis, somewhat agitated in mien, who requested my immediate presence in the car park. I arrived outside to find Said Saif and Fazil spread-eagled face down over the bonnet of a battered blue Ford Sierra. Their interrogators were a couple of German nationals in sports shirts and blue jeans –Starsky and Hutch types. In my politest German I enquired of the pair who they were and what they were doing. "*Autobahn Polizei, und wer sind Sie?*" "Oman National trainer" I told them. The two backed off reluctantly and demanded ID all round. This was 1987, and the PLO threat was still palpable throughout Europe following the attacks on the Rome and Vienna International Airports some eighteen months previously. Most of the team wore national dress when travelling – the *dishdasha,* a white ankle-length, long-sleeved gown. Said and Fazil were wearing this gear and were assumed to be potential terrorists... . We arrived that evening at Bad Lippspringe to be greeted by Commandant Tom Oxley and Chief Instructor Bob Charters, and got to work the following morning. We were joined a few days later by the CO, *Muqaddam* Nasser Sultan, who flew into Hanover International, accompanied by the adjutant. Tom organized the Islander, flown by Patrick Long, to pick them up from the airport. This earned us a few brownie points from the *Muqaddam,* who had decided to combine travel to Europe with the team and visits to the MOD in the UK.

After two weeks we flew down to Vienna for the Invitation Meet; at the airport the whole team, wearing national dress, once again were detained and searched by armed security forces by dint of their Middle Eastern identity. Eventually we were collected by an Austrian army officer and driven to Pinkafeld, a small township some fifty odd miles south of the capital. Despite the rural setting, this was a first class meet, which attracted seventeen teams. Rico Deutsch and Johan Volk were running the show, ex-Golden Knight jumper Bob Donahue was also on site and I joined them on half a dozen Siki jumps from the Porter, in between judging the Style. The *Muqaddam* had rejoined us from the UK; we then spent two days in Vienna before flying back to Germany for the RAPA competition. The team performed exceptionally well and finished ahead of the UAE Abu Dhabi team to take the Gold medals in Team Accuracy. We finished our European season with a final visit to Netheravon for the APA Meet.

Back once more in Rostaq, I decided it was time to review my options. My contract was up for renewal, and I had been asked to stay. On the other hand, I had already had six years separation from my family, and thirty-three years in uniform. The family was the overriding factor and accordingly I handed in my notice to take effect on the 31st of December. We had just had a great season and it was time for a new challenge. Jake had also decided to call it a day, Bill Cook was gone and had been replaced by ex-Falcon Dave Ross. Jake and I carried out our last recce together in the September, checking out an exercise DZ down south at Barzaman, in the Sharqiya (Eastern area). Jake went at the end of September. I was winding down, and one weekend I took the section Landrover to drive the five hours over the border to Al Ain to spend some time with my eldest daughter, who was working in the UAE at the local hospital with her husband. Back at Hazm, I spent my final weeks jumping with the team, working with the jumpers who had been my life for the previous six years. The final act came in the shape of a demo jump onto the airstrip, just outside the base. This was the climax of a special pageant enacted by the local townspeople; Chris and I ran the DZ while the team took the Skyvan to ten thousand feet completely self-contained, built a six-way, took it down to four thousand then split into a bomburst right overhead, before obliterating the target cross with overlapping canopies. This was indeed a parachute demonstration *par excellence*, the culmination of Chris's efforts going back to the Watayah stadium night jump seven years previously, plus my own input over the last five. The team were in great shape, had proven themselves against international opposition, and were ready to move forward under their own steam.

My final jump in the Oman was at Hazm on the 22nd December; the team signed up my logbook, we enjoyed a meal on site and the CO presented me with a *Khanjar,* a traditional Omani ceremonial dagger, which remains to this day one of my most-prized trophies. My few possessions were shipped out in two crates and I flew out from Seeb International for the last time on New Year's Eve 1987. From my window seat as we travelled westward over the Mediterranean, absorbed as always in the panorama thirty thousand feet below, I reflected that this was but the end of another chapter in my life, a waystation on the odyssey. I had no firm plans beyond the certainty that parachuting would remain my animating spirit for the foreseeable future. I touched down at Heathrow later in the evening, to be greeted by my entire family. Supportive beyond words; these memoirs are, above all, dedicated to them.

259

**144.** *British Delegation 21st World Parachute Championships Trieben, Austria 1992.* Back row: *Williams, Hitchen, Ballard, King, Carroll, Andrewes, Chandler.* Seated: *Fran Shaskova, Debbie Card, Katherine Andrewes, Cheryl Smyth, Esther Reynolds. I am kneeling in front.*

**145.** *Team Accuracy Winners at the British National Championships at Hinton in September of 2002. With Nicky Johnstone and Glen Stephenson.*

146. *Jumpmaster at Hinton in 1999.*

147. *Keeping in touch as Hinton Club Chief Instructor in 2007.*

*Photo Matt Abram*

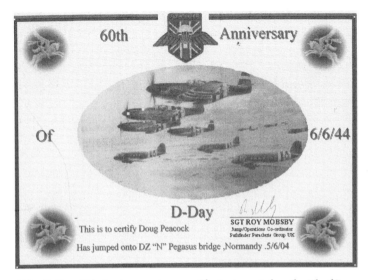

**148.** *D-Day 60th Anniversary jump certificate, presented on the 5th of June 2004.*

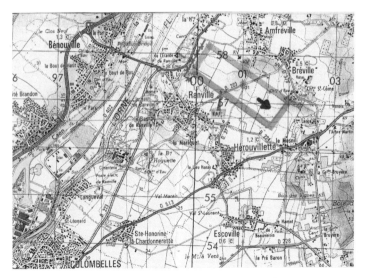

**149.** *The Pegasus Bridge Drop Zone, showing the run-in direction.*

**150.** *Dakotas at the mounting airfield, Le Havre Octeville before the Ranville drop.* *Photo Terry Crawley*

**151.** *With Ian Marshall and troops in the Dakota prior to takeoff.*
    *Photo Terry Crawley*

**152.** *Geoff Wood over Hinton with tandem student in 2013.*
*Photo Eamonn Fairhead*

**153.** *Mike Browne exits the Hinton PAC.*      *Photo Eamonn Fairhead*

**154.** *Eamonn films Geoff Wood over the Hinton Drop Zone in 2013.*
*Photo Paulo Ya Braz*

**155.** *Breakoff. Eamonn on his way down.*          *Photo Paulo Ya Braz*

265

156. *The War Cemetery at Ranville.*

# *Epilogue*

Twenty-six years later…

I gave Michel a good two seconds, then followed him out of the left hand door of the Huey at 3,300 feet directly over the western frond of the Palm. Dipped the left shoulder a couple of inches, eased into a 180 turn, and watched his pilot chute appear some eight seconds later. Simultaneously threw my own and checked the canopy as the slider rattled my knuckles. Settled in the harness and turned to face the Drop Zone, some eight hundred metres downwind. The unmistakable spoon-shaped peninsula below me was the home of Skydive Dubai, site of the 4th Dubai International Championships. I was back in the Emirates for the fourth successive year; my job was Head of Manifest, and I made sure I was on the Siki load. It was the 1st of December 2013, and I was still in business…. .

Back home from the Oman in 1988, I needed a job, and was fortunate enough to be taken on as a freelance proofreader by Hope Services, a family typesetting company with an extensive client portfolio, including the Oxford University Press and Blackwell publishing. Hope Services were great people to work for, extremely supportive, and I gained valuable insight there into basic computer technology, which was to prove very useful further down the line. In the event, I was to remain with Hope for a further eight years. At the same time, I had taken a long look at the UK parachuting scene, and decided to set up as Parachute Training Services (PTS, what else?). I was convinced that the era of the round canopy was rapidly fading, and in April 1988 I went down to Swansea to meet up with Dave Howerski and Andy Houston. Dave was pioneering the Ram Air Progression System in the UK, and I worked with him and picked his brains for a couple of weeks. My next stop was Netheravon, where Commandant Jim Steele and Chief Instructor

Pete Lambson agreed that I could start jumping my students, the payback being that the APA would use my experience when they converted to RAPS at some future date. I purchased six Zerox/Manta student assemblies and set up a training base in Abingdon. From there, I ran courses most weekends for students from Reading, Brunel, Portsmouth and Southampton universities, plus any other local groups or individuals who signed up. My premise from the outset was that these were my personal students and I guaranteed individual coaching all the way to Category 10 for any jumper who was prepared for this level of commitment.

Bob Card took over as Commandant at Netheravon the following year, with Keith Skelley as his Chief Instructor. Bob was chairman of the BPA Competition Committee at the time and he asked me to take the British Team to Austria for the 21st World Parachute Championships as Team Manager. I relished this opportunity to return to the international competition arena after a five-year absence. We fielded two full teams, male and female; John Hitchen was Head of Delegation, with Bob King as Accuracy Event Judge. During the following years I expanded my student operation and went full time in 1996. I continued at Netheravon with some success right up until early 1999 when the Army Parachute Association introduced a policy change which precluded outside agencies operating there. I had had ten successful years at Netheravon, and I maintained excellent relations with the Committee and staff. Nonetheless I was professionally homeless, and turned to the Hinton Skydiving Centre for assistance. It turned out to be one of my better decisions.

I had jumped there once or twice in 1993 when Mike Bolton was running the Drop Zone; in 1998 Mike Browne and Geoff Wood took over the business and developed the Hinton club into a full-time commercial Centre. Mike was a former RAFSPA Instructor, whilst Geoff had served full time at Brize and Weston as an RAF PJI. The Chief Instructor was Dave Emerson, also a former PJI who had jumped with the Falcons for three seasons. Dave was a highly qualified Instructor/Examiner, Tandem and AFF; we had known and respected each other from my time at the Parachute School. PTS became integrated with the Hinton student operation seamlessly, and I became an ever-present Club instructor from then onwards. In September 2002 we hosted the Classic British National Championships and I decided to enter, forming a team with Jeff Chandler, Nicky Johnstone, Glen Stephenson and Ivan Rossington. We won the team event over eight rounds, putting me in the medals again after a quarter of a century since my last competition.

In June 2004 I enjoyed the unique privilege of jumping into one of the Normandy battlefields. The occasion was the 60th anniversary of the D-Day landings and Ian Marshal invited me to assist in the dispatching of four Dakota lifts onto the Pegasus Bridge Drop Zone at Ranville. The jumpers were from the Pathfinder Parachute Group UK, and included Hinton jumper John Gibbs (Gibbo) and veteran BPA member Terry Crawley. We ran in that day from the sea, over the Sword invasion beach, across the Caen canal and the Orne river onto the open fields to the east of the town. The weather was absolutely perfect as we flew behind the stream of Hercs at one thousand feet. The green came on as we crossed the DZ boundary, and I started dispatching the stick as we came abeam a small wood on the port side. We returned three times to the mounting airfield at Le Havre to pick up more jumpers before the final lift when we took the C47 up to 4,000 feet on the last pass, and followed out; it was an unforgettable experience to walk out of the door and watch the historic aircraft with its black and white invasion stripes lift away into a cloudless blue sky. After the jump we visited the Ranville War cemetery, the final resting place of more than two thousand British and Commonwealth troops, including many from the 6th Airborne Division. An unforgettable experience, certainly; and humbling in the extreme.

In October of the following year, Mike and Geoff invested in a new aircraft; they purchased a PAC 750 from New Zealand. This made perfect sense, although it also heralded the end of the Hinton RAPS operation; AFF was definitely the way forward, demand for RAPS was declining and the PAC was not economically viable in the static line role. We flew a few sorties early in 2006 and then terminated the operation. In May of that year the situation changed somewhat rapidly when Dave Emerson moved on to pastures new. Hinton were without a Chief Instructor, so Mike and Geoff asked me to fill the position until a replacement could be found. The original deal was for three weeks, which eventually became extended to three years. It turned out to be another great job; I thoroughly welcomed the challenge, although with the professional backup I had from the staff we had there, it was probably the easiest post I had ever had. Easy because Mike and Geoff took care of the tandem operation, along with aerial cameramen Eamonn Fairhead, Graham Meggison, Matt Abram and Steve Park. Easy because of the quality of our supporting tandem instructors, Dave Luke, Brian Poole *et al*; and easy because of the equally outstanding calibre of the other staff members – Maddy, Sandy, Justine, Natalie, Matt Gardner, Kris Sheppard, and rigger Dave Gould. I received nothing less than one hundred percent support from everybody all the time I worked there until May 2009; and it was with extremely mixed feelings that I decided it was time to move on and hand over to Stuart Meacock, son of John, my old friend and colleague of the 1970s. Hinton gave me a great double send-off, with a midweek dining-out for Helen and myself, followed by a champagne farewell at the Club bar after the weekend's jumping.

Later that year I had a phone call from another old friend, Helmut Schlecht. Helmut was the Meet Director for the forthcoming 1st Dubai International Parachute Championships and he invited me to join his team to run the Manifest. The other members of his technical team were Chief Judge Dr. Rainer (Exi) Hoenle and Accuracy Judge Günter Berendt. The four of us were together from the outset and the team ethic was outstanding; it was a real pleasure and education to work with these continental professionals and I was soon back up to international speed. The Manifest setup was pretty basic at that time, and was expanded year on year in line with the ever-increasing numbers of competitors. The 2010 Manifest team consisted of myself, Camille Jardel and her husband Franz, with erstwhile UAE competitor Abdullah Murad in charge of the loading area. I also met old friends that year, as the Omanis entered their national team. In 2011 Colonel Gernot Rittenschober of the Austrian Army joined us for the second Championships. Gernot was, and is, the current President of CISM and he applied his massive international and administrative experience to the Registration procedure. He then organized the Skydive Dubai staff to run his half of the Manifest with effortless aplomb.

Since 2010 we have organised five consecutive Championships at Skydive Dubai under the patronage of the Crown Prince, Sheikh Hamdan, himself an active skydiver. By the third Championships we were dealing with over one thousand competitors and operating two drop zones and the Manifest staff was expanded accordingly. In 2012 Skydive Dubai hosted the Mondial World Parachuting Championships with fifteen events and 1400 competitors from fifty-eight countries. We operated three Drop Zones simultaneously with a fourth as alternate, utilizing five fixed wing aircraft and two helicopters. This was a far cry from my first international competition at Leutkirch back in 1961, and I felt privileged indeed to be participating at this level half a century later.

The story (to date) ends at the Parachute School, where it began, when Wing Commander Wayne Loxton presented me with the PJI Lifetime Achievement Award at our annual reunion, an honour of which I am extremely proud. Jimmy Blyth's original six months has been extended more than one hundred fold, and the brevet has taken me many times around the globe over the past fifty-seven years. Parachuting is first and foremost where my passion lies. It has given me a great life, many friends, and countless unforgettable experiences. Would I do it all again? Every time.

157.  *Hinton Chief Instructor Stuart Meacock, with tandem student.*
*Photo Eamonn Fairhead*

158.  *Dave Emerson in action at Hinton.*          *Photo Eamonn Fairhead*

272

**159.** *Mike Browne landing approach at Hinton Skydiving Centre* c. *2006.*
*Photo Helen Spratley*

**160.** *Geoff Wood enjoys this one. Hinton* c. *2006.*
*Photo Helen Spratley*

**161.** *The Manifest Team at the 1st Dubai International Parachute Championships in 2010. Abdullah Murad with Camille and Franz Jardel.*

**162.** *The Manifest Centre at the 4th Dubai International Championships, four years later.*

**163.** *With the Oman National Team at the 1st DIPC in 2010.*

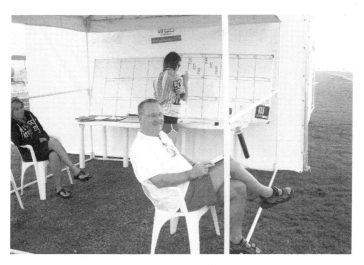

**164.** *Friend and colleague Gernot Rittenschober at the 2nd DIPC. Camille is sitting on the left.*

275

**165.** *Three wise men. Chief Judge Exi Hoenle, Accuracy Event Judge Günter Berendt with Assistant Meet Director Helmut Schlecht. 3rd DIPC December 2011.*

**166.** *With Dubai Crown Prince Sheik Hamdan and loadmaster Casi Thiel at the 3rd DIPC in December 2011.*        *Photo courtesy Carsten Thiel*

**167.** *On the Siki load, 4th DIPC December 2013. Jürgen is by the door, with Colonel Saeed Al Ghaithi nearest to the camera.*     *Photo Michel Jara*

**168.** *Standby to exit the Huey behind Michel Jara over the Dubai Palm in December 2013.*     *Photo Jürgen Barth*

169. *On target at the 4th DIPC in December 2013. Michel has just landed.*
*Photo Jürgen Barth*

170. *PJI Lifetime Achievement Award, September 2013. Presented by Wing*
*Commander Wayne Loxton, OC Airborne Delivery Wing, RAF Brize Norton.*

# *Appendix 1*

## REPORT ON 11th WPC TALEQUAH USA 1972

"The 1972 World Championships were concluded here at six in the evening of Thursday 17th August, but British medal aspirations died some sixty minutes earlier as the immaculate Czechs totaled 16 centimetres on their final jump to edge Great Britain into fourth place by a margin of 14 centimetres. The subsequent Russian jump of 0.97m which brought the Soviets the silver medal was of academic interest only as their ability to score inside 1.93m in the perfect accuracy conditions prevailing was never in serious doubt and the Swiss gold was already secure thanks to a classic 17 centimetre total achieved on a fourth round rejump. Thus ended the eighth British incursion into the World arena: 4th place in Team Accuracy and 7th place overall.

The road to Talequah started some three months earlier at Weston on the Green on the occasion of the British National Championships. Selected from this competition, the top ten jumpers were invited to attend team training at Royal Air Force Abingdon. In the event, only seven of our parachutists came under serious consideration as Dale, Cathro, and Wright were unable to make sufficient qualifying descents owing to military commitments. This left Meacock, King, Savage, Hiatt, Kemley, Mapplebeck and Standring in contention for the six available slots and on 25th June, after some 30 further jumps, Hiatt was the unlucky seventh man and arrangements for the five week trip proceeded apace.

Contact had already been made with the (American) South-East Conference Director, Gene Thacker, for the British contingent to set up a training camp at his Raeford Drop Zone and the party left Heathrow on Saturday 15th July. The decision to train at Raeford was possibly the major factor in the results subsequently achieved in Talequah. Facilities here were first class, with exclusive use of a Cessna 182, a good deep pea gravel pit, voice tape recorder on the telemeters, rigging facilities, air conditioned accommodation, excellent home cooking by Gene's wife Billie and continuous help and encouragement from Gene Paul himself. The team quickly settled down to a routine of six and seven jumps per day with a break from midday until four when temperatures soared into the nineties Fahrenheit with a relative humidity approaching eighty percent. Emphasis was laid on Style training as this event was considered the key to a high overall placing and after some 25 jumps performances showed a pleasing consistency with corrected averages ranging from 8.8 sec (Meacock) to 10.5 sec (Mapplebeck). Accuracy conditions were tricky in the humid atmosphere and the tree-shrouded drop zone with average results varying from 0.29cm (King) to 1.34cm (Meacock). In all, 200 accuracy jumps were made plus 20 team accuracy and 155 style jumps. Parachuting was interspersed with a little graded physical training and at the end of two weeks and some 70 jumps apiece the top five jumpers for Talequah were named. Meacock and Kemley were in to turn style, King and Standring primarily for accuracy and Mapplebeck was to lead the team stack. Savage was nominated as Team alternate. On Monday 31st July the team boarded the 737 of Piedmont Airlines thoroughly acclimatized, relaxed and confident.

The thousand miles to Tulsa, via Washington, passed pleasantly enough thanks to the comfort and efficiency of the American internal airline system and the final sixty-odd miles from Tulsa to Talequah were covered in a school bus laid on by the Organisers. Accommodation was provided at the North-eastern State College in town some three miles from the Airport. Next morning the team visited the Drop Zone anxious to make some familiarization jumps to be confronted with a farmer's field containing a tarmac strip, a couple of hangars and a somewhat tatty heap of gravel which was the World Championship pit. National Guard helicopters were, however, provided and the team made a couple of accuracy jumps before going swimming in the afternoon, nursing a distinct sense of anti-climax. Head of Delegation Doc Johnson arrived in the evening together with Target Trust representatives Ian Sampson and Ian Dunning.

Further practice jumps were made during the week and as the days went by various impedimenta appropriate to a parachute Meet, such as windsock, telemeters, and anemometer began to arrive and were assembled in the vicinity of the pit. The National Guard erected a field kitchen and a spectators' stand was put up to augment the plentiful bales of hay. Much in evidence also were the American national team with their highly vocal entourage who had, presumably all together, been training on site for the previous four weeks and who were displaying impressive accuracy with Papillons and Mk 3 Para Commanders in national colours. Spectre at the feast was American National Style Champion Roy Johnson compete with plaster and crutches, having contrived to break a leg in training the previous week

On Friday evening the hosts suffered a further setback when the World Championships Friendship Saloon was raided by the local constabulary in the middle of a welcome party, State alcohol regulations apparently having been contravened, and the Assistant Meet Director, Lenny Potts, was incarcerated in the local nick. This unfortunate occurrence detracted somewhat from the festivities but it was confidently asserted that the Opening Ceremony on the morrow would fully vindicate the Organisation and bring some sense of order to the proceedings. Alas to relate, the said Opening Ceremony passed off unnoticed by ninety percent of the teams, perspiring dutifully in their tracksuits and waiting in vain for someone, anyone, to tell them what was going on.

The serious business began on Sunday 6th August with the first round of Team Accuracy in marginal conditions with winds at altitude in excess of 20 metres/sec and the met information over one hour old. Undisturbed by the spectacle of the American women's team fast disappearing over the brow of a nearby hill, Meet Director Heaton attempted to order the British team aboard the helicopter with the met now 90 minutes overdue. His suggestion was, however, firmly resisted until the necessary details arrived to indicate opening points of 1200 and 2400 metres for first and fourth respectively with fifteen degrees variation to boot. This information was superbly exploited by the team who opened their bid for honours with consecutive dead centres from Mapplebeck, King and Standring with Meacock a shade short on 1.12m.

Clear skies the following morning presaged the start of the Style event. Top British scorers were Mapplebeck with 8. 8sec and Kemley with 10.0. Mapplebeck was immediately the victim of a particularly harsh decision which gave him a 3.5 arrow penalty out of his final loop. Style continued the next day until mid-afternoon when jumping was suspended because of increasing winds. Meacock and Kemley were again the most impressive with 8.7 and 9.0 respectively, Mapplebeck (9.9) Standring (10.2) and King (10.8) backing up well. On Wednesday, with midday temperatures in the 100's, four rounds of style were completed; Kemley turning an immaculate 8.6 left series to equal the fastest British time in international competition. At this stage the pattern was beginning to emerge with best times of 6.5 from Armaing (France), 6. 8 Pospichal (Czech), 7.2 Ossipov (USSR), and 7.4 Schoeppele (USA). Thursday 10th saw the completion of three accuracy rounds. This day was the watershed as far as our individual accuracy was concerned; Kemley undershot for a disastrous 7.80 metres and Standring collected 1.56 metres of his subsequent 2.65 ten-round total. Meacock was awarded a rejump and improved two and a half metres to 1.31m.

Friday was the rest and recreation day spent at the lakeside with the water skiers; Saturday was blown out and on Sunday jumping recommenced at 06.30 with accuracy in light winds. Parachuting continued through midday temperatures of 110 degrees and by nightfall the team had pulled back a few places with dead centres from Standring (two), Kemley and King with Mapplebeck totalling 19 centimetres for two jumps. Of the other competitors at this stage Kumbar (Czech) had five consecutive discs, Majer (Czech) had totaled 9 centimetres and Sutton (Canada) had already collected his 19 centimetres which was to earn him second place. The only

Cloud* in the sky was that of US alternate, Bill Hayes, who so far had amassed seventy centimetres on three jumps. Monday saw a further round of individual accuracy with Kemley continuing his revival with 0.08, Standring being awarded 0.06 for a clean strike and Mapplebeck taking his first disc in the individual event. In the sizzling midday heat Team Accuracy recommenced with the team totaling a fighting 0.76m (Mapplebeck 0.03, King 0.33, Standring 0.00 and Meacock 0.40). After this effort the team went back to the College to rest in air-conditioned comfort for a couple of hours before returning at six o'clock to complete Round 3 Team accuracy and go into first place with an immaculate stack and 0.70 total (Mapplebeck 0.00, King 0.00, Standring 0.04, Meacock 0.66).

On Tuesday 15th the final round of style was completed, Armaing of France clinching the title with a final right set of 7.3 sec to give him an average of 7.18, one tenth of a second ahead of Pospichal (Czechoslovakia). Third was Schoepelle (USA) who averaged 7.7 for the five jumps. The two latter provide an interesting contrast between Eastern and Western schools of thought, Pospichal using pulse turns with long arm and leg configuration while Schoepelle turned tight with minimal arm movement and good leg control. Armaing gained consistently over his rivals by virtue of lightning transition between manoeuvres. The day continued with Round seven accuracy, King slipping a little through an off-line 2. 20m while the rest all scored inside one metre. Wednesday followed with Rounds eight and nine, and with the Meet virtually over the British continued to consolidate their overall position with consistent scoring from Mapplebeck (two dead centres), Standring (0.06 and 0.00) and Meacock (0.04 and 0.00).

The Meet was concluded on Thursday 17th August with the final round of individual accuracy and two dramatic rounds in the Team event. Great Britain entered Round 4 as leaders for the first time in World competition as surface windspeeds in the heat of the afternoon fluctuated between two and five metres per second

* ParaPlane Silver Cloud.

with pronounced thermal activity. Team after team fell victim to the unstable conditions and fell out of the running. The Swiss scored over 14 metres, the Canadians over 15 while the Czechs totalled 2.91 and the Russians an ominous 0.08m. For the first time in the competition the British stack was untidy with Meacock and Standring at the same level and unable to resolve the situation. Mapplebeck and King scored their customary dead centres, then in a salvage situation Standring reached desperately for 0.83 and Meacock, having been forced out to the last second crashed home for a most worthy 1.46 metres. Hasty calculations put the Russians in the lead with 3.87, ourselves second on 4.87 metres and the Czechs third with a 5.50 total. The rest were nowhere. The issue was left wide open again however as the Swiss were awarded a rejump. In nil wind conditions they made no mistake to score 0.17m and go into the lead at this fourth round stage with a mere 3.03m total. The fifth round proceeded apace under cooling skies and fading winds. First to score were the Swiss with a Gold clinching 0.76 metres. Now under pressure were the British team who responded with a copy book stack and a repeat of their opening jump, with three dead centres from Mapplebeck, King and Standring with Meacock trying to make sure and falling short for 0.93. This left the Czechs with 30 centimetres slack which they exploited with deadly precision and we were out of the medals.

Thus ended what was undoubtedly the toughest World competition to date. New standards in accuracy and style were set and it now seems probable that times for the present style format will be improved upon only marginally. Rather one envisages a raising of standards among the less favoured parachuting nations with a consequent levelling of times around and below eight seconds as the norm. First class accuracy was achieved by jumpers using Papillons, Mk 3 Para Commanders, PTCH8's and the new Soviet UT15. The much vaunted Cloud was jumped six times by Hayes who totaled 4. 06 metres in the process and three times by Stratziota of Venezuela who then gave up in disgust. With the development of a more sophisticated control system the Para Plane Cloud will doubtless appear as the accuracy machine of the future with a tremendous bonus of slow landing speed to facilitate the task of the judges. When the stage is reached that the parachute canopy is the deciding factor rather than the sheer skill of the jumper, then separate classes for separate canopies will have to be considered. At the moment the truism remains that the canopy is only as good as the jumper using it, and for my money the performance of the Meet was that of Kumbar using a PTCH 8 for his nine consecutive Dead Centres in the individual accuracy event.

What of the British Team? Arguably the strongest combination to leave these shores, the team undoubtedly consolidated the position of Great Britain in World rankings in face of considerably improved opposition. It was particularly pleasing to note that without exception the jumpers improved upon their training performances under the stress of competition. The Group Precision in particular brought out the best in Mapplebeck and King with four Dead Centre strikes apiece from the five jumps. Meacock confirmed his ability as National Champion with the highest overall placing (28th) followed immediately by Standring (29th) whose consistent accuracy earned him 19th position in the individual event. Kemley thrived in the international atmosphere and finished with a respectable 9.6sec style average while Savage provided invaluable backup assistance all along the line. In all, a solid team performance which augurs well for the national and international future of our Sport. "

**Doug Peacock – BPA Magazine December 1972**

*(With the perspective imposed by the forty intervening years, several comments on the above seem appropriate. This was a very respectable performance by the British Team; we had dropped one place in World rankings since 1968, but this was a much larger competition and from a technical standpoint our own first round performance in Team Accuracy should not be underestimated; the canopy handling skills were superb. With upper winds in excess of forty knots and the top man opening a mile and a half from the target, we scored three*

*dead centres and a 1.12 metre strike – and this on round canopies. On the wider scene, ram air canopies were soon universally adopted as accuracy machines; the 12th WPC in Hungary two years later was the last occasion on which a round canopy would win a World accuracy event, whilst the 1976 WPC in Rome saw the final appearance of Para Commander types. The electronic scoring pad was introduced in the Hungarian Meet; and the dead centre disc was reduced progressively from ten to five, then three, and is now only two centimetres in diameter. Style judging remained on telemeters for another full ten years before ground to air video was to be used in Czechoslovakia 1982).*

# *Appendix 2*

## THE 1978 RHINE ARMY CHAMPIONSHIPS
## (OR UNCLE TOM OXLEY AND ALL)

"The Rhine Army Parachute Centre at Bad Lippspringe is generally held to be one of the most hospitable and productive establishments within the Association. To the North and West of the Drop Zone lie miles of heathland, utilised as firing and mortar ranges and populated by the itinerant soldiery of many nations. Directly to the South and East is the town of Bad Lippspringe, a health resort populated by physiotherapists, doctors and nuns and frequented by the middle class hypochondriacs of the Northwest German plain. The DZ itself contains a polo pitch, sundry football pitches and a golf course. The ranges may not be overflown, nor the health resort; the horses may not be frightened nor the golfers disturbed. They still average about fifteen thousand jumps a year, using their own Islander and a tame Dornier 27. They also run a highly entertaining annual Open Championships which this year attracted some one hundred and thirty four competitors.

The Army, naturally, were there in force. There were also Dutchmen, Danes, Germans and miscellaneous Belgians. There were novices and champions, soldiers and civilians, relative workers and females. Pete Sherman brought his team all the way from Dubai to add a further touch of colour. There was an Accuracy Event, a Style Event and an RW Event. They had the Islander, the Dornier and a German Army Huey. They had cooks, field kitchens, beer, caravans, tents, a windsock, anemometer, telemeters, video, air traffic control, met and an electronic disc. They had Jock Manson. They had the lot. Jock Manson is a pilot and, as his name implies, is from Scotland. He likes aeroplanes and the people who jump out of them. He dislikes hot gravy on his lap during takeoff and jumpmasters who give corrections on jump run. He is in the Royal Air Force and bound by Queens Regulations; despite these twin handicaps he flies the Islander incessantly and superbly. When he is not flying the Islander he may be found critiquing canopy approaches and raking the pit. Jock, in short, is totally integrated into the jumping scene and a complete professional. Jock's alter ego is Roy, who will change the plugs, fix the brake pads, cure the hydraulics, operate the radio, operate the video and provide fuel for the aircraft and coffee for Jock as and when required, seemingly simultaneously if necessary. Roy is a friendly soul to whom no problem is too complex for his ability nor too small for his attention. Between them they ensured continuous operation of the Islander at the drop of a hat whenever it was required.

It was, in fact, required all day and every day from Sunday until Friday for the temperature reached the mid eighties and the wind stayed down most of the time. It had been decided to combine Individual and Team within one accuracy event; this combination, normally acceptable, gave rise to certain technical problems when the wind blew off the ranges. The competitors had agreed to accept crosswind runs within the DZ boundaries, a feasible proposition which rapidly deteriorated when the fourth jumper in one team light heartedly made a late exit followed by a ten second delay only to find himself halfway up the range road a thousand meters cross wind from the target. Upper lips quivered, rejumps were demanded and harsh words directed at the judging staff who referred the attention of the complainants to their own jumpmaster. Meanwhile, Mark IIIs and Papillons continued to bomb the target from all angles. Accuracy proceeded apace, interrupted only by the odd dull thud of a novice landing on the runway.

The week was not entirely without incident. Pete Santagoeds threw his hand deploy between his legs to his considerable discomfort and Jock Manson spilled an excellent lunch over his lap whilst accelerating down the runway during the fifteenth of his thirty seven sorties that day. Cloud base came down to six thousand feet, the Relative Workers paused momentarily in their endless Indian war dances and the word went forth that the Style Event was to begin. The Judge, having arrayed the telemeters, stopwatches and scoresheets to his entire satisfaction, was standing by the pit casting a benign eye upon the feverish activity around him and mentally computing the penalties for major and minor undershoots. His reverie was interrupted by the arrival of one Chandler, who, mentally standing respectfully to attention, felt it his duty to report that a member of the load was boarding the Huey, in his opinion, inadequately shod. Bootless, in fact. A small wisp of steam arose from the thinning pate of the Judge. Carefully handing his half smoked duty free cigar to a minion, he proceeded to the aircraft to verify this startling intelligence for himself. The miscreant, a comely youth with shoulder length hair cascading gently over his shoulders from beneath a pale fawn ribbed French helmet and the offending off-white toes peeking coyly out from under outsize off-white bell bottoms stood waiting questioningly. The Judge spoke, quietly and sadly. "Do you understand English, young sir?" The youth's face broke into a beatific smile. "Yes indeed", said he. "Then you've thirty seconds to get some effing boots on, otherwise you're zapped", responded the Judge reverting to character and, turning on his heel, strode off to resume his cigar and contemplation of the hired hands scratching about ineffectively in the pit.

The Style Event was concluded that same evening with two re-jumpers turning a cross set on a heading illuminated by car headlights. Before they had landed the telemeters had been struck, the scores collated and posted on the board and two crates ordered. The outright winner was Nadolny of the German Airborne with an average of 8.3 for the three sets. For reasons best known to himself he insisted on jumping a reefed Stratostar securely packed in a bag, which anachronistic juxtaposition earned him two total malfunctions within the space of four jumps. He left the DZ the following day clutching his trophies and a slider. First Rhine Army competitor was veteran Crab Ken Mapplebeck who also took the Rhine Army accuracy title and the first Open Overall, a worthy finale for a consistent and uncompromising competitor.

The four man RW event was conducted from the Huey and provided an interesting workout for the 27 Luftlande Brigade, German Army who were, however, closely pushed by the Lott in the guise of the British Army Team and by Quadriga of the Rhine Army who finished joint second. The Germans concentrated on flying a linked pair and two singles from the door, a technique which allowed for some impressive close flying once the initial formation had been built. The Meet was in fact a complete success for the 27 Luftlande Brigade who swept the board in the RW event, Team Accuracy, Individual Accuracy and Individual Style— a result which cast prophetic shadows for within a few weeks the full German Army Team were to finish third overall nation in the 14th Classic WPC in Zagreb.

The competition ended on Thursday evening with the traditional disco. Friday morning was bedevilled by low cloud and hangovers, Friday afternoon taken up with prizegiving and the striking of tents. Five days dawn to dusk operation made possible by the competitors, pilots and the willing tireless efforts of the Rhine Army Parachute Centre staff, headed by Mr perpetual motion McQueen ably backed up by George Clark, Ron Lutz, Ann Fowler and Gaby, Jack Fowler, Bob Card, Wally Wallace and the British Army Team who most professionally judged all the accuracy. Proceedings were directed by David Ward, that most understanding of diplomats and conducted by impresario supreme Tom Oxley, that most thoughtful of all DZ potentates. The farewells were spoken, the addresses exchanged, the deals concluded, the arguments abated and the trophies distributed. Next year will be even bigger and better, Jock Manson will order chicken and chips for lunch and Pete Santagoeds will buy himself a handle. Pondering these and many other thoughts, the Judge assigned his expenses to his Swiss bank, lit another duty free cigar, climbed into his yellow Rolls Royce and headed West towards the autobahn. "

**Doug Peacock– BPA Magazine October 1978**

# Glossary

| | |
|---|---|
| AFF | Accelerated Free Fall. Training system with student controlled by two instructors. c/f RAPS |
| AMO | Air Ministry Order. Four-jump courses for selected personnel under the relevant directive |
| AQM | Air Quartermaster, subsequentlyAir Loadmaster |
| APJI | Assistant PJI. Army Instructor, qualified to despatch from the balloon |
| APA | Army Parachute Association |
| A& AEE | Aeroplane and Armament Experimental Establishment Boscombe Down |
| B4 | Type of US Air Force back-type parachute container and harness |
| Bergen | Rucksack for personal equipment and weapons carried by jumper and attached by carrying straps |
| BETAP | Base École des Troupes Aéroportées. French Airborne School |
| BOC | Bottom of Container. Position of hand-deployed pilot chute |
| BPA | British Parachute Association |
| C9 | 28 foot flat circular US Air Force parachute canopy |
| Capewell | Device to disconnect risers from main harness |
| CIP | Commission International du Parachutisme. See IPC |
| CISM | Conseil International du Sport Militaire. International Military Sports Council |
| CYPRES | Cybernetic Parachute Release System. Automatic activation device, usually on the reserve parachute |

| | |
|---|---|
| DZ | Dropping Zone |
| DZSO | Dropping Zone Safety Officer |
| EFA | Études et Fabrications Aéronautiques French-based Parachute Manufacturers |
| FAI | Fédération Aéronautique Internationale. International Air Sports Governing Body |
| FXC | Automatic Activation device either on main or reserve parachute |
| Golden Knights | United States Army Parachute Team |
| GQ | British parachute manufacturing company founded by James Gregory and Sir Raymond Quilter in 1932 |
| HALO | High Altitude Low Opening. Military freefall tactical insertion |
| Hitefinder | Automatic Activation device on main parachute |
| IPC | International Parachuting Commission |
| Irvin | Parachute manufacturing company founded in the UK by Leslie Irvin in 1926. Now Irvin-GQ following merger with GQ in 2001 |
| Met. | Meteorological |
| NEAF | Near East Air Force |
| PWC | Personal Weapons Container. Now superseded by the Bergen rucksack |
| PFO | Physical Fitness Officer |
| PTS | Parachute Training School |
| RAFSPA | Royal Air Force Sport Parachute Association |
| RAPA | Rhine Army Parachute Association |
| RAPS | Ram Air Progression System. Basic sport parachute training with first jumps static line. c/f AFF |
| Red Devils | Parachute Regiment Freefall Display Team |
| RW | Relative Work, now Formation Skydiving |
| SAS | Special Air Service |
| Siki | Wind jumper or Wind Drift Indicator. French/Algerian origin, relating to a weighted dummy |

| | |
|---|---|
| | thrown from the aircraft to determine the wind conditions |
| SOAF | Sultan of Oman's Air Force |
| SOPR | Sultan of Oman's Parachute Regiment |
| Static line | Line attached to aircraft strongpoint to open the parachute |
| STC | Safety and Training Committee of the BPA |
| TAP | Tactical Approach Parachute (GQ) |
| Telemeters | Tripod-mounted $10 \times 80$ observation binoculars Pre-WW2 German military origin |
| Track | Horizontal movement in freefall. Also verb |
| T10 | US Military static-line parachute |
| TU | Type of modification, by removal of gores, of a round canopy to produce  forward speed. Also single blank, double blank and double L. See photos 12, 25, 26 and 31 |
| USPA | United States Parachute Association |
| WDI | Wind Drift Indicator. See Siki |
| WPC | World Parachuting Championships |

# Bibliography

Hearn, Peter, *Parachutist* (Robert Hale, London, 1976)

Hearn, Peter, *Falcons* (Grub Street 1995)

Poynter, Daniel, *The Parachute Manual* (Daniel F. Poynter 1972)

Reilly, Mike, *Alone in the Sky* (Robert Hale 1963)

Suire, André, *Chute libre* (Arthaud 1958)

Valentin, Léo, *Bird Man* (Hutchinson 1955)

Willans, T W, *Parachuting and Skydiving* (Faber and Faber 1964)

# *Acknowledgements*

Many people have assisted in the compilation of this book; first and foremost I must thank Peter Hearn for his unstinting encouragement and practical advice. I am also deeply indebted to BPA archivists Andrew Hilton and Graham Spicer who willingly provided me with background information at every turn.

I also owe a big thank you to John Saxby, Bob Souter, and Chris Lyall for their individual contributions to the text, which vividly recount the dramatic parachuting moments they lived through.

For assistance in jogging my memory, and filling in much detail, I thank many friends and colleagues, both past and present: Geordie Charlton, Dave Cobb, Bill Cook, Terry Cooke, Joe Featherstone, Barry Furness, Mike Hand, John Hitchen, Dave Howerski, Alan (Doc) Johnson, Peter Keane, Bob King, George Long, Henry MacDonald, Jake McLoughlin, Ken Mapplebeck, Scotty Milne, Ron Mitchell, Ronnie O'Brien, John Parry, John Robinson, Charlie Shea-Simonds, Pete Sherman, Jackie Smith, Stevie Stephenson and Ray Willis.

For photographic contributions I thank Matt Abram, Jürgen Barth, Paulo Ya Braz, Eamonn Fairhead, Mike Hand, Dave Hayward, Michel Jara, Chris Lyall, Jake McLoughlin, Helen Spratley, Carsten Thiel and Ray Willis; I also thank Terry Crawley for the Ranville photographs. Where photographs remain unattributed, every effort has been made to contact the source.

Finally, grateful thanks are due to Sally, Suzy and Mark at Hope Services for their great support and professional expertise in putting these memoirs together.